11/86

SMILEY'S CIRCUS

A Guide to the Secret World of John le Carré

SMILEY'S CIRCUS

A Guide to the Secret World of John le Carré

David Monaghan

A Thomas Dunne Book
St. Martin's Press New York

SMILEY'S CIRCUS — A GUIDE TO THE SECRET WORLD
OF JOHN LE CARRÉ

First published in Great Britain 1986 by Orbis Book Publishing
Corporation Ltd. A BPCC plc company.

Library of Congress Cataloging-in-Publication Data
Monaghan, David.
  Smiley's circus.
  1. Le Carré, John, 1931- —Handbooks, manuals,
etc. 2. Le Carré, John, 1931- —Characters—
George Smiley—Handbooks, manuals, etc. 3. Smiley,
George (Fictitious character)—Handbooks, manuals,
etc. 4. Spy stories, English—Handbooks, manuals, etc.
I. Title.
PR6062.E33Z79   1986   823'.914   86-6447

ISBN 0-312-73014-4

First U.S. Edition
10 9 8 7 6 5 4 3 2 1

Contents

Introduction 7
THE CIRCUS
History of Major Operations 12
Chronology of Major Operations
The Fennan Case 28
The Fiedler–Mundt Operation 30
The Haydon Case 32
Operation Dolphin 35
The Karla Case 38
Hierarchy of the Circus 41
Cambridge Circus Headquarters 48
WHO'S WHO
Biographies of People, Places and Particularities
in the Secret World of John le Carré 51
Appendix: Notes on the 'Circus' Series of Novels 194
Index to THE CIRCUS Chapter 198

List of photographs

(between pages 64–65)
1 The Berlin Wall
2 Outdoor Chess Game at The Platform, Berne
3 Carne Abbey, Dorset
4 Circus Headquarters, Cambridge Circus, London
5 The Fennan Case: Battersea Bridge, London

(between pages 96–97)
6 The Haydon Case: Hotel Islay, Paddington
7 Hong Kong: Operation Dolphin
8 The Haydon Case: The Lock Gardens Safe House, Camden Town

(between pages 128–129)
9 London: South End Green, North Hampstead
10 London: Trumper's of Mayfair
11 London: The Travellers' in Pall Mall
12 Oxford: Recruiting Ground for Circus Talent

(between pages 160–161)
13 Smiley's London Home: 9 Bywater Street, Chelsea
14 Ann Smiley's Home Ground: Marazion, Cornwall
15 General Vladimir's Flat: 6B Westbourne Terrace, Paddington
16 Hampstead Heath – Scene of Vladimir's murder

List of Maps (within the WHO'S WHO A–Z section)
Berne; East Germany and Czechoslovakia (with inset of Berlin);
Hong Kong and Hong Kong Central District; London; South East Asia

Author's Acknowledgements

Many people have helped me in bringing *Smiley's Circus* to completion. These include Margaret Tang, who provided invaluable information on the shifting topography of Hong Kong: Marilyn Congdon, who gave tangible form to my vague artwork ideas; Charles Merullo, whose enthusiasm helped convince Orbis to publish the book; Judith A. Kavanagh, who typed two drafts of the manuscript; and the staffs of the British Library and the Killam Library of Dalhousie University, who helped locate maps.

My greatest debts, however, are to Andrew Best, my agent, for never losing faith in the book; Jorge Lewinski, for his sensitive realization of my photographic ideas; and Marie-Jaqueline Lancaster, my editor, for her grasp of detail, compendious knowledge, and unfailing patience.

Source References

The **Circus** book titles given as source references throughout the text are indicated by the following initials within brackets:

(CD)   –   *Call for the Dead*
(HS)   –   *The Honourable Schoolboy*
(LW)   –   *The Looking-Glass War*
(MQ)   –   *A Murder of Quality*
(SC)   –   *The Spy Who Came in from the Cold*
(SP)   –   *Smiley's People*
(TT)   –   *Tinker, Tailor, Soldier, Spy*

Introduction

The special department of the British Intelligence Service known as 'the Circus' may not exist but we believe that it might . . . Many of us have stayed at London's Hotel Islay, even if for some reason it was masquerading under a different name, and few of us would be surprised to see George Smiley emerge blinking from Chelsea's Bywater Street. We hesitate while crossing Cambridge Circus and try to identify which of the ring of buildings is the Circus itself, and wasn't that Peter Guillam returning from a late lunch, at Chez Victor no doubt?

The creation of a world which captures readers so completely is no easy task. Le Carré has allowed himself seven books in which to accomplish the feat, but space in itself is no guarantee of success. Recurring settings and characters are a staple of popular fiction. Yet we can visit the world of James Bond or Lord Peter Wimsey again and again without it ever achieving more than two dimensions. This is because the serial works of Ian Fleming and Dorothy L. Sayers are characterized by repetition rather than development or elaboration. Even where books do introduce detail and documentation, it is often in self-contained lumps which refuse to blend with the main body of the action, and so do little to help a fictional world to achieve imaginative credibility. The American spy-thriller writer and one-time CIA operative, Charles McCarry, may be well qualified to talk about the realities of espionage but, because of the manner in which he incorporates factual material, his novels are almost entirely devoid of the air of authenticity which so richly pervades le Carré's work.

Le Carré is able to achieve this elusive quality of authenticity because he has the nerve to refrain from imprinting directly on his stories the complex blueprint of the Circus – its history, organization, physical presence and personnel – which clearly exists in his imagination (assisted by the necessary file cards he updates and the photographs he uses for reference). Instead, he plunges his readers directly into the centre of his world and lets them experience its infinite variety for themselves without benefit of the author's pointing finger or potted summary. In this aspect le Carré's novels, with the exception of his apprentice piece of 1961, *Call for the Dead* (which opens with an informative but dramatically stultifying précis of Smiley's background and of the history of the Circus), deserve comparison with William Faulkner's Yoknapatawpha County series, Jane Austen's depiction of late eighteenth-century society or, to remain within the sphere of genre fiction, Dick Francis's horse-racing stories. The price readers must pay for the satisfaction of living in, rather than merely learning about, the world of the Circus is frequent confusion. Their task, as they struggle to move from the flux of experience to the stability of knowledge, is to recreate le Carré's imaginative blueprint. It is in response to the acknowledged difficulties of some readers in achieving such a transformation that this book has been written.

The fictional world with which we have to come to terms is an evolving one that does not acquire its definitive shape until *Smiley's People* (the last of the Circus novels to date) has been completed. *Call for the Dead* and *A Murder of Quality* introduce the reader to the history of the Circus, to one central figure, George Smiley, and to aspects of a London landscape. *The Spy Who Came in from the Cold* and *The Looking-Glass War* provide more history, particularly of the 1950s, as well as taking the narrative on into the 1960s; they add further figures, most notably Control and Alec Leamas, expand the landscape into East Germany, offer brief insights into the complex organizational structure of the Circus, and give some inkling that spies speak a private language of their own.

The process of broadening and deepening is expanded enormously in the interconnected trilogy which completes the present series: *Tinker, Tailor, Soldier, Spy*, *The Honourable Schoolboy*, and *Smiley's People*. Here the history of the Circus between the 1930s and the 1960s is fleshed out as well as being brought right up to the late 1970s. Significant attention is finally focused on its hierarchy, and the headquarters building in Cambridge Circus acquires a tangible physical presence, while more and more dimensions are added to the biography and personality of George Smiley. Fringe figures from earlier novels, such as Peter Guillam, are moved to centre stage and fully developed and a host of new characters, major and minor, are introduced. The London landscape is mapped out in exhaustive detail and other settings, covering much of Europe and parts of South East Asia, are added. At the same time, the specialized vocabulary of the spy world is significantly expanded.

Le Carré's final creation is extremely diverse and complex and to analyse its component parts is to discover, not so much a blueprint as a microcosm, that is, a miniature but three-dimensional and completely functioning world. We may often feel lost in the labyrinth of the Circus but in fact, as the anatomy carried out in this book shows, le Carré has provided all the tools necessary to explore its every nook and cranny. So much information exists on the history of the Circus that relationships can be established between events which occur years apart. Thus we understand why, in the conduct of the Haydon case in 1973, Smiley several times refers to the authority of Steed-Asprey, a man who had given up any involvement with espionage as far back as 1945. Similarly, because we know the role of Oxford in the pre-war history of the Circus we can recognize the special poignancy of Smiley's visit to that city as he prepares for his final battle with Karla in 1978.

By gathering together scattered pieces of information, it is possible to grasp quite precisely how the complex organizational structure of the Circus works. Starting with a simple hierarchy of Minister responsible for Intelligence matters, the Minister's Adviser and the head of the Circus, we work our way downwards and outwards through an ever more complicated network of authority which embraces functions as varied in importance and prestige as the operation of overseas networks, the resettlement of retired agents, training in unarmed combat, pay and pensions, blackmail and murder, tea-making, code-breaking, and the maintenance of radiators.

A third major aspect of the Circus, the building which provides it with a headquarters, is no less accessible. Armed with the multitude of clues provided, especially in *Tinker, Tailor, Soldier, Spy* and *The Honourable Schoolboy*, it should not be difficult – given the right 'pass' – to find your way from the lobby to the head's office on the fifth floor or, starting from the men's lavatory on the fourth floor, to get coffee from the machine near the elevator and then carry it to someone in Banking Section. Registry, Housekeeping, the senior secretarial pool, the offices occupied by Smiley, Guillam, Connie Sachs and Bland, the duty-officers' room and the fifth-floor conference room are all equally easy to find. Belief in the reality of the Circus building derives not just from knowledge of its layout but from the precise sense given by a mass of descriptive details of how it feels to be in the headquarters of a budget-starved department of British Intelligence. There is an intensely tactile quality to the smell of stale, cheap scent and dust in the duty-officers' room, to the claustrophobia of the endless narrow, winding corridors, the discomfort promised by a night spent on the divan reserved for the night duty-officer, the contrast between the bustle and excitement of life on the fourth floor and the funereal quiet of the fifth where even typing is done softly.

Similar techniques are used in the creation of the landscape at the centre of which the Circus stands. London in particular acquires a complete identity built out of a combination of precise geographical details and frequent evocations of the personality of place. So long as care is taken not to be distracted by the occasional fictional place or changed name, it is easy to follow the routes taken by Dieter Frey as he flees from Hammersmith Broadway to the Thames and by Guillam as he hastens from his towpath

observation point to Lock Gardens (actually St Mark's Crescent in
Camden Town). Similarly, restaurants and pubs such as Scott's, the
White Tower, the Sherlock Holmes and the Eight Bells, favourite haunts
of spies, are all open to the inquisitive visitor. Equally important on this
journey would be the acute sense acquired of the atmosphere of decayed
grandeur and contemporary nihilism which pervades all of le Carré's
London settings. No other parts of the fictional landscape are as complete
but they can be experienced in similar ways. Thus, with a map of Hong
Kong Central in hand it is possible to trace quite precisely the circuitous
route taken by Westerby as he walks to Frost's bank. Every Hong Kong
location is characterized by a richly ambiguous combination of colonial
dullness, Chinese vitality and almost magical natural beauty.

Important as these aspects are, the credibility of le Carré's fictional
world derives ultimately from the cast of characters with which he
populates it. The first need is for that cast to be large enough to lend a
human dimension to the bare facts of the Circus history and structure. Le
Carré meets this challenge totally and his Circus, past and present, has an
identifiable staff of over eighty. His real achievement is in giving so many
of his characters sufficient personality to bring them alive. Most completely recognizable, of course, are major figures such as Smiley, Guillam,
Westerby and Control. By the time they have completed their several
fictional appearances we are aware of what they look like, what kind of
personality they have, what they believe in, and are fully acquainted with
the details of their careers and personal relationships, their cover names
and nicknames, their tastes in clothes, food, drink and sexual partners,
their hobbies, and their idiosyncrasies. Even much less important figures
often acquire a sharply defined identity. White hair, a red face, slowness
and an unctuous whining manner imprint on the memory the briefly-met
janitor, Bryant, while the archivist 'Sal', with her plump figure, good
nature, and tolerant cynicism about Guillam's claims to virtue, combined
with her interest in judo and youth clubs, becomes an individual in her
own right.

The world beyond the confines of the Circus is no less thickly populated
or particularized. Other branches of intelligence and foreign secret
services such as 'the Department', 'the Cousins' and 'Moscow Centre' also
possess staff, however skeleton, many of whom exist as far more than
names. In the course of their intelligence activities and private lives,
Circus personnel come into contact with a multitude of different and often
very striking people, ranging from fully developed characters such as the
enigmatic and adventurously promiscuous Ann Smiley to those who need
only a few moments to take hold of our imaginations. Who could forget,

for example, Beckie, an American diplomat's wife encountered briefly by Westerby in Phnom Penh, as she struggles to cope honestly with the demands of Cambodian culture while longing for her New England home, or the boy waiter who horrifies Smiley with his nonchalant disregard for the proprieties of serving burgundy?

The final important element in the creation of le Carré's world is the invention of a language of spying. Authenticity is rooted in thoroughness because, rather than simply introduce a few terms designed to give a flavour of espionage 'jargon', le Carré offers nearly two hundred words and phrases. What makes his jargon truly convincing is the inventiveness, wit and occasionally poetic inspiration which goes into its creation. Thus, amongst his forty or so terms used to describe types of spies are such felicitous titles as: 'little ships', 'secret whisperers', 'burrowers', 'coat trailers', 'Golden Oldies', 'ju ju men', 'lamplighters', 'pavement artists', 'shoemakers', 'vicars'. Elsewhere, to be cleared of suspicion is to be 'graded Persil' and to threaten and bribe simultaneously is to carry out a 'stick-and-carrot job'.

Because le Carré simultaneously creates a world which is complex and wide-ranging yet refrains from revealing it in every detail, this guide to his secret world is designed for both new readers as they grapple with the complexities of Operation Dolphin or of the Smileys' marriage, and for those familiar with le Carré's books who will find here the answers to some puzzles, the chance to make fresh connections or simply to experience the pleasure of seeing familiar personalities and events from new angles. Its value is to be judged on the extent to which it assists readers in gaining access to – and pleasure from – the challenging but marvellously inventive Circus novels of John le Carré.

THE CIRCUS
History of
Major Operations

The known history of the Circus goes back as far as 1918, when Ben
Thruxton passes himself off as a Latvian dissident in order to mingle with
the revolutionaries in the streets of Moscow, although a coherent picture
of its activities does not begin to emerge until 1928. At this time espionage
activities are officially centred on a terraced house in Knightsbridge,
London, but are largely controlled by a small group of Oxbridge
academics, the most notable being Steed-Asprey, who is probably head of
the service, Jebedee, Adrian Fielding, and Sparke of the School of
Oriental Languages at Oxford. Working together under the guise of the
Overseas Committee for Academic Research these men recruit likely
candidates for espionage work, including George Smiley whom they
interview in July 1928. (An alternative dating of 1937 seems unlikely in
the light of evidence about Smiley's espionage activity during the 1930s.)
(*CD; TT*)

Such talent-spotting activities continue throughout the 1930s. In 1936–
37, for example, the Oxford tutor Fanshawe recruits the undergraduates
Bill Haydon and Jim Prideaux and in 1938 Control recruits Connie Sachs.
Similar efforts on the part of Soviet Intelligence seem to have gone
unnoticed. Nothing is known of the Soviet agent Karla's visit to England
in 1936 until much later and the most important of his achievements – the
recruitment of Bill Haydon – remains secret until 1973. This lapse on the
part of British Intelligence must be attributed to its concern with the
much more obvious threat posed throughout the 1930s by the growth of
Nazism. Efforts to penetrate German territory and to establish espionage
networks begin well before the outbreak of war. The role played by
George Smiley is of particular note. Working under cover as an *englischer
Dozent* (lecturer in English), he directs a number of his students towards
British Intelligence. (*CD; TT*)

Once the war begins, the range of Circus activities increases enormously. Smiley returns to Germany to manage the networks he has helped
to create. Bill Haydon recruits agents in the Chinese ports of Wenchow

and Amoy, runs French fishing smacks out of the Helford estuary in Cornwall and, aided by Jim Prideaux, establishes courier lines across southern Europe. Prideaux also assists partisan groups in Czechoslovakia, while Alec Leamas works in Norway (1941–43) and Holland (1943–45). Millie McCraig spies in Mozambique and Hamburg under cover as a Bible School teacher. Further recruitment in China is carried out by Doc di Salis. Peter Guillam's father spies for a Circus *réseau* (network) in France. Given the dangerous nature of this kind of wartime field work losses are inevitable, the most significant being that of Jebedee who disappears during a train journey from Lille in 1941. A number of new staff are taken on at the Knightsbridge headquarters to service this intensified activity in the field. Maston is transferred from the Civil Service; Lord John Landsbury is put in charge of coding. Serving under him are Ailsa Brimley, Peter Guillam's mother and, temporarily, Roddy Martindale. Ailsa Brimley also works as Adrian Fielding's secretary and Lady Ann Sercombe as Steed-Asprey's. Ben Sparrow, later of the Special Branch police, is another who works in Intelligence during the war. (*CD; SC; TT; HS*)

The peace of 1945 and the beginning of the Cold War bring with them drastic changes in British spying. Not only do staff who were recruited for the war leave, but so do many whose involvement goes back to the 1930s and earlier. Fielding, Steed-Asprey, Smiley, Prideaux and Leamas are, for example, all lost. The intensification of the Cold War leads to the return of Smiley, Prideaux and Leamas, but the Intelligence Service has altered markedly during their absence. Operations are now centred in London at a building in Cambridge Circus – hence the nickname 'the Circus'. The head is the former civil servant, Maston, and a complex bureaucratic machinery is established. New agents recruited in the period from 1945 to 1955 include Percy Alleline, Sam Collins, Peter Guillam, Ricki Tarr, Brian de Gray, de Jong, Haverlake, and, as an 'Occasional', Jerry Westerby. Circus Operations range over a wide geographical area in the years following the war. Sam Collins works under cover in Borneo, 1953–56, and Burma, 1956–62; Ricki Tarr takes part in 'scalphunter' missions in Malaysia and Kenya; Alleline establishes networks in South America; and Bill Haydon is involved in the Middle East. However, major attention is now focused on the communist enemy. (*CD; SC; TT; HS*)

Although the secret conflict with the Soviet Union must have assumed major proportions by the 1950s, only two events of importance have been recorded. First, in 1955 Smiley travels extensively to negotiate the defection of Soviet agents threatened by a 'Moscow Centre' purge. This mission brings him into contact for the first time with Karla. Second, Bill

Haydon begins to fulfil his obligations to Karla. From 1950 to 1956 he betrays only the Americans but after the Suez crisis he places no restrictions on his commitment to the Soviet cause. Much better documentation exists for activities directed against East Germany. Responsibility for planning operations rests with 'Satellites Four', a special department concerned with Soviet satellite countries, and staffed before 1951 by Smiley, Leamas and de Gray and later by Guillam, de Jong and Haverlake. Major field successes occur as a result of the efforts of the networks established by Leamas, Hackett, Sarrow and de Jong in East Berlin between 1951 and 1961. Amongst those they recruit are, Ländser, Viereck, Paul, Saloman, a girl from Wedding in Berlin's French sector who is used for courier jobs, and Frau Marthe who looks after a 'safe flat' on the Dürer-Strasse. Between 1954 and 1956 their most useful East German source is Fritz Feger, second man in the DDR Defence Ministry, and from 1959 to 1961 Karl Riemeck of the SED (East German Communist Party) Praesidium. (*SC; TT*)

The secret conflict with East Germany becomes particularly intense in the period between 1959 or 1960 and in 1962. The long sequence of events which is to end disastrously at the Berlin Wall in late April 1962 begins at Walliston, in Surrey, just outside London, with the apparent suicide of Samuel Fennan, a civil servant, on Tuesday, January 3, 1960 (1959 according to another account of the incident). Maston, who is still head of the Circus, is content to accept the evidence provided by a suicide note that Fennan took his own life while in a distressed state following questioning by Smiley about possible communist connections. Smiley, however, disagrees with Maston, partly because his interview with Fennan was conducted in a friendly spirit and partly because he quickly uncovers several clues pointing to foul play. In order to be free to conduct an investigation, Smiley resigns from the Circus. He retains access to police sources through Inspector Mendel, and to Circus material (illicitly) through Peter Guillam. (*CD; SC*)

Smiley's first line of investigation involves tracing the car parked outside his house by an intruder whom he encounters immediately after his resignation. This takes Smiley to Adam Scarr's used-car lot and ends in a brutal attack made on him as he examines the vehicle. Scarr is later murdered but, under questioning by Mendel, has already given information which links the driver of the car, known to him as 'Blondie', with the East German Steel Mission and connects the dates the car was used to the visits of Fennan's wife, Elsa, to her local Weybridge Repertory Theatre. Enquiries made by Mendel at the theatre following Smiley's recovery three weeks later further establish that there is a close similarity between the descriptions of Blondie and of Elsa Fennan's theatre companion, and that both Elsa and her companion carried music cases to performances. Mendel also discovers that on the night of Fennan's death, Elsa left her music case at the theatre where it was later claimed by her companion. A simultaneous investigation conducted by Peter Guillam reveals that 'Blondie' is Hans-Dieter Mundt of the East German Steel Mission, which closed down immediately following Fennan's death, and that his superior at the Mission was Dieter Frey, formerly a member of Smiley's network in wartime Germany. (*CD*)

Armed with this information and released from hospital Smiley questions Elsa Fennan. She admits to handing secret material over to Mundt by means of an exchange of music cases at the theatre, but claims that she was simply acting out of loyalty to her husband who had been recruited as an East German agent by Frey five years earlier. According to her version of events Mundt murdered Fennan, covering up with a fake suicide note, because Dieter Frey, having seen him with Smiley, had concluded that he was under suspicion. Shortly after this Guillam informs Smiley that Mundt has finally made good his escape from England. The discovery made by Guillam's assistant, Felix Taverner, that none of the files taken home by Fennan in the last six months was secret causes Smiley to doubt Elsa's story. It also appears odd to him that Frey's name is recorded quite openly in Fennan's diary and that Mundt did not leave England until some time after murdering Scarr. Re-examination of the information available to him leads Smiley to the conclusion that Elsa Fennan is in fact the spy and that Fennan was killed to prevent him exposing her. In order to take the case further Smiley needs to reactivate contact between Elsa and her controller. Thus, acting on the assumption that Dieter Frey will not have changed his 'tradecraft', Smiley employs their old wartime technique for arranging emergency meetings. His trick works and Dieter joins Elsa in the stalls of the Sheridan Theatre in Hammersmith on February 15. Discovering that he is the victim of deception, Dieter Frey murders Elsa Fennan and is subsequently killed by Smiley while resisting arrest. (*CD*).

This dramatic incident does not, however, bring the sequence of events involving East German Intelligence to a conclusion. In 1961 Alec Leamas's hitherto successful Berlin network is systematically destroyed by the Abteilung (East German Intelligence) under the leadership of Hans-Dieter Mundt, a process which is completed by the shooting of Karl Riemeck as he tries to escape to West Berlin in October 1961. After Leamas's return to England in March 1961, Control, who succeeded Maston as head of the Circus following the Fennan case, invites him to take part in a plan to eliminate Mundt. In its essentials Control's scheme is simple. Leamas will pretend to be completely disaffected with the Circus in the hope that East German Intelligence will consider him a potential traitor. Once recruited, Leamas will supply information on an Operation entitled Rolling Stone which will discredit Mundt by proving that he is working for the British. (*SC*)

After an elaborate charade during which Leamas leaves the Circus in disgrace and descends into drunkenness and poverty before eventually being imprisoned for a brutal attack on a grocer named Ford, the East Germans make their approach in the spring of 1962. Initial contact is made by Bill Ashe and Leamas is then taken by a more senior operative, Kiever, to Holland, where he is questioned by the seasoned professional, Peters. The first indication that all is not as Leamas assumes is given when he discovers that Control has listed him as wanted for offences under the Official Secrets Act. This causes Peters to insist that the interrogation be transferred to East Germany. Puzzled as he is by the turn of events, Leamas continues to act according to Control's instructions. The East Germans are convinced by Leamas's account of Operation Rolling Stone and so Fiedler, the Head of Counter Intelligence for the Abteilung, takes steps to bring Mundt, whom he has long suspected of treachery, to justice. During the trial Mundt is able to produce as a witness Leamas's former girl friend, Liz Gold, who provides evidence of extensive involvement by the Circus in Leamas's affairs long after he supposedly lost all contact with the organization. Now that his collusion with Control has become obvious Leamas confesses in the hope that Liz Gold might be spared punishment. As a result Fiedler rather than Mundt is discredited. (*SC*)

At this point Leamas realizes Control's actual intentions. Far from escaping from England after murdering Fennan and Scarr, Mundt had been captured by British Intelligence and persuaded to act as a double-agent. He passed information through Riemeck, having recruited him specifically for this role. Mundt's subsequent success in destroying Leamas's networks was the result of information given to him by Control who was anxious to increase his double agent's prestige and hence his access to East German secret material. However, Fiedler's suspicions quickly endangered this most valuable source and Control concocted a plan by means of which Leamas, while trying to destroy Mundt, would actually discredit Fiedler. The planting of information which would prove Leamas's complicity with the Circus was not dependent on him actually becoming involved with Liz Gold. A Circus agent at the Labour Exchange named Pitt ensured that Leamas took a job that brought him, at least briefly, into contact with Liz. After that an affair could have been invented and Circus contacts with Liz still be made. She was chosen for this role in Control's plans because, as a member of the Communist Party, she would be likely to accept the invitation to visit East Germany that made her available for the trial. (*SC*)

Because Mundt is in the employ of the British he arranges for Leamas's escape from East Germany. At Leamas's insistence he also allows Liz Gold to go free but as they try to cross the Berlin Wall, Liz Gold is shot down, presumably because she is a potential source of embarrassment to the Circus. Now totally disillusioned with British Intelligence and its expedient tactics, Leamas also allows himself to be shot. (*SC*)

During the rest of Control's reign, which lasts until 1972, the Circus continues to direct its energies towards a wide variety of targets. Alleline moves from South America to India, where he has some success in recruiting agents, and then in 1965 to Egypt as Haydon's replacement. Collins continues to operate in South East Asia and spends five years in Northern Thailand and three in Vientiane, Laos. After completing his tour of duty in the Middle East, Haydon becomes involved in negotiations with the Americans. During the early 1960s Peter Guillam develops networks in French North Africa. Blackmail and bribery operations take the 'scalphunter', Ricki Tarr, to Brazil in 1964 and Spain in 1965. Smiley's talents are largely subdued by the demands of schemes devised by Control. Nevertheless, in 1966 he manages to buy a report from the Toka (Japanese Intelligence) which is later to prove very useful in identifying Karla's techniques for employing deep-penetration agents. New recruits help to broaden still further the scope of Circus operations. Roy Bland, functioning as Smiley did in the 1930s under academic cover, spies for eight years in Poland, Czechoslovakia, Bulgaria, Hungary and the Soviet Union, and sets up networks which include Aggravate (in Czechoslovakia), Plato (Hungary) and Contemplate (Georgia and the Ukraine). Concern with the emergence of the Communist Chinese threat inspires the recruitment of agents, including Phoebe Wayfarer in about 1962, charged with breaking into the 'Peking–Hong Kong shuttle' and so getting a foothold on the Chinese mainland. Toby Esterhase, employed initially as a 'watcher' and 'listener', is first found in action in 1965 working with Peter Guillam against Belgian arms dealers in Berne. The effort against the East Germans continues under the leadership of Paul Skordeno. (*TT; HS*)

Despite all this activity the Circus enjoys little success during the time Control is head. Alleline's involvement in an abortive American-inspired coup brings to an end his efforts in the Middle-Eastern sphere; Guillam's French North African networks are blown in 1965; and in the early 1970s Roy Bland's Belgrade network is wrecked and the best Soviet Source in

East Berlin is killed. This series of failures is compounded by a scandal in
Portugal and the collapse of the despatch box system used for Operation
Gadfly. (*TT*)

Blame for the poor performance of British Intelligence is directed
largely at Control. There is some justification for this in that he often
seems more interested in conducting private feuds than in collecting
intelligence. In the mid-1960s, for example, Control becomes involved in
Operation Mayfly, a rather inglorious plot to destroy 'the Department', a
rival but feeble branch of the Intelligence Service with a mandate to attack
military targets. There is also a suggestion that Control's hand lies behind
the disastrous conclusion of Percy Alleline's Egyptian adventures.
Certainly he directs considerable energy towards the frustration of
Alleline's efforts to function effectively as Operational Director, a position
he occupies in the late 1960s and early 1970s. However, as becomes
evident only after Control's death, the repeated frustration of British
Intelligence initiatives during the 1960s is mainly the result of Bill
Haydon's treachery. Although overseas postings limit Haydon's opportunities between 1961 and 1965, he is particularly active after then and
passes information through Polyakov, a 'Moscow Centre' agent operating
under diplomatic cover. Haydon is presumably responsible for the failure
of the North African and Belgrade networks and the death of the Circus's
East Berlin Source. His own intelligence efforts, as Smiley notes later,
always promise more than they accomplish and it is obvious that he travels
to Washington with the intention of sabotaging rather than fostering
British–American relations. One of the most damaging of all Haydon's
betrayals occurs when he takes advantage of the alterations of 1966 to plant
hidden microphones throughout the Circus headquarters. He further
weakens the Service by encouraging the promotion of incompetent
officers such as Tufty Thesinger and by contriving to hinder or destroy
the careers of those who pose a threat to his subversive efforts. Guillam is a
notable victim of Haydon's efforts. (*LW; TT; HS*)

Control eventually realizes that there is a traitor within the ranks of the
Circus and, although slowly dying, he takes on the task in 1971 of
discovering his identity. It is this knowledge rather than his long-
established antipathy towards Percy Alleline that explains Control's lack
of enthusiasm for the apparently invaluable intelligence material entitled
Witchcraft that Alleline begins to receive from Source Merlin at the end of
1971. As Control correctly assumes, the Soviet mole within the Circus has
created Witchcraft to serve his own ends. Witchcraft is useful to Haydon
because it increases the likelihood that the manipulable Alleline will be the
next head of the Circus, gives 'Moscow Centre' control of all material

received by British Intelligence, promises future access to American secrets, and facilitates meetings with Polyakov who functions at once as Haydon's own link with Karla and the source of the Witchcraft product. Control can do little to halt Alleline's cultivation of Source Merlin without revealing his suspicions of treachery within the ranks of the Circus and so he allows Witchcraft to grow throughout 1972 while pressing on with his own investigations. (*TT*)

By October 1972 Control has narrowed his list of suspects to Alleline, Bland, Esterhase, Haydon and Smiley. Before he can make further progress, Haydon, who has managed to keep in touch with his investigations, devises a scheme to destroy Control's career and thereby remove the threat of discovery. The plan centres on a Czech general named Stevcek who, Control learns, has become disillusioned with the Soviet Union and wishes to provide information on the identity of the mole operating within British Intelligence. On October 21, 1972, Control dispatches Jim Prideaux, assisted by Max Habolt, on Operation Testify with instructions to establish contact with Stevcek near Brno, Czechoslovakia. Soviet troops are waiting there for Prideaux. The scandal which follows his capture, which is compounded by the execution of all members of the Aggravate and Plato networks, forces Control to resign. He dies in December of that year. (*TT*)

Control's resignation is accompanied by a considerable reorganization in the Circus, master-minded by Haydon to promote his own interests. Intelligent and loyal officers are either dismissed, like Smiley, Collins, Connie Sachs and Westerby, or removed to fringe positions, like Guillam who is exiled to the 'scalphunter' headquarters at Brixton in South London. A combination of guilt and friendship forces Haydon to arrange Prideaux's repatriation but he is not allowed to rejoin the Service. Alleline, as Haydon has planned, becomes head of the Circus, and he works closely with a small élite, known as 'London Station', which is led by Haydon, Bland and Esterhase and also includes Mo Delaware, Phil Porteous, Paul Skordeno, Spike Kaspar and Nick de Silsky. Under Alleline, the Circus intelligence efforts are limited almost entirely to the development of Witchcraft. The 'lamplighters', who collect Witchcraft material, and the Adriatic Working Party, which processes it, are the only sections of the Circus to grow during this period. By the end of 1973 there are sixty-eight members of the AWP and 308 reports have originated from Source Merlin. The purchase of a 'safe house' in Lock Gardens in April 1973 facilitates meetings with Polyakov who passes along the Witchcraft material carefully prepared by 'Moscow Centre' and collects the genuine secrets provided by Haydon. (*TT*)

'Moscow Centre' and its mole, Bill Haydon, remain in effective control of the Circus until November 1973 when Ricki Tarr, who had supposedly defected in April, turns up and tells Lacon, the Minister's Adviser on Intelligence, Guillam and Smiley a most disturbing story about his encounters with Irina, a Soviet agent, in Hong Kong. The likelihood that Irina's claims are true and that there is a mole in British Intelligence serviced by Polyakov gains support from the failure of the Circus to respond to Tarr's attempts to communicate his findings. Thus, Lacon calls on Smiley, assisted by Mendel and Guillam, to discover the identity of the traitor.

Smiley begins his investigation by checking the accuracy of Tarr's story. An examination of the duty logbooks undertaken surreptitiously by Guillam confirms that Tarr's telegrams were indeed suppressed and Smiley's own interview with Connie Sachs provides corroboration of Irina's claim that Polyakov is really Colonel Viktorov, a graduate of Karla's private training school for spies. A review of Circus files provided by Lacon then gives Smiley a complete picture of the development of Operation Witchcraft and reveals the existence of a 'safe house' in London through which the product is transferred. By comparing Witchcraft files and information on Polyakov's movements Smiley is next able to demonstrate to his own satisfaction that the mole's contact is also the filter through which Witchcraft material passes. Before making use of this crucial information, Smiley examines files and interviews Collins, Habolt, Westerby and Prideaux, in order to paint for himself a complete picture of Operation Testify. He is able to confirm that Prideaux was betrayed, that Polyakov was involved, and that Haydon had advance knowledge of the mission. In one sense this final discovery is crucial in establishing the identity of the mole. In another it advances Smiley's efforts very little because he has always known in his heart that Haydon is guilty. The task now facing Smiley is to trap him. (*TT*)

The interrogation of Guillam at a 'London Station' meeting about his knowledge of Tarr's whereabouts tells Smiley that the mole is unaware that he has already returned to England and communicated his findings. This fortuitous piece of information provides Smiley with the basis for a plan of action. First, he dispatches Tarr to Paris. Then he blackmails Esterhase into revealing the location of the 'safe house'. When Tarr reaches Paris he holds up the Circus 'resident', Steve Mackelvore, and forces him to cable a demand for a meeting with Alleline. As Smiley anticipates this causes Haydon to arrange a 'crash' meeting with Polyakov at the 'safe house', where Smiley, Guillam and Mendel lie in wait for him. After his capture Haydon is confined at 'Sarratt' awaiting deportation to the Soviet Union. However, before the transfer can be arranged he is murdered, almost certainly by Prideaux in revenge for his own betrayal during Operation Testify. (*TT*)

The unmasking of Haydon is followed by the professional ruination of those he deceived. Alleline is sent on extended leave while Bland, Kaspar and de Silsky are dismissed. Esterhase, however, survives, perhaps because he changed sides at the crucial moment. Smiley becomes acting head of the Service and he rehabilitates Guillam and Connie Sachs. Others who serve under his administration include Fawn, who proved his loyalty while guarding Ricki Tarr, and the expert on China, Doc di Salis. Smiley has few resources with which to work as he begins his reign. All funding is frozen in the wake of the Haydon débâcle; the Circus staff has been reduced by three-quarters; overseas outstations, including High Haven, the Circus headquarters in Hong Kong, are closed; every Soviet and Eastern European network is presumed to be blown; domestic outstations are now considered insecure; the Circus itself is torn to pieces by efforts to uncover the listening devices planted by Haydon. (*TT; HS*)

Faced with this situation, Smiley relies on documentary sources to provide him with intelligence data. His technique is to take what he calls 'back-bearings', which involves searching through the files for evidence of intelligence initiatives suppressed during the Haydon years because they posed a threat to Soviet interests. The value of this approach is confirmed in mid-1974 when Connie Sachs uncovers evidence that Haydon halted Sam Collins's investigation into a Soviet 'laundering' operation which moved clandestine funds to the Banque de l'Indochine in Vientiane, Laos. An interview with Collins reveals that the next destination of the money was Indocharter, an air company staffed by Lizzie Worthington and the pilot, Tiny Ricardo, who is now believed to be dead. Payments began in January 1973, rose sharply but were cut off after Collins filed his report. A subsequent search reveals that Haydon went to extraordinary lengths to bury all material connected with the case. (*HS*)

Having confirmed Connie's original suspicions, Smiley begins what is now called Operation Dolphin by tracing the route followed by the 'gold seam' established to replace the one discovered by Collins to its ultimate destination in a numbered account at the South Asian and China Bank in Hong Kong. At this point Jerry Westerby, an 'Occasional' and therefore one of the few agents not blown by Haydon, is sent to Hong Kong under journalistic cover. Once there he blackmails Frost, a bank employee, into revealing that the account in question is a trust fund with a balance of half a million American dollars, beneficiary unknown, opened by Drake Ko, a leading Hong Kong citizen. Smiley's conclusion is that the fund is being used to fund a mole, perhaps Ko himself. Westerby also reports having seen Ko in the company of a blonde European woman. Although she has changed her name to 'Liese Worth', this woman is soon identified as Lizzie Worthington, formerly of Indocharter. Phoebe Wayfarer provides Craw, the journalist and Circus agent, with further information on Lizzie. (*HS*)

After manipulating the Intelligence Steering Committee into providing him with the funds needed to take the case further, Smiley focuses his investigations on Lizzie Worthington. Lizzie's former husband, Peter Worthington, and her parents, Nunc and Cess Pelling, provide him with complete details of her background. Smiley also discovers from the Pellings that, while in Vientiane, Lizzie worked in a secret capacity for Sam Collins. Armed with this knowledge Smiley is able to persuade Collins to admit that Lizzie carried drugs for him as part of a low-level intelligence operation. In the hope that Collins's earlier relationship with Lizzie Worthington will prove useful, Smiley allows him to rejoin the Circus. A parallel investigation is made of Drake Ko. An interview with the Reverend Hibbert, a former missionary to Shanghai who was virtually a father to Ko in his childhood, not only yields considerable information on Ko's background but also uncovers the existence of a brother, Nelson. (*HS*)

At this point, an element of urgency is introduced into the case. American narcotics agents inform Smiley that they wish to investigate Ko for smuggling drugs into Red China and are willing to hold off for only ten to twelve weeks while British Intelligence conducts its enquiries. Although they put his Operation into jeopardy, the narcotics agents also prove useful to Smiley by telling him that Ricardo, who was hired by Ko to pilot his plane into China but failed to complete the mission, is still alive and by inadvertently providing evidence that, not only is Nelson Ko, rather than his brother, Karla's mole but that Drake is trying to get him out of China. Smiley's theory that Ricardo's flight to China involved the rescue of Nelson rather than drug-smuggling gains support from the subsequent discovery that Tiu, Ko's right-hand man, visited Shanghai – where Nelson lives – six weeks before the intended date of the flight and did not purchase the Beechcraft in which the journey was to be undertaken until two weeks later. Complete confirmation is received when di Salis's investigations turn up Nelson's full history. Two facts are particularly significant. First, Nelson was recruited for Soviet Intelligence by Karla's 'talent spotter', Bretlev, while studying in Leningrad. Second, the payments to Drake Ko began immediately after Nelson's rehabilitation from the disgrace he suffered during the Cultural Revolution and grew as his access to secret information increased. (*HS*)

Smiley's first response to the pressure put on him by the narcotics agents is to increase his strength on the front line by sending Collins to Hong Kong. However, his main problem is to persuade Drake Ko to take action before the deadline imposed by the Americans. In order to begin to 'shake the tree', as he calls it, Smiley directs Jerry Westerby to establish contact with Lizzie Worthington. In the course of his meeting with Lizzie, during much of which Tiu is also present, Westerby reveals a knowledge of Ricardo's continued existence, of the Beechcraft and of the 'gold seam'. The subsequent murder of Frost demonstrates that Westerby's ploy has indeed succeeded in disturbing Ko. To maintain the pressure Smiley next sends Westerby on a journey through South East Asia in pursuit of Charlie Marshall, whom Lizzie Worthington has accidentally revealed as Ricardo's friend and fellow pilot with Indocharter. After trailing him through Bangkok in Thailand and Phnom Penh and Battambang in Cambodia, Westerby eventually runs Charlie Marshall to ground in an opium den in Phnom Penh. The main point of questioning Marshall is to discover Ricardo's present whereabouts and to provide Ko with more grounds for concern, but Westerby also acquires considerable information about the relationship between Charlie Marshall, Ricardo and Lizzie Worthington, about the proposed flight into China, and about the agreement whereby Ko spared Ricardo from the consequences of failing to complete his mission into China so long as Lizzie agreed to be his mistress. He further learns for the first time of Lizzie's past connection with Sam Collins. (HS)

Although Circus 'listeners' are able to report that Charlie Marshall has told Tiu of his encounter with Westerby, nothing happens for five weeks. Then Ko takes to the water. To ensure that Ko remains firm in his apparent decision to act, Smiley sends Westerby to North East Thailand where he makes contact with Ricardo. Under the pretence of wishing to involve Ricardo in a plot to blackmail Ko, Westerby makes it obvious that he has a full knowledge of the past attempts to get Nelson out of China. At this time Smiley also instructs Sam Collins to blackmail Lizzie Worthington into agreeing to work against Ko. (HS)

Tiu's almost immediate departure for mainland China demonstrates the success of Westerby's efforts and his role in the Operation is now complete. He is instructed to return to London while Smiley, Guillam and Fawn travel to Hong Kong where, with the assistance of American Intelligence under the leadership of Martello, they hope to bring the case to its conclusion. However, affection for Lizzie Worthington and the conviction that she is in a most vulnerable position persuade Westerby that he must disobey orders and go back to Hong Kong. The discovery of the body of his friend Luke, obviously killed by Tiu in mistake for himself, confirms Westerby's growing conviction that too many innocent people have been sacrificed to the goals of the Operation and he quickly makes contact with Lizzie Worthington in an effort to save her. He is captured by British Intelligence at Lizzie's apartment but escapes soon after armed with the information, let slip by Peter Guillam, that plans are afoot to seize Nelson Ko as he enters Hong Kong. Questioning of Lizzie Worthington provides Westerby with the information Collins has extracted from her: Ko plans to bring his brother out of China by fishing junk and to make a landing on Po Toi, the most southerly of the Hong Kong islands, during the festival of Tin Hau on May 4, 1975, thus repeating the method by which he (Drake) escaped from China himself in 1951. (*HS*)

Westerby travels out to Po Toi where, after disabling Tiu, he offers Ko a deal: he will represent Nelson's interests with British Intelligence if Ko will release his hold on Lizzie Worthington. Ko is agreeable, but there is no hope of Westerby's plan working because British and American Intelligence are aware not only of Nelson's progress to Po Toi but also of Westerby's. As Nelson lands, their agents descend from helicopters to seize him and one of them, probably Fawn, shoots and kills Westerby. At this point it emerges that while Smiley has been concentrating on the capture of Nelson Ko, Saul Enderby, officially a Whitehall linkman with the Circus, has been plotting with the Americans to give them the first opportunity to interrogate Nelson Ko in return for their support for his ambitions to be head of the Service. Consequently, at the moment of his greatest success Smiley is ousted from office. Connie Sachs soon follows him into retirement and Guillam returns to exile with the 'scalphunters' in Brixton. Collins, however, who seems to have been involved in the plot against Smiley, profits from the change of leadership and becomes Enderby's Operational Director. (*HS*)

Although Smiley's major efforts during 1974–75 are concentrated on Operation Dolphin, he also pays some attention to Karla's activities on another front. Oleg Kirov, a Soviet diplomat transferred to the Paris Embassy in June 1974, is soon identified by General Vladimir, a Circus agent and member of the Riga Group of Baltic nationalists, as Oleg Kursky, a man with a history of intelligence activities. Otto Leipzig, a freelance agent of Estonian background who was friendly with Kursky during their student days before being betrayed by him, is given the task of renewing their relationship. His goal is to blackmail Kursky and, although he does not get an opportunity to do this, he does receive some interesting information. While drunk Kursky admits that he was sent to

Paris by Karla to prepare a false biography for a female agent to be infiltrated into France. The case is an intriguing one because the use of Kursky, a foolish man with little grasp of espionage technique, seems to confirm recent reports that Karla has been behaving erratically. However, in April or May 1975, while Smiley is absent in Hong Kong, Enderby gives orders to abandon the case. (*SP*)

Little is known of Circus activities during its first three years under Enderby's leadership. The success of Operation Dolphin leads to an increase in funds and both the 'scalphunters' and the 'lamplighters' are revived but an unsympathetic Labour Government brings to a halt the kind of enterprises in which these two groups specialize, such as blackmail, 'listening', and surveillance, and by 1978 they are virtually defunct. Operations aimed at Soviet and Commonwealth targets are also greatly restricted by Government policy and Enderby's main energies seem to be directed towards fostering a closer relationship with the Americans. However, on August 4, 1978 the case suppressed by Enderby in 1975 resurfaces. (*HS; SP*)

On this date Kursky approaches a Russian *émigrée*, Maria Ostrakova, and offers to arrange a reunion with the daughter she left behind in the Soviet Union. Arrangements are made but Ostrakova is soon convinced that the girl in question is not her daughter. Therefore, she writes to her dead husband's old friend, General Vladimir, seeking help. Vladimir is now living in London under the name Miller and has retired from intelligence work. Nevertheless, the letter reaches him through the medium of a fellow Estonian freedom-fighter, Mikhel. The connection with Kursky's activities of three years ago is obvious and Vladimir enlists Otto Leipzig to re-establish contact with Kursky. Leipzig entices Kursky into a 'honey-trap' at a sex club in Hamburg run by his friend Kretzschmar. Photographs taken of Kursky in sexually compromising situations persuade him to give a full account of his intelligence activities which is taped. Otto leaves the tapes and a copy of Ostrakova's letter, which Vladimir has forwarded to him, with Kretzschmar and gives instructions that they are to be handed over only if the claimant can produce the other half of a postcard which he also gives to his friend. A negative of the blackmail photograph is carried to London by Villem Craven, a long-distance lorry driver and friend of Vladimir. (*SP*)

After receiving the negative on October 13, Vladimir phones the Circus to arrange a meeting with Smiley, his former case officer. Smiley has, of course, retired and Vladimir's call is not taken seriously. Nevertheless, a young probationer, Mostyn, is assigned to meet Vladimir at a 'safe flat' near Hampstead Heath in North London. While walking across the Heath to keep his rendezvous, Vladimir is murdered by 'Moscow Centre' agents. It seems likely that he was betrayed by Mikhel, who must have opened Ostrakova's letter. Ostrakova herself is the target the next day of an unsuccessful assassination attempt. Vladimir's death is the source of some embarrassment to the Circus since contacts with members of exile groups are banned under the restrictions imposed by the Labour Government. Therefore, Lacon calls on Smiley to dispose of the affair quietly and unofficially but because a conversation with Mostyn reveals that Vladimir claimed to have two pieces of evidence damaging to Karla, Smiley decides to begin investigations of his own. (*SP*)

His initial efforts are aided by a receipt for a minicab journey found on Vladimir's body and a second letter from Ostrakova delivered to Vladimir's flat the day after his death. Returning to the scene of the murder, Smiley quickly discovers the photographic negative which is one of Vladimir's proofs. Before developing it he traces the cab ride to its destination at Villem Craven's house. Villem directs him on to Mikhel and Mikhel to Esterhase. Smiley visits Esterhase after developing the negative. From Villem Smiley learns that the negative originates from Hamburg and from Mikhel he finds out about Ostrakova's first letter. Esterhase, however, proves to be the most useful source of information. He tells Smiley that Vladimir tried to recruit him for the task eventually performed by Villem Craven and revealed to him during their meeting that Karla is trying to 'make a legend' for a girl and is once again behaving erratically. This information, of course, immediately alerts Smiley to the events of three years ago. Esterhase also identifies Otto Leipzig as the source of the negative and as one of the male figures in the photograph. It seems obvious to Smiley at this point that Kursky is the other. Smiley completes his domestic investigations by visiting Connie Sachs in order to refresh his knowledge of the earlier Operation directed against Kursky and to develop his theory that, far from being an agent, the girl that Karla is trying to infiltrate into the West is his own daughter, who has a history of mental illness. (*SP*)

Smiley's next destination is Hamburg where Kretzschmar supplies details of the 'honey-trap' and directs him on to Otto Leipzig's houseboat. When Smiley reaches Otto at a water camp outside Hamburg he is already dead, brutally murdered by Karla's agents. He is able to discover, however, what they missed: the torn half of the postcard which, in accordance with the techniques used by Vladimir's networks in the past, will provide access to hidden information. Since Kretzschmar's manner during their meeting had indicated that he was reluctantly holding back evidence, Smiley visits him once again, and hands over the half postcard.

It matches the half held by Kretzschmar and he therefore gives Smiley the package containing the tapes and Ostrakova's letter. (*SP*)

Anxiety about Ostrakova's safety sends Smiley to Paris where, after removing her from danger, he cables his findings to Enderby. At a subsequent meeting with Enderby in London, Smiley reviews the evidence of the tapes. These reveal that a Soviet diplomat in Berne, named Grigoriev, receives money paid by Karla to finance a mysterious girl, code name 'Komet'. Smiley does not express his conviction that she is Karla's daughter but points out that they now have considerable evidence that Karla has been acting in an extremely irregular way and has become susceptible to blackmail. He then persuades Enderby to mount an operation designed to gather still more evidence of Karla's unofficial activities with the intention of forcing him to defect. Some weeks pass while Smiley completes his preparation and Esterhase, recalled from retirement, puts together a team of 'pavement artists'. Smiley then travels to Berne where, after collecting evidence of his illegal receipt of funds, he blackmails Grigoriev into providing final proof that the girl called 'Alexandra Ostrakova', whose financial affairs he is managing, is in actuality Karla's daughter, Tatiana, and not Maria Ostrakova's daughter, Alexandra. After visiting Tatiana at the clinic near Berne where she is being treated for mental illness, Smiley moves on to Berlin where he observes Karla respond to the demand that he defect. It is now mid-December of 1978 and, with this major intelligence victory over the Soviet Union, information about the history of the Circus terminates. (*SP*)

Chronology
of Major Operations

The following chronologies of the five major Circus operations provide a greater understanding of how the Circus – and its enemies – plan their various moves and interpret the day-to-day events. These detailed chronologies cover the Fennan Case (from *Call for the Dead*), the Fiedler–Mundt Operation (*The Spy Who Came in from the Cold*), the Haydon Case (*Tinker, Tailor, Soldier, Spy*), Operation Dolphin (*The Honourable Schoolboy*) and the Karla Case (*Smiley's People*).

THE FENNAN CASE

Evidence about the dating of this case is quite detailed but sometimes contradictory and there is even some question about the year in which it occurs. These minor discrepancies do not suspend belief in the general documentation given. Elsa Fennan's claim that her association with Dieter Frey, which began in 1955, has lasted five years clearly places the case some time in 1960. During the Fiedler–Mundt Operation Leamas states that Mundt left England in 1959. Reference to the perpetual calendar chart in *Whitaker's Almanac* is no help in this instance because January 2 did not fall on a Monday, as claimed, in either 1959 or 1960. Because of the lack of definitive evidence, Elsa Fennan's version will be accepted since she is closer to the events under consideration. The dates at which the case begins and ends can be firmly fixed. Smiley interviews Samuel Fennan on January 2 and Dieter Frey kills Elsa Fennan on February 15. However, if January 2 had been a Monday, February 15 must have been a Wednesday, not a Tuesday or a Thursday as stated at different times. In between these dates there are a number of major problems of chronology. First, if Smiley remains in hospital for three weeks prior to being allowed visitors and Scarr is murdered on that day (thus, January 25, 1960), he cannot have died three weeks before Mundt leaves England since this must occur around February 6. Second, based on the evidence available it would seem that the investigation conducted by Guillam and Mendel as Smiley lies in his hospital bed is completed in one day and that Smiley is released from hospital on Saturday, January 28. His subsequent interview with Elsa Fennan and the sequence of events which follows, terminating in him realizing she is a spy, sending her the 'code' postcard and observing her response, seem to cover only two days. This is of course impossible if Elsa's meeting with Frey, which takes place five days later, occurs on February 15. Because of these various discrepancies in dating the following chronology is extremely tentative for events occurring after January 25 and is based on the assumption that the documents available to us gloss over a number of time lapses.

January 1955	Dieter Frey recruits Elsa Fennan for East German Intelligence.
1956	The East German Steel Mission is established.
	Mundt begins his car-rental arrangement with Adam Scarr.
?Monday, January 2, 1960	Smiley interviews Samuel Fennan; Frey sees them together.
Tuesday, January 3	The East German Steel Mission closes.
	Samuel Fennan sends a letter to Smiley requesting a meeting on January 4.
	Elsa Fennan attends the Weybridge Repertory Theatre.
	Samuel Fennan requests an early morning call from the telephone exchange.
	Mundt murders Samuel Fennan and collects the music case left by Elsa at the Weybridge Rep.
Wednesday, January 4	Frey leaves England.
	Smiley interviews Elsa Fennan and answers Samuel Fennan's early morning call.
	Samuel Fennan's letter arrives at Smiley's office.
	Smiley resigns.
	Smiley encounters an intruder in his house.
	Smiley and Mendel visit Scarr's garage where Smiley is attacked and Mendel learns about Scarr's car-rental arrangement with 'Blondie'.
Saturday, January 7	Mendel retires from the police force.
Wednesday, January 25	Smiley recovers sufficiently to see Mendel.

Thursday, January 26	Smiley talks to Guillam about the East German Steel Mission.
	Scarr's body is discovered in the Thames.
Friday, January 27 to	Mendel visits the Weybridge Rep.
Friday, February 3	Guillam supplies photographs that identify Smiley's attacker as Mundt, a member of the Steel Mission, and his superior, Frey, as Smiley's wartime intelligence colleague.
Saturday, February 4	Guillam visits Weybridge Rep. and identifies Elsa Fennan's companion as Mundt.
	Smiley, now released from hospital, dines with Mendel and Guillam and recounts his past acquaintance with Frey.
Sunday, February 5	Smiley interviews Elsa Fennan who indicts her husband as a spy.
Monday, February 6	Mundt leaves England.
Tuesday, February 7	Guillam discovers that Fennan has been taking home only unclassified files.
Friday, February 10	Smiley sends a 'code' postcard to Elsa Fennan as if from Frey.
Saturday, February 11	Elsa Fennan responds to the card by sending a ticket for the Sheridan Theatre to Frey.
Wednesday (referred to as a Tuesday or Thursday), February 15	Elsa Fennan and Frey meet at the Sheridan Theatre where he kills her.
Thursday, February 16	Smiley kills Frey.
Sunday, February 19	Smiley, Mendel and Guillam meet again for dinner and Smiley reviews the case.

THE FIEDLER–MUNDT OPERATION

As with the Fennan case so there is some confusion about the dating of events during the Fiedler–Mundt Operation. Most striking is the account of Mundt's career given by Leamas because it fixes the date of his exit from England as 1959 rather than 1960 as suggested in the Fennan case. Information on dates is generally less precise than during the Fennan case, particularly for the period that Leamas spends playing his down-and-out role. He tells Ford, the grocer whom he attacks, that he has lived in the

Bayswater area for four months but evidence that the entire operation is completed by the end of April 1962 makes this unlikely. The list of dates given here takes at face value Leamas's account of Mundt's career and assumes that Liz Gold travelled to East Germany on April 23, 1962, as proposed in her invitation. Any inaccuracies caused by the latter assumption can amount to no more than a day or so. Similarly, the few days Fiedler and Leamas are in Mundt's hands are taken quite arbitrarily to be four. Again, this can be assumed to be accurate within one or two days.

February 6, 1959	Mundt returns to East Germany after agreeing to work for British Intelligence.
1959	Mundt recruits Karl Riemeck as his go-between with British Intelligence.
March or April 1960	Mundt becomes head of the Ways and Means Committee of the Abteilung.
December 1960	Mundt becomes deputy director of Operations for the Abteilung.
January to March 1961	Mundt destroys Leamas's Berlin network.
March 1961	Riemeck is shot while escaping to West Berlin.
	Leamas returns to London.
March to September 1961	Leamas works in the 'Banking Section' of the Circus.
October 1961 to (approx.) January 10, 1962	The period of Leamas's decline. He works for two periods of one week as a personnel manager and an encyclopedia salesman and is employed by the Bayswater Library for Psychic Research for five weeks. He is ill during one of these weeks. The rest of the time, about seven weeks, he is either unemployed or awaiting trial for his attack on Ford.
January 10 to April 10, 1962	Leamas serves his jail sentence.
April 5	Elvira, Riemeck's mistress, is murdered.
April 10	Leamas is released from jail.
	Ashe makes contact with Leamas on behalf of the Abteilung.
	Leamas meets Control.
April 11	Ashe passes Leamas on to Kiever.
April 12	Leamas flies to The Hague where he is interrogated by Peters.

April 13	The interrogation by Peters continues.
April 14	Leamas flies to West Berlin and then travels into East Germany by car. Smiley and Guillam call on Liz Gold.
April 15	Fiedler interrogates Leamas.
April 16	Leamas writes to the banks supposedly involved in Operation Rolling Stone.
April 23	Leamas and Fiedler are arrested by Mundt. Liz Gold travels to Leipzig.
April 27	Leamas and Fiedler are released. Liz Gold is taken to Görlitz to be a witness at Mundt's tribunal.
April 28	Mundt's tribunal is held.
April 29	Leamas and Liz Gold are shot at the Berlin Wall.

THE HAYDON CASE

There are no serious contradictions in the dating of this case but two aspects of it cause problems. First, nowhere in material directly concerned with the Haydon case are the years stated in which Operation Testify takes place and in which Smiley seeks out the mole 'Gerald'. Only by examining material from Operation Dolphin is it possible to establish that they occur in 1972 and 1973 respectively. Reference to *Whitaker's Almanac* supports this dating in that October 21, 1972 and March 31, 1973 do indeed fall on Saturdays as claimed. Second, although clear dates are given for prior events, it is not possible to locate with certainty even the month in which Smiley tracks down Bill Haydon. Separate references to Tarr's trip to Hong Kong as being 'six' and 'seven months ago' place it in October or November. A relevant garage bill places it later than October 9. Because of a number of allusions to Christmas it seems most likely that Smiley's investigation occurs at the end of November. This conclusion is supported by documents relating to Operation Dolphin.

There is considerable information on the sequence of days during which Smiley pursues his quarry and it seems that he actually completes the investigation too quickly to accommodate all the stages described. Beginning on a Friday and establishing the connection between 'Gerald' and Witchcraft the following Tuesday late in the evening, Smiley cannot meet Lacon and Sercombe on the next day and then Collins, Habolt and Westerby on the day after, unless he meets Prideaux on the Friday. However, it is claimed that he meets Prideaux on Thursday. It is possible, but highly unlikely given the general intensity of his actions, that Smiley meets Lacon and Sercombe on Tuesday, one week after establishing the link between 'Gerald' and Witchcraft. It is much more likely, and quite plausible given his speed of movement, that Smiley actually meets Collins, Habolt and Westerby on the same day he meets Lacon and Sercombe. There seems to be a further error in the suggestion that Roach observes Prideaux dig up his gun on Sunday because Prideaux states that it was Tuesday. Since Mendel does not begin the investigations which disturb Prideaux until Tuesday, there seems no reason why he should have retrieved the weapon earlier. Dating for the Haydon case is therefore precise except for the sequence of events covering the final investigation about which there must be an element of deduction.

Summer 1971	Haydon has an affair with Ann Smiley.
October	Haydon draws Alleline into Operation Witchcraft.
April 1972	Witchcraft is firmly established. Control is well embarked on his investigation into the identity of the mole, 'Gerald'.
May	Smiley interviews Esterhase and Bland about their involvement in Witchcraft.
A Tuesday or Wednesday in May or June	Smiley interviews Haydon.
The Monday following	Control flies to Vienna in connection with Stevcek's proposed defection.
Sunday, October 15 (probably)	Control recruits Prideaux to make contact with Stevcek in Czechoslovakia.
Monday, October 16	Prideaux recruits Habolt to help him with the mission.
Thursday, October 19	Control persuades Collins to do 'duty' for Saturday, October 21.
Saturday, October 21	Prideaux travels to Czechoslovakia where he is captured by Soviet troops.
Sunday, October 22	Haydon conducts a cover-up operation.
Tuesday, October 24	Habolt returns safely from Czechoslovakia.
October 26 or 27	Habolt is dismissed from the Service.
November	Control is forced to retire, and Alleline is made head of the Circus. Hankie photographs Polyakov and Connie

	Sachs is dismissed as a result.
	Smiley is dismissed.
December	Collins is dismissed.
	Westerby is dismissed for suggesting Prideaux was betrayed.
December 24	Control is cremated.
February 27, 1973	Approval is given for the purchase of the Witchcraft 'safe house'.
Late March	The house is bought.
March or April	Prideaux is released from captivity.
Saturday, March 31	Tarr flies to Hong Kong to check on a possible Soviet agent.
Sunday, April 1	Tarr observes Boris, his suspect.
Monday, April 2	Tarr makes contact with Irina, Boris's wife.
Wednesday, April 11	Tarr telegraphs the Circus about Irina's offer of information.
Thursday, April 12	Irina is forcibly returned to the Soviet Union.
Saturday, April 14	Tarr finds Irina's diary and flees to Kuala Lumpur, Malaysia.
Late May	Prideaux begins to teach at Thursgood's school.
July	Boris, Irina and Brod ('Ivlov') are executed.
A Friday in November, probably November 17	Tarr tells his story to Lacon, Guillam and Smiley.
Saturday, November 18	Smiley moves into the Hotel Islay.
Saturday, November 18 to Tuesday, November 21	Smiley studies the files.
Monday, November 20	
afternoon	Guillam secretly examines the duty logbooks.
evening	Smiley visits Connie Sachs.
	Mendel locates Prideaux.
Tuesday, November 21	
morning	Mendel goes to Thursgood's.
	Guillam steals the Operation Testify papers from the Circus archives.
late morning	Alleline accuses Guillam of meeting Tarr.
evening	Guillam and Smiley interrogate Tarr

	about his use of passports.
	Smiley tells Guillam about Karla.
	Prideaux digs up gun.
late evening	Smiley connects Witchcraft to the mole 'Gerald'.

Wednesday, November 22

morning	Smiley meets Sercombe and Lacon to reveal his discovery.
lunchtime	Smiley questions Collins about Testify.
early afternoon	Smiley questions Habolt about Testify.
afternoon	Smiley questions Westerby about Testify.
evening	Smiley reads the Prideaux file.

Thursday, November 23

| evening | Smiley questions Prideaux about Testify. Guillam takes Tarr to Liverpool. |

Friday, November 24

morning	Smiley meets Lacon and Sercombe again to discuss the capture of 'Gerald'. Prideaux is absent from school.
afternoon	Smiley forces Esterhase to reveal the location of the 'safe house'. Tarr telegraphs Alleline from Paris.
evening	Smiley traps Haydon in the Lock Gardens 'safe house'.

Saturday, November 25 and Sunday, November 26	Smiley is in limbo.
Monday, November 27 and Tuesday, November 28	Smiley questions Haydon at the 'Nursery', Sarratt.
Tuesday, November 28 evening	Haydon is murdered by Prideaux.

OPERATION DOLPHIN

This case presents only one major problem of dating. If Sam Collins was dismissed from the Circus in December 1972, as is stated in documents concerning the Haydon case, he cannot have been involved in an investigation into an illicit bank account opened in January 1973. Otherwise the general progression of the case is fairly clear and consistent despite a paucity of precise dates and some vagueness about the time lapse between certain events. The detailed chronology of events occurring between Smiley's meeting with American narcotics agents and the capture of Nelson Ko is constructed around two firm dates (the telegram sent to

Craw on February 15, 1975 and Nelson Ko's entry into Hong Kong waters on May 4, 1975) and some precise statements about the number of days lapsing between events. However, some speculation has been necessary and parts of the reconstruction of the entire operation may not be accurate to within a day or so. The dating of Westerby's arrival at the American air base in North East Thailand is based on the claim that this occurs more than a week before his return to Hong Kong on May 3, 1975. In doing this the problem posed by Captain Masters's statement to Westerby that the evacuation of the American Embassy in Saigon (an event which occurred on April 29, 1975) has just taken place has to be ignored. The dating of Nelson Ko's departure from China, which is a consequence of Westerby's activities in Thailand, as April 25 supports the decision to ignore Masters. It can only be presumed that Masters is referring to an earlier stage in the evacuation of Saigon since the complete operation took a number of days.

1972	Lizzie Worthington works in a secret capacity for Sam Collins.
January 1973	Nelson Ko's rehabilitation begins in China.
	A bank account for Nelson Ko is opened in Vientiane, Laos.
January (probably)	Charlie Marshall is employed as a pilot for Indocharter.
February	Marshall refuses to undertake a mission into China for Tiu.
March (probably)	Lizzie Worthington is employed by Indocharter.
July and August	Collins investigates the Vientiane bank account until halted by Haydon.
	The account is closed.
July 6	Tiu meets Nelson Ko in Shanghai.
Early July	Ricardo is engaged for the China mission.
July 20	Tiu buys a Beechcraft.
August 21	Ricardo disappears during his flight into China.
September 2	Ricardo tries to sell information and opium to an American narcotics agent.
Late November	Smiley becomes head of the Circus.
Late Spring 1974	Connie Sachs uncovers evidence of Haydon's interference in Collins's

	investigation into the Vientiane bank account.
June or July	Smiley questions Collins.
September	Hong Kong is identified as the final destination of the 'gold seam'.
	Westerby is called back from his Tuscan home in Italy.
October (probably)	Westerby blackmails Frost.
	Drake Ko's relationship with Lizzie Worthington is discovered.
	Smiley obtains funds to carry the investigation further.
October or November	Craw interviews Phoebe Wayfarer about Drake Ko.
December	Smiley interviews Peter Worthington and her parents, the Pellings, about Lizzie Worthington.
Mid-January, 1975	Connie Sachs and di Salis interview Hibbert about Drake Ko.
Monday, January 13 or 20	Collins re-joins the Circus.
February 7	Smiley and Guillam meet Martello and the American narcotics agents.
February 9	Craw finds out about Tiu's trip to Shanghai in July 1973.
February 11	Esterhase uncovers Tiu's purchase of the Beechcraft.
February 12 to 14	Esterhase travels to the Western Isles in Scotland to investigate Ricardo and Lizzie Worthington's involvement in a scheme to sell whisky.
February 15	Smiley decides on his plan of action and cables Craw.
February 17	Collins leaves for Hong Kong.
Monday, February 24 (probably)	Westerby contacts Lizzie Worthington and begins to 'shake the tree'.
February 28	Westerby sees Collins.
March 3	Di Salis discovers Nelson Ko's complete history.
	Frost is murdered.
March 4	Westerby is ordered to find Charlie Marshall.

	Westerby flies to Bangkok, Thailand.
March 5	Westerby flies to Phnom Penh, Cambodia.
March 6	Westerby makes contact with Charlie Marshall in Battambang, Cambodia, and completes his questioning in Phnom Penh.
March 7	Westerby cables the Circus and flies to Saigon, South Vietnam.
March 8	Charlie Marshall phones Tiu.
March 10	Drake Ko goes to a fortune-teller.
April 16 to 21	Drake Ko takes to the water.
April 21	Westerby meets Ricardo in North East Thailand.
April 22	Westerby contacts the Circus from an American air base in North East Thailand.
April 23	Tiu arranges to visit Shanghai.
April 25	Nelson Ko leaves China.
	Tiu returns to Hong Kong.
	Smiley travels to Hong Kong.
May 3	Westerby returns to Hong Kong.
May 4	Nelson Ko is captured.
	Westerby is shot.
May 18	The 'safe house' (the 'Dolphinarium') prepared for Nelson Ko in Maresfield in Sussex is abandoned.
May or June	Enderby succeeds Smiley as head of the Circus.

THE KARLA CASE

There is a good deal of information on the events that lead up to and follow the murder of General Vladimir and, with some help from *Whitaker's Almanac* calendar references, it is possible to construct a fairly precise chronology. It is much less easy to provide any but a rather general timetable for the second stage of the operation during which Smiley prepares and then executes the plan to force Karla to defect. The precise dates given in this chronology may not be the right ones but the actual days of the week and the time-lapse between events are correct.

| June 1974 | Kursky arrives in Paris. General Vladimir |

	and Leipzig begin an attempt to blackmail him.
April 1975	Enderby orders action against Kursky to cease.
May or June	Vladimir and Leipzig appeal to Smiley for help. Smiley retires from the Circus.
December	Vladimir is expelled from Paris and takes up residence in London.
August 4, 1978	Kursky approaches Ostrakova about a reunion with her daughter, Alexandra.
Early September	Grigoriev is asked by Karla to take care of the affairs of Tatiana ('Alexandra') during her stay at the clinic near Berne.
September 2	Ostrakova writes to Vladimir.
September 4 or 5	Vladimir receives the letter and sends a message to Leipzig in Hamburg through Kretzschmar.
September 5 or 6	Leipzig receives a copy of Ostrakova's letter.
September 8	Leipzig speaks to Vladimir on the telephone.
September 14	Leipzig travels to Paris where he speaks to Ostrakova and re-establishes contact with Kursky.
September 18	Leipzig entices Kursky into a 'honey-trap' in Hamburg and then blackmails him. He gives most of the information to Kretzschmar.
October 1 (probably)	Vladimir tries to persuade Esterhase to make contact with Leipzig in Hamburg.
October 2	Vladimir borrows £50 from Mikhel.
October 4	Kursky is recalled to Moscow.
Monday, October 9	Vladimir recruits Villem Craven to make contact with Leipzig.
October 12	Villem picks up the negative from Leipzig in Hamburg.
October 13	Villem gives the negative to Vladimir. Vladimir is murdered on his way to a meeting with Mostyn. Leipzig is murdered.

October 14	Smiley is called in to perform a cover-up operation. He receives Ostrakova's second letter, finds the negative, interviews Villem and Mikhel, develops the negative. Ostrakova is attacked by Soviet agents.
October 16	Smiley interviews Esterhase and Connie Sachs.
October 17	Smiley travels to Hamburg where he interviews Kretzschmar.
October 18	Smiley discovers Leipzig's dead body and the torn half of the postcard required by Kretzschmar before he will release Leipzig's evidence. Smiley receives the tapes and letter held by Kretzschmar on behalf of Leipzig. Smiley travels to Paris where he rescues Ostrakova and cables Enderby.
October 19 (probably)	Smiley meets Enderby in London.
December 7 (probably)	Smiley travels to Berne, Switzerland.
Friday, December 8	Smiley and Esterhase execute the plan to photograph Grigoriev making his transaction at the bank in Thun. Then they observe his visit to Tatiana.
Sunday, December 10	Grigoriev is blackmailed by Smiley and Esterhase.
Friday, December 15	Smiley visits Tatiana. Smiley sends a letter to Karla demanding his defection.
A few days later	Karla defects.

Hierarchy of the Circus

Little is known of the organizational structure of the Circus before and during the Second World War. All the indications are that a spirit of inspired amateurism prevails and that there is little formal demarcation of function between Steed-Asprey, who is probably the head, and Fielding, Sparke and Jebedee, the Oxbridge academics in charge of Operations. During the war Fielding and Steed-Asprey run a training school near Oxford attended by new recruits such as Alec Leamas. This is presumably a precursor of the 'Nursery' at Sarratt. Nothing is known of other departments or outstations during this period, except for the 'wranglers' whose staff during the war includes Bill Magnus. Once the war is over, however, a much more precise structure emerges which, with variations, particularly after 1974, continues to the present day. Ultimate responsibility for intelligence matters rests with a member of the Cabinet who employs a senior civil servant to keep him closely in touch with the Circus. The Circus itself is organized hierarchically. At the top is a single head, sometimes also known as the Minister's Adviser or the chief. Working closely with him is a small group of senior intelligence officers who are responsible for the functioning of a number of departments and out-stations, of both an operational and bureaucratic nature, which provide back-up services for agents in the field. (*CD; SC; TT*)

Maston's intense concern with the wishes of the Minister suggests that tight governmental control of Circus activities is introduced in the early post-war years. Detailed information on how the government monitors its Intelligence Service is not available until the early 1970s when Miles Sercombe is identified as the Minister responsible and Oliver Lacon, of the Cabinet Office, as his liaison with the Circus. Although Sercombe presumably loses his position as power shifts from Conservative to Labour, Lacon's role as 'head prefect' continues throughout the 1970s. After the Haydon scandal Government attention to the functioning of the Circus intensifies and Smiley, as head, is compelled to deal not just with Lacon but with an Intelligence Steering Committee. The mandate of this committee is to define the scope of Circus activities and it comprises representatives from the Foreign Office led by Saul Enderby, and including Luff, a Parliamentary under-secretary who is a trade union appointment, and Roddy Martindale; the Colonial Office, led by Chris Wilbraham, and including an unnamed Colonial Office lady and a young man called John; the Security Service in the figure of Pretorius; Defence which has two members; and two Treasury bankers including Hammer, a Welshman. By 1978 this committee has been superseded by the Inter-Ministerial Steering Committee, known colloquially as the 'Wise Men', made up of a combination of Westminster and Whitehall interests. (CD; TT; HS; SP)

The first post-war head of the Service is clearly a product of the increased entanglement of the Circus in the machinery of Government, for Maston is a civil servant with no background in intelligence. The limitations of such a choice become evident during the Fennan case and he is replaced in 1960 by Control, an experienced caseman. The next two heads of the Circus, Percy Alleline (November 1972 to November 1973) and George Smiley (November 1973 to May 1975) are also men with considerable experience in espionage. However, Smiley's successor is Saul Enderby, a career ambassador and member of the Foreign Office, who first becomes connected with the Service as a Whitehall linkman. (CD; SC; TT; HS; SP)

Under Maston and Control a good deal of authority is assigned to the senior officers responsible for the major geographical regions between which the Circus espionage activities are divided. These are the Soviet Union, China, 'Satellites' or 'Satellites Four' (other Iron Curtain countries), Africa and South East Asia. Control ensures that the heads of each region keep in close communication with each other and with him by supplementing weekly meetings with continuous informal discussions. Once Alleline becomes head of the Service regionalism is abandoned in favour of lateralism. Under this system a small group of senior officers, known as 'London Station', has a collective responsibility for all operations. The Commander of 'London Station' is Haydon, Bland is second in command and Esterhase is third. The other members are Mo Delaware, Porteous, the head 'housekeeper', Paul Skordeno, and two 'legmen', Spike Kaspar and Nick de Silsky. While this group works closely with Alleline, the head of the Service, it has virtually no communication with other areas of the Circus. (CD; TT)

George Smiley has little use for a system of governance which he recognizes as being created to serve Haydon's treacherous goals; neither does the impoverished state into which the Circus has fallen by the time he becomes head make a revival of regionalism practical. Instead, Smiley returns to something like the informal model of organization with which he is familiar from his pre-war service with the Circus. Power is placed in the hands of those who can meet the needs of the moment – researchers such as Connie Sachs and di Salis, the most skilled of all the 'lamplighters',

Esterhase, intelligent and imaginative newcomers such as Molly Meakin, and men of proven loyalty and dedication such as Guillam and Fawn. Final authority clearly resides in Smiley himself but in most respects this group operates as a team of equals, every one of whom is willing to change his function as required. There is evidence that a more formal structure continues to exist alongside this informal one – the posts of director Western Europe and director Soviet Attack are both identified – but because they have nothing to contribute to the task at hand, such people play no role in directing the affairs of the Circus during Operation Dolphin. (*HS*)

Little is known of the shape the upper reaches of Circus government assume after Enderby becomes head. Sam Collins is his Operational Director but the post seems to be a token one given as a reward for services rendered during Enderby's campaign to oust Smiley. The fact that another of Enderby's supporters, Lauder Strickland, has risen close to the top suggests that, at this stage of its history, the Circus may have become something of a dictatorship and that the second level of administration is occupied by a group of sycophants. (*SP*)

Beneath these higher echelons of government, the Circus is divided into a bewildering number of sections, operational and bureaucratic, which are located at headquarters, in outstations and overseas.

MAIN OPERATIONAL SECTIONS IN BRITAIN

Scalphunters The official name of the scalphunters is Travel and they are formed by Control at Haydon's suggestion to handle 'hit-and-run' jobs too risky for the 'resident' agents. Typical tasks set them include murder, 'crash' blackmail, kidnapping and bribery. Up until 1972 Jim Prideaux is head scalphunter and he is succeeded by Peter Guillam. The scalphunters number about twelve in all including Karl Stack, Ricki Tarr, Cy Vanhofer, Pete Sembrini, Pete Lusty and Fawn. The scalphunter headquarters is an old schoolhouse in Brixton, South London. The importance of the scalphunters declines during Alleline's time as head of the Circus because much of their function is taken over by Toby Esterhase's 'lamplighters', and they are completely abolished as part of the general cutbacks which follow the Haydon scandal. The upswing in the Circus fortunes after Operation Dolphin sees the revival of the scalphunters, again under Guillam, but they cease to have any role to play in the restricted espionage environment created by the Inter-Ministerial Steering Committee known as the 'Wise Men'. (*TT; HS; SP*)

Lamplighters The function of the lamplighters, whose headquarters are at the 'Laundry' in Acton, West London, is to provide support services such as 'watching', 'listening' (electronic surveillance), 'baby-sitting', transport, 'post boxes', and 'safe houses' for 'mainline operations'. At their peak they are a large organization. In 1973, for example, they service 'safe houses and flats' in Lambeth, St James's, Kensington, Camden Town and Hampstead, all in London, and in 1975–76, in their role as 'postmen', they are involved in as many as forty meetings and pick-ups a week. The head lamplighter is Toby Esterhase and those working for him include Max Habolt, Teddie Hankie and Ferguson, the manager of the transport pool. Lamplighters who specialize in surveillance (known as 'pavement artists') include Canada Bill, Harry Slingo, the Sartor brothers, and the Meinertz-hagen girls, a plump female 'watcher', and a stern-looking woman with a son named Edward. The best-known 'listener' is Millie McCraig. The important position occupied by Esterhase in Alleline's administration of 1972–73 ensures a significant increase in the prestige of the lamplighters but they are abolished along with the 'scalphunters' after the fall of Haydon. Only Esterhase, Millie McCraig and a few 'pavement artists' retain their positions. The lamplighters experience a second rise and fall with the success of Operation Dolphin and the introduction of the 'Wise Men'. Only Ferguson survives the cuts imposed by the 'Wise Men'. Whether this situation will continue is made uncertain by the enormous success of the *ad hoc* team of 'pavement artists' gathered together by Esterhase to assist Smiley in the blackmailing of Grigoriev.

The Nursery, Sarratt Located between Rickmansworth and Watford, this is a large country house called Sarratt in the village of that name in Hertfordshire. The training of new recruits and the briefing of agents takes place here. Training includes aspects of 'tradecraft', such as memorization of phone numbers, word codes, contact procedures, use of 'dead letter boxes', relationships with local agents, maintenance of courier routes, as well as combat techniques. The 'charm-school' run by Thatch is particularly concerned with the 'tradecraft' and psychological preparation required by deep-penetration agents and includes amongst its graduates, Roy Bland. The other major function of the Nursery is interrogation and its inquisitors deal with Circus agents returned from missions abroad, such as Max Habolt, defectors, such as Stanley, and captured enemy agents, such as Haydon. Haydon is questioned by a tall limping man and a flabby man with ginger hair. Apart from Thatch and the two inquisitors, only two members of the Sarratt staff have been identified: Craddox and Cranko who are head of Sarratt and reception respectively in 1974. From time to time permanent staff are supplemented by visiting field officers including Smiley, who lectures on 'Agent-Handling in the Field' and Craw, whose topic is 'Agents Who Recruit Themselves'. As part of their cover Sarratt staff live on a housing estate in Watford. The Nursery has a long history and is well-established during the Cold War. However, by 1973 it is in serious decline. The buildings and grounds are falling into decay and discipline is so poor that the staff fail to protect Haydon from Prideaux's fatal attack. Following his discovery of Karla's mole Smiley considers Sarratt to be insecure. Nevertheless, it continues to function and in 1974 provides Westerby with training and briefing prior to his South East Asian mission. (*TT; HS*)

Banking Section This term is not to be confused with Accounts. Whereas the latter department is concerned with everyday Circus finances – salaries, pensions and so on – Banking deals with the financial aspects of espionage activity. Apart from financing agents and operations, it arranges for secret payments to sources abroad and the 'laundering' of dirty money. Because the work of Banking is secret its staff often includes former field agents, such as Alec Leamas. Other members of Banking in 1961 are two women named Thursby and Larrett. In 1973 Lauder Strickland occupies a senior position amongst the Banking staff. (*SC; TT*)

OTHER OPERATIONAL SECTIONS

These sections include the **experimental audio laboratory** in Harlow, Essex; the **stinks-and-bangs school** in Argyll, Scotland; the **water school** on the Helford estuary in Cornwall; the **long-arm radio transmission base** at Canterbury, Kent; the **wranglers** (code-breakers) at Bath, Avon, whose staff includes Bill Magnus. At the Cambridge Circus headquarters other sections cover **coding**, whose staff includes Lord John Landsbury, Ailsa Brimley and Roddy Martindale during the war and later Molly Purcell, Oscar Allitson and Hilary; **interpreters**; **transcribers**, whose head in the late 1970s is a blimpish man; **special travel**, which is concerned with the preparation of false identities; **nuts and bolts** (technical and scientific services); **shoemakers** (forgers), whose staff includes Hyde and Fellowby; **research**, whose staff includes Haggard, the head, and Thruxton, Doolittle, Sachs, di Salis and the scholarly sort who traces Operation Dolphin back to the British seizure of Hong Kong in 1841; **vetting**, for whom Molly Meakin works in 1974–75; **Oddbins**, which is headed by a negligent man in 1978 and whose staff – probationers awaiting overseas postings – includes Mostyn; **duty-officers**, who include Geoff Agate and Mary Masterman; **tradesmen** (outsiders on call for special services) such as Lark the chemist who provide professional assistance as required. (*TT; HS; SP*)

MAJOR NON-OPERATIONAL SECTIONS

Service Departments In order to service an organization of the magnitude of the Circus there is a need for a large number of departments whose role is purely bureaucratic. They concern themselves with the daily functioning of the Cambridge Circus headquarters, pay and pensions, the personal problems of agents, and the storage of documents. The most important of these departments is **Housekeeping** which has responsibility for co-ordinating all bureaucratic activity within the Circus. The issuing of pay cheques, the monitoring of agents' false documents, the enforcement of internal security regulations, and the recording of agents' movements in and out of the Circus are all tasks that fall within the jurisdiction of Housekeeping. The head of the Department is Phil Porteous and his assistant is Diana Dolphin. **Registry** is also a large department since it is responsible for the housing of all case papers and for the safe-keeping of subscription files. The staff of this Department include Miss Bream in 1961 and in 1973 Sal, Juliet and Molly Meakin. A marine named Alwyn is responsible for security. (*SC; TT*)

OTHER NON-OPERATIONAL DEPARTMENTS

Included here are **Special Despatch**, which keeps agents' records; **Resettlement**, which finds jobs for retired agents; **Personnel**, whose staff includes Fawley in 1961; **Accounts**; the **janitors**, who are responsible for monitoring movements within the Circus and whose staff includes Mellows (head in 1973), McCall, MacFadean, and Bryant; the **Mothers**, who include Control's secretary, Ginnie; **secretaries**, including Mary, who works for Guillam, and Ellen, who works for Prideaux; **maintenance**, whose staff includes Astrid; the **shuttle**, which is responsible for transporting documents between Cambridge Circus, Brixton, Acton, Sarratt and the Admiralty. The Circus banks with Blatt and Rodney and employs a doctor who is located in Manchester Square. (*SC; TT; HS*)

The final purpose of all those departments, both operational and bureaucratic, is to provide support to intelligence officers working in the field. In 1974 there are 600 field agents including 150 behind the Iron Curtain. They can be divided into the following categories. (*HS*)

Legal (above-the-line) Residents These are agents who operate abroad under the official or semi-official protection of a position with a British embassy or consulate, the BBC, or British Airways. Circus agents who work under diplomatic cover include Steve Mackelvore and Peter Guillam, both head resident in Paris, Tufty Thesinger in Hong Kong,

Peter Jensen in Helsinki, Ben, a radio operator in Paris, and Anstruther, Guillam's clerk in Paris. (*TT; HS; SP*)

Illegal (below-the-line) Residents Such agents lack the protection of an official position and have to rely on the plausibility of their cover identity for protection. They include at various times George Smiley, operating as a lecturer in Germany, Sam Collins as a trader in South East Asia, Craw as a journalist in Hong Kong, and Roy Bland as a lecturer in Eastern Europe. (*CD; TT; HS*)

Occasionals A group of part-time agents who carry out their secret duties under cover of their regular occupations. They include the journalist, Jerry Westerby. (*HS*)

Local Agents Part of the task of Circus agents working abroad is to create networks of foreign nationals who will have access to information not available to outsiders. Such networks include Leamas's Berlin networks in the 1950s, and three created by Roy Bland: Aggravate and Plato, which operate in Hungary and Czechoslovakia, and Contemplate, which is based in Georgia and the Ukraine. The Czech members of Aggravate are Pribyl, his wife and his brother-in-law and of Plato, Landkron, Eva Krieglova and Hanka Bilova. Contemplate is led by a husband and wife, the Churayevs. Individual local agents include Phoebe Wayfarer, who works for Craw in Hong Kong.

Freelance Agents Although they lack any official connection with the Circus, freelance agents can be a useful source of information. There are problems of loyalty and reliability associated with their use, however. The most notorious of the freelance agents employed by the Circus is Otto Leipzig. (*SP*)

Cambridge Circus
Headquarters

The Circus headquarters have been located at Cambridge Circus in London since 1945. The exact building is not identified but agents' patterns of entry suggest it is the one which runs along Charing Cross Road with its front on Cambridge Circus and its back on what was New Compton Street (no longer an actual street). However, the physical characteristics of the Circus – its five floors of corner turrets – are closer to those of one diagonally opposite on the curve between Charing Cross Road and Shaftesbury Avenue and now housing the Midland Bank. In 1960 the interior of the Circus is bright and well-maintained but by 1972 it has become scruffy. Its run-down condition is evident as soon as one enters the dingy lobby with its mouldering telephones, dated posters and old, rattling lifts. The condition of the building deteriorates still further in 1974 as a result of the destruction wrought during attempts to uncover microphones planted by Haydon. (*CD; TT; HS*)

In accordance with the generally hierarchical organization of the Circus, the offices of the head and his closest advisers are to be found at the top of the building on the fifth floor, with other senior officers on the fourth floor. The importance attached to location is made very clear by Collins's insistence that his office be moved from the fourth to fifth floor when he rejoins the Circus during Operation Dolphin. Similarly, the fact that Guillam is given an office on the first floor in 1972 is an indication of his declining prestige within the service. (*TT; HS*)

The most important room on the fifth floor, the head's office, is long and narrow. During Control's occupancy and Smiley's the door is unmarked and the interior bare. Alleline, however, adds a grandiose chair and a conference table in an attempt to give the room some dignity. Immediately outside this office is a long, low-ceilinged, brown-carpeted ante-room, where the head's secretaries work. The office occupied by Smiley prior to Operation Testify also opens onto this Secretariat. His is a plain room decorated with old prints of Oxford. Other rooms on the fifth floor include the conference or rumpus room and the senior officers' lavatory. These both open onto a long corridor with several turns which runs from the ante-room to the top of the stairs leading down to the fourth floor. (*TT; HS*)

The fourth floor is busy and crowded except during the time of 'London Station' when access is restricted by a janitor stationed at the lift. The famous hexagonal pepper-pot room occupied for many years by Haydon can be found near the lift, just beyond the coffee machine introduced in 1973. Further on in a last narrow corridor stands what is Bland's office until his dismissal, 'Banking Section' and the offices of Porteous and his assistant Diana Dolphin of 'Housekeeping'. The men's toilets are close to Diana's office and opposite them is the duty-officer's room which doubles in the daytime as a women's rest-room. During Operation Dolphin Guillam, di Salis and Connie Sachs all have offices on the fourth floor. The second floor is given over mainly to the 'wranglers' and to radio and code rooms, but it is also the home of 'Satellites Four' in 1961. Guillam's office is on the first floor in 1972 prior to his exile to the 'scalphunters' at Brixton. (*SC; TT; HS*)

In the early 1960s Registry and its archives are on the fourth floor but by 1972 they have been moved to the back of the building on the first floor. Access is by a separate front door in Charing Cross Road which leads into a lobby housing a telephone and a security desk and then, up four steps, into the reading room. The main hall where files are held is at the far end of the reading room. By 1974 Registry has either moved or expanded into the basement which at this time also provides space for Millie McCraig, the head 'listener'. (*SC; TT*)

Note

The Circus chapter – History, Chronology, Hierarchy and Headquarters – on pages 12–49 is indexed separately (*see* page 198). Entries in this **Who's Who** biographical section for which additional information is given in the **Circus** chapter are indicated with the following cross-reference: [CIRCUS INDEX].

The Circus book titles given as source references are indicated by their initials within brackets. *See* **Source References** note on page 6.

Jargon terms are marked with an asterisk and a complete list of such words appears under 'jargon' on pages 102–104.

WHO'S WHO

Biographies of People, Places and Particularities in the Secret World of John le Carré

*above-the-line Intelligence officer (known as a legal resident) who operates in a foreign country under the protection of an official or semi-official position, usually in an embassy, national airline or similar institution. (*HS*)

Abteilung Although officially titled the Department for the Protection of the People, the East German Intelligence Service is usually referred to as the Abteilung. Little is known of its activities prior to 1956. However, it is generally accepted in the intelligence world that the Abteilung pursues only insignificant targets and that possibilities for more ambitious enterprises are hindered by the use of a cumbersome operational procedure by means of which agents in the field take their orders from a controller who remains in East Germany. The limitations of this thesis become evident in 1956 when the Abteilung mounts a significant espionage operation against Britain. Two agents, Dieter Frey and Hans-Dieter Mundt, are introduced into the country under cover as members of the East German Steel Mission, located in Belsize Park, London. Their task is to assist Elsa Fennan in supplying Foreign Office material to East Germany. The operation flourishes until 1959 (or 1960), at which time it is exposed and destroyed by George Smiley during the Fennan case [CIRCUS INDEX].

The fortunes of the Abteilung suffer a serious decline as a result of the Fennan case because the agent Mundt is captured and turned* by the Circus before his return to East Germany. Mundt's subsequent rise to the position of second man in the Abteilung provides British Intelligence with extensive access to East German secrets. Jens Fiedler, head of Counter Intelligence, comes close to exposing Mundt but the Fiedler-Mundt Operation [CIRCUS INDEX] mounted by Control in 1961–62 removes this threat. Further information about the Abteilung is lacking but it can be assumed that the continued presence of a mole within its highest echelons severely limits its future effectiveness.

Apart from Frey, Mundt and Fiedler, known members of the Abteilung are: Jahn, head of the Ways and Means Committee; Stammberger, whose position is senior but undefined; the agent who directs Leamas to the

Berlin Wall; the hotel manager of the Le Mirage Hotel at Scheveningen who provides Leamas with accommodation in Holland. Local agents recruited by Frey and Mundt during their time in London include, in addition to Elsa Fennan, William Ashe and Sam Kiever. (*CD; SC*)

Adam, Miss Gloria Proprietor of the Fountain Café in Walliston, Surrey. Her origins are obscure and although she refers to her father as 'the Colonel' his rank may have been earned in the Salvation Army. The Fountain Café is run with an air of genteel amateurism, under cover of which customers are liable to be robbed. Miss Adam's coffee is reputed to be the worst south of Manchester. (*CD*)

*alimony Payments held in a safe place for an agent during the time when he is operating in hostile territory. (*HS*)

Alleline, Percy Son of a Presbyterian minister, Alleline is born in the Lowlands of Scotland in 1926. He takes a degree at Cambridge where, rumour has it, he is Control's pupil, and works for a company in the City before joining the Circus. Esteemed only by his original sponsor Maston, Alleline finds himself exiled into distant postings for much of his career. The 1950s are spent in Argentina and after that he moves to India and, finally, Egypt. To everyone's surprise, Alleline is remarkably successful in creating agent networks* in South America and India, but disgraces himself in Egypt after becoming involved without authorization in an American plot to overthrow a local ruler. Pressure from his supporters in the Conservative Party forces Control to make Alleline Operational Director after he returns from Egypt, but the position lacks any real power. His fortunes take a dramatic turn after he begins to develop Source Merlin in 1971 and, following Control's resignation in November 1972, Alleline becomes head of the Circus and is knighted. The discovery a year later that he has been the unwitting tool of Haydon's treacherous schemes brings Alleline's career to a sudden end.

Percy Alleline lives in Buckingham Palace Mansions, London, is a member of the Travellers' Club and has two 'wives', both alcoholics. His London-based 'wife' is named Joy. Alleline is a large man with rich, black hair, a weather-beaten face and whiskery cheeks. His heavy-handed manner matches his appearance. Concealed behind a cloud of smoke sent up by his enormous pipe, Alleline bludgeons his way through all situations with an unremitting stream of bullish banter and heavy *bonhomie*. Although there are those in clubland and Whitehall, such as his fellow Scot, Lilley of naval intelligence, who warm to Alleline's style, in general people dislike it. A tendency to vanity, which manifests itself in the gesture of massaging his double chin in the hope of reducing it, and a meanness about whisky and tips add to his unpopularity. Control seems to capture the essence of the man's appearance and personality when he calls him 'a parade horse'. (*TT*)

Alvida, Juan First of Ann Smiley's post-marital lovers. Alvida is a Cuban racing driver who includes amongst his successes a race at Monte Carlo. He has repulsively hairy arms and a falsely warm manner. (*CD*)

Alwyn, — Effeminate marine who guards the entrance to the Circus archives. While diligent enough in the execution of his duties, Alwyn does not seem to have his heart in his job and talks only of weekend activities. (*TT*)

American diplomat The senior diplomat and Cousin* in Phnom Penh, Cambodia, who serves as Westerby's contact. He is married to Beckie and owns land in Vermont. Despite the competition offered by his silk tartan jacket, the American's most notable features are his intelligent and mysterious brown eyes. His manner is excessively respectful and part of his code of politeness is to tell stories against himself. He is as angry as Westerby at the delay created by 'John', the British counsellor, in passing on information regarding Charlie Marshall's whereabouts. (*HS*)

American Drug Enforcement Administration Sol Eckland succeeds Ed Ristow as the senior member based in South East Asia. (*HS*)

American Intelligence Service *See* Cousins, the*

'Amies' Cover name used by Alec Leamas for a pick-up by Circus personnel during the Fiedler–Mundt Operation [CIRCUS INDEX]. Amies comes from Hounslow, in Middlesex. (*SC*)

Andrewartha, Willy Friend of Roddy Martindale who claims to have seen Control at Johannesburg airport long after his death. He is a fat man who suffers from the heat. Although more than willing to circulate Willy's stories, Martindale acknowledges that Andrewartha is an inveterate liar. (*TT*)

'Angel, Alan' Cover name used by George Smiley for a meeting with Toby Esterhase at his Bond Street art gallery during the Karla case [CIRCUS INDEX]. (*SP*)

*angels Local security services. (*HS*)

—, Anna Young girl of about eighteen with whom Fred Leiser has a brief affair while on the run in Kalkstadt, East Germany. She works at the Old Bell Hotel and occupies Apartment 19 in the Hockhaus, which is to be found behind the Friedensplatz. Nothing is known of Anna's past except that she has lived in Kalkstadt for two years. Anna is heavily built and has a pretty face marred by bad skin. The oppressions of the East German system have made her slightly insane and desperate for any experience that will make her feel free. (*LW*)

Annexe, the Cousins jargon for their own intelligence section of the

American Embassy in Grosvenor Square, London. (*HS*)

'Anselm' Cover name used by Toby Esterhase when contacting Smiley at the Bellevue Palace in Berne during the Karla case [CIRCUS INDEX]. (*SP*)

Arpego, — Wealthy Filipino friend of Drake Ko who is reputed to own half of Manila. Given his prominent paunch and rude manner, it is presumably Arpego's wealth rather than his personal qualities that attracts the beautiful girl who is always by his side. (*HS*)

'Arthur' Cover name used by Mendel when making contact with Guillam during the Haydon case [CIRCUS INDEX]. (*TT*)

Ashe, William Little is known for certain about William Ashe, or Bill, as he prefers to be known, except that he is an agent for East German Intelligence recruited by Frey and Mundt in London some time after 1956 and rents a flat in Dolphin Square, Pimlico, under the name Murphy. His status within the Abteilung is clearly low as he is entrusted only to make the first contact with Alec Leamas and plays no part in attempts to convince him to betray his country. Ashe tells Leamas that he once worked for the BBC in Berlin and that he has pursued a career in journalism since then. He also claims a mother in Cheltenham, Gloucestershire. Liz Gold knows Ashe as a member of the Cultural Relations Department of the Communist Party. Little of the above personal information is likely to be true. Ashe is tall, with curly hair and has an effeminate and petulant manner. He dresses in rather flamboyant colours. It seems that he has few strong views and in social intercourse he readily conforms to the opinions of others. (*SC*)

Astrid, — Maintenance man at the Circus who soon tires of the task at hand and takes refuge in his daily newspaper, the *Sun*. (*TT*)

Avery, John Somerton As a student Avery attends a College in the Turl, Oxford (thus Exeter, Jesus or Lincoln) where he reads German and Italian. After graduation he works in publishing but at the age of twenty-eight switches to intelligence work and joins the Department.* Four years later he has reached the position of aide to Leclerc, the Director. It seems likely that Avery will resign from the Department* following his unpleasant experience of a mission to Norway and the disastrous termination of Operation Mayfly. Avery meets his future wife, Sarah, at Oxford. On leaving their flat in Chandos Road, Oxford, the Averys move to Prince of Wales Drive in Battersea, London. They have one child, Anthony. Avery is a tall, bespectacled man whose unassertive manner reflects a very real uncertainty about his relationship to the world around him. Occasional bursts of affection cannot conceal a general dissatisfaction with his marriage and his love for the Department* becomes strained during times of crisis. Friendship with Fred Leiser seems likely to bring Avery closer to maturity. However, the casual manner in which Leiser is sacrificed to further the petty ambitions of others leaves him in a greater state of turmoil than ever. (*LW*)

Avery, Sarah A fine student during her days at Oxford, Sarah has achieved very little since. Marriage to John Avery has simply made her dependent and the tension expressed by her face reflects a general anxiety about the future. Lacking friends or pursuits and despising her husband, Sarah has only her mother to whom she can turn for support. (*LW*)

Avilov, — Moscow Centre's resident member in Hong Kong. (*TT*)

*baby-sit To guard an agent while he or she is involved in an operation. (*HS*)

*back-bearings Investigative technique based on working through files and documents in search of patterns created by the deliberate removal of material. (*HS*)

*back door Emergency escape route prepared by an agent prior to commencing an operation. (*SP*)

Baltic Independence Movement *See* Vladimir, General

Bardin, Colonel — Graduate of Karla's secret training school for spies. Later he changes his name to Sokolov and then Rusakov and is posted to the Soviet Delegation to the United Nations. Bardin probably services a mole* but his cover is impenetrable. (*TT*)

'Barraclough' Cover name used by George Smiley while staying at the Hotel Islay in London during the Haydon case and at the Bellevue Palace in Berne during the Karla case [CIRCUS INDEX]. (*TT*; *SP*)

Bayswater Library for Psychic Research An endowed library with a large but incompletely catalogued collection. One section is devoted to archaeology and includes *Archaeological Discoveries in Asia Minor*, Volume IV. The librarian is Miss Crail and the staff is made up of Liz Gold, Alec Leamas (temporarily) and an old curator shell-shocked during the First World War. Higher authority resides in the hands of the possibly fictional Mr Ironside. The library operates in accordance with a set of eccentric rules formulated by Miss Crail. These concern, amongst other things, limitations on the right to ink in card entries, a ban on staff shopping bags, the assignment of coat pegs and a rigid definition of working hours. (*SC*)

Bayswater South Branch of the Communist Party The Bayswater Branch is significant only because Liz Gold's membership of the group persuades Control that she can play a useful part in his scheme to free his East German double agent, Mundt, from the threat of exposure. The

Bayswater South Communists lack even a permanent base and hold their meetings in locations as various as the back rooms of pubs, the Ardena Café and a school classroom. The members are not characterized by any great enthusiasm and prefer to pay for copies of the *Daily Worker* themselves rather than struggle to sell them on the street. The election of female officers is likely to have as much to do with the candidates' sexual charms as their ideological fervour. Apart from Liz Gold, who is secretary, the members of the group include George Hanby, the treasurer, Bill Hazel, a schoolteacher, and a man called Mulligan. (*SC*)

bearleaders Sarratt staff who brief an agent prior to an operation. (*HS*)

Beatitude, Sister Nurse at the clinic near Berne where Karla's daughter, Tatiana, is a patient. (*SP*)

—, Beckie Wife of a senior American diplomat in Phnom Penh, Cambodia. She is big and speaks in an emphatic style. As if to differentiate herself from her fellow countrymen, who make no concessions to local custom, she dresses in a colourful array of Asian clothes and wears hand-beaten silver bought at the market. Nevertheless, her conversation indicates that she is more concerned with re-establishing her American roots than with adapting to a life in exile. (*HS*)

below-the-line Agent (known as an illegal resident) who operates in a foreign country without the protection of official cover such as that provided for above-the-line legal residents by positions in embassies, national airlines or similar institutions. (*HS*)

—, Ben Coding clerk who works under Steve Mackelvore at the Paris Embassy and who transmits Ricki Tarr's message to the Circus during the Haydon case [CIRCUS INDEX]. He is tall, wears spectacles over unblinking eyes and gives the impression of being simultaneously good with figures and silly. (*TT*)

'Benati, Mr' Name adopted by Toby Esterhase for his career as an art dealer. (*SP*)

'Bennett, Stephen' Cover name used by Alec Leamas for setting up a bank account in Helsinki during the Fiedler–Mundt Operation [CIRCUS INDEX]. Bennett is a marine engineer from Plymouth. (*SC*)

Berg, — The master spy who may have been at one time head of the Thirteenth Directorate branch of Moscow Centre. (*TT*)

Berlin A Circus safe flat* is located at 28A, Albrecht Dürer-Strasse, next to the Museum and a meeting between Control and Karl Riemeck takes place on Schurzstrasse. Riemeck introduces Leamas to his girlfriend Elvira at the 'Alter Fass'. One of Leamas's agents is a girl who lives in Wedding, a district in the French sector (*SC*). *See* map on page 77

Berlin Wall The area around the Berlin Wall is the location for three important events in the history of the Circus. In 1961 Karl Riemeck is shot down while attempting to cross from East to West, thus completing the destruction of Leamas's Berlin network;* in 1962 Alec Leamas and Liz Gold are shot and killed while climbing the Wall at a spot north of Griefswalder and Bernauerstrasse near the Pankow district; and in 1978 Karla defects via a crossing in the Turkish quarter. The area around the Wall is ugly, cold, bleak and ruined. The dirty Wall built of barbed wire dominates everything; its searchlights provide a hideous illumination and its pillboxes a sense of being under continuous observation. Only the poorest immigrants live here. (SC; SP)

Berlin Wall, agent at Young member of the Abteilung who directs Leamas and Liz Gold to the spot where they can climb the Berlin Wall at the end of the Fiedler–Mundt Operation [CIRCUS INDEX]. His cold and precise manner fails to conceal his nervousness at the danger of the situation in which he has been placed. (SC)

Berne Two Circus operations take place in Berne, one minor and the other major. In 1965 Guillam and Esterhase travel to Berne to foil the efforts of two Belgian arms dealers and in 1978 Smiley and Esterhase combine forces to blackmail Grigoriev of the Soviet Embassy into giving the information needed to force Karla to defect. The location of the Belgians' house is not known but Esterhase passes his spare time at the Chikito and the Bellevue Palace. During his visit to Berne in 1978 Smiley stays first at the Bellevue Palace and then the Arca in the old town. His target Grigoriev lives on the ground floor of Brunnadernrain, 18 in the Elfenau district. Other Soviet diplomats live in the Muri district. Esterhase's hotel is unidentified but he conducts his business from the sun pavilion in the ornamental garden (the Kleine Schanze) next to the Bundeshaus. When Esterhase drives Smiley around Berne at the beginning of the operation they start from the Nydegg Bridge, travel into the Elfenau, along Brunnadernrain, then past the British Ambassador's Residence and up to the Soviet Embassy. They end the journey near the Thunplatz. Although Grigoriev also works at the Soviet Trade Delegation at Schanzeneckstrasse, 17, Esterhase does not take Smiley there. Grigoriev is kidnapped while watching a game of chess played with giant men on The Platform which is close to the Cathedral. His interrogation takes place in a house on the Länggas-strasse behind the University.

Berne's diplomatic ghetto is leafy and grandiose, and is full of large houses with huge gardens that contain swimming pools and expensive cars. In contrast to the ostentatious materialism of the Elfenau district is the old city with its cobbled streets, ancient fountains and medieval buildings. The old city is built between the Kirchenfeld and Kornhaus

Bridges, within the horseshoe created by the curve of the river Aare, and climbs upwards to the Cathedral, a late-Gothic triumph, and The Platform with its public chess games, benches and ornamental trees. The southern edge of The Platform stands a hundred feet (thirty metres) above the river. Berne's old city is one of the few places in the modern world capable of winning the affection of George Smiley. (*TT; SP*)

Berne, clinic near Interdenominational Christian theosophist institution specializing in the treatment of mentally ill young women of international origins. The director of the clinic is Mother Felicity, the psychiatrist Dr Rüedi, and the staff includes Sister Beatitude and Sister Ursula as nurses and Kranko, a porter. Amongst the patients are girls from France and the USA as well as Karla's daughter, Tatiana, known in the clinic as Alexandra Ostrakova. The clinic has an elevated, rural setting and from a distance it looks like a castle but this impression is dissipated at closer range by the presence of an incinerator, an orchard, and modern outbuildings. Tatiana's experience does not encourage confidence in the clinic's therapeutic methods since it suggests that attention is paid to the wishes of those who commit the patients rather than to the needs of the patients themselves. Furthermore, despite the presence of Dr Rüedi the

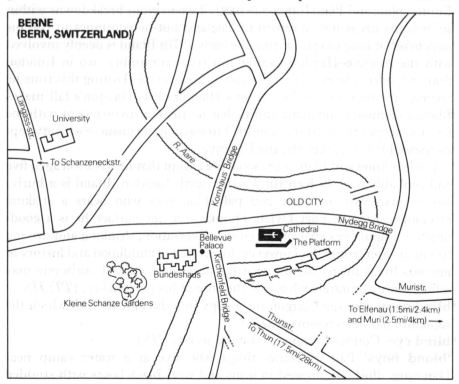

major therapeutic techniques seem to be based on good food, strict
routine, confinement and the threat of removal to the mental hospital at
Untersee. (*SP*)

—, Betty Clerk at a bank managed by Mr Dawnay, and Fred Leiser's
mistress. Betty speaks in a style that reflects her generally grudging
approach to experience. Her love-making is sullen and she responds
ungraciously to Leiser's dinner invitations. (*LW*)

*Big Moo Journalistic jargon for the Governor of Hong Kong. (*HS*)

Bland, Roy Son of a docker who opposes his educational ambitions,
Bland nevertheless wins a place at Oxford and becomes a don at St
Antony's College. While still an undergraduate, Bland is recruited for the
Circus by George Smiley and spends his vacations at Sarratt* learning the
fundamentals of espionage technique. By developing a Marxist façade and
making use of his father's left-wing connections, Bland is eventually able
to secure a position as an assistant lecturer in economics at the University
of Poznan in Poland. Later he teaches at the Budapest Academy of
Sciences, Hungary, and in Prague, Czechoslovakia, Sofia, Bulgaria, and
Kiev, USSR. During the nine years he spends behind the Iron Curtain,
Bland creates a number of espionage networks* including Aggravate,
Contemplate and Plato [CIRCUS INDEX]. Two nervous breakdowns within
six months necessitate a return to England but he continues to run his
networks* at long range. During the early 1970s Bland is deeply involved
with the Alleline–Haydon faction and rises to number two in London
Station* after Alleline becomes head of the Service. During this time he
receives mention in the New Year's Honours list. Haydon's fall makes
Bland's dismissal inevitable and he has no further involvement with the
Circus except for a brief recall in 1974 to assist in the unsuccessful attempt
to rescue his former agents, the Churayevs.

   Little is known of Bland's personal life except that he has a son aged five
and probably lives in Kentish Town, North London. Bland is a burly,
sweaty man with red hair and pale blue eyes who bears a striking
resemblance to the poet Dylan Thomas. On the surface he is a good-
hearted, impulsive extrovert given to conversation, drinking and driving
fast in his Mercedes 190. However, his wretched childhood and history of
nervous breakdowns suggest that his occasional cynical outbursts may
reflect more accurately what is at the core of his personality. (*TT; HS*)

blind copy Cousins jargon for a copy of a document from which the
signature has been removed. (*HS*)

blind eye Cousins jargon for totally secret. (*HS*)

'blond boys' Pair of young thugs who live at a water camp near
Hamburg. Both are dressed in jeans and wear black boots with studded

love-daisies. Their expressions suggest a criminal and inhuman mentality which manifests itself in the damage they do to Smiley's car. The humorous double act in which they engage does nothing to modify their menace. (*SP*)

'Blondie' Cover name used by Hans-Dieter Mundt in his dealings with Adam Scarr. (*CD*)

***Bloomsbury Group** Four pay and personnel officers employed to deal with problems of reorganization after the fall of Haydon. They are located, as might be anticipated, in Bloomsbury, London. (*HS*)

***blown** Term used to describe an agent whose cover has been penetrated by the enemy. (*HS*)

—, Boris Moscow Centre agent born in Minsk in 1946. In April 1973 Boris is operating in Hong Kong under cover as a trade delegate. His job is to recruit businessmen as local agents and to pass on secret messages for the Soviet Residency. Depression caused by the deteriorating relationship with his fellow agent and common-law wife, Irina, drinking and a liking for dancing girls combine to reduce his professional effectiveness. Boris is executed along with Irina in the Lubianka in July 1973 as part of the reprisals for her betrayal of the mole* Gerald to Ricki Tarr. (*TT*)

'box-office girl' Employee of the Sheridan Theatre in Hammersmith, London, but probably also a student. She is on duty the night that Dieter Frey murders Elsa Fennan. Although harassed by the demands of the job, tired and careless about her appearance, she nevertheless rouses herself to flirt with Peter Guillam. (*CD*)

***branch lines** Agent's contacts. (*TT*)

'Brandt, Martin' Cover name used by Karla when posing as a German journalist in Japan during the 1930s. (*TT*)

Bretlev, Ivan Ivanovitch Formerly a Russian revolutionary and Moscow Centre agent in Shanghai, China, Bretlev is now a member of the shipbuilding faculty at the University of Leningrad and a talent spotter* for Karla. Nelson Ko is almost certainly one of Bretlev's recruits. (*HS*)

Brimley, Ailsa During the Second World War Ailsa Brimley works in intelligence as Adrian Fielding's secretary and as a coder under Lord John Landsbury. After leaving the Circus, she becomes editor of the *Christian Voice*, a position she still holds in 1960 when she involves Smiley (who has temporarily left the Circus) in the Rode murder case at Carne School. Besides editing the paper, Miss Brimley writes an advice column under the name Barbara Fellowship. By 1973, at age sixty, she is running the safe house* in Suffolk which accommodates Ricki Tarr on his return from Hong Kong. Ailsa Brimley has a firm, intelligent face and is neat in appearance. She is a person of admirable personal qualities, including an essential humanity which is evident in her treatment of children and in her concern that Smiley be comfortable and properly fed during his journey to Carne. Her other virtues include punctuality, a good memory, calmness in the face of emergencies, such as the discovery of blood-stained clothes in a refugee parcel, and a sense of loyalty, both to old friends and her newspaper. A more acerbic side of her nature reveals itself when confronted with officious telephone operators. (*MQ; TT*)

British diplomat at Phnom Penh, Cambodia *See* John

British Intelligence Service *See* Circus chapter, pages 12–49

British liaison Cousins jargon for the British Intelligence Service. (*HS*)

Brod, — Moscow Centre agent who operates under the cover name Ivlov in London and Moscow. For several years up until late 1972 Brod works as Polyakov's legman* in London under cover as an embassy driver and assistant coding clerk. His workname* is Lapin. Later Brod is based in the filing department of the Trade Ministry in Dzerzhinsky Square supervised by Irina. During a brief affair with Irina, conducted in the apartment of his wife's cousin, a Moscow University professor, Brod reveals the existence of the mole* Gerald. He is executed in July 1973 along with Irina and Boris for his indiscretion. Although attractive to Irina, who likes his blond hair and kindness, Brod is not particularly appealing and his personality is best summed up by his workname* Lapin – a rabbit. He is weak, insecure and given to following girls he is too scared to approach. It is a pathetic desire to impress that causes Brod to commit the insecure act for which he is executed. (*TT*)

*brush over the traces To conceal evidence of espionage activity. (*HS*)

Bryant, P. Janitor stationed in the lobby of the Circus. He is a red-faced, white-haired man who moves slowly and likes to complain. (*TT*)

*burn To blackmail. (*TT*)

*burrower Researcher. (*HS*)

*buy for stock To cause the defection of enemy agents of no great intelligence value with the intention of later selling them to or exchanging them with another intelligence service. (*TT*)

cache Sarratt jargon for to hide. (*SP*)

Cale, Sally Sixty-year-old lesbian antique dealer, pimp, and heroin-pusher who lives in Hong Kong. Sally Cale introduces Lizzie Worthington to Drake Ko with whom she is involved in illegal gold-trafficking. She is reputed to keep Alsatians and chimpanzees. (*HS*)

Cambodian Press Agent Employee of the governor in Battambang, Cambodia. Westerby approaches him while acting out his journalistic cover. Although he has some qualifications for his job, including the ability to speak French beautifully, this Press Agent appears to owe his position mainly to the fact that he is a general's son. Apart from his official responsibilities he manages the Battambang branch of his family's opium business. There are several signs that this tiny man thinks well of himself. He has equipped his office with an enormous desk, loves to hear himself speak and has an unjustifiably high opinion of his poetry. (*HS*)

*camel Agent responsible for transporting secret material. (*SP*)

—, Camilla Music student and one-time mistress of Peter Guillam. Camilla is tall and beautiful with a sad expression. Although she is only twenty, her hair is streaked with grey. Considerable mystery surrounds Camilla's past but it appears that she has been married and divorced. Besides Guillam, she sometimes takes Dr Sand, her music teacher, as a lover. Although she practises a number of self-imposed restrictions and will not eat meat, drink alcohol or wear leather, Camilla refuses to be limited by the wishes of others. Her flute practice times are, for example, chosen without any regard for the neighbours. (*TT*)

'Canadian cowboy, the' Journalist based in Hong Kong. He is noted for his Mexican-style revolutionary moustache and his ability to seduce two girls at once. His journalistic experience includes covering the Tet offensive and student riots in Bangkok, Thailand. (*HS*)

*car coper Agent skilled at interfering with car engines. (*SP*)

Cardew, Mr — Minister of the Baptist Tabernacle in Carne. Although physically large, Cardew is free of the forbidding air usually associated with nonconformist clergymen of North Country origins. He is a sensible and down-to-earth man who possesses the practical intelligence needed to see through Stella Rode's virtuous façade. (*MQ*)

'Carmichael' Cover name used by George Smiley when making contact with Max Habolt during the Haydon case [CIRCUS INDEX]. Carmichael is a fussy man seeking a place for his new Rover in the parking garage run by Max. (*TT*)

Carne Town in Dorset near Dorchester famous for its public school, Abbey and beautiful Abbey Close. Other buildings of note are the Sawley Arms, Carne's major hotel, the town hall and the police station, all of which stand in the Victorian municipal part of the town, a red-brick Tabernacle, and the run-down local Carne High School. There is also a vast area of playing fields running alongside North Fields Lane, Lammass Land near the Tabernacle, and small houses in Bread Street. Sawley Castle and the ancient village of Pylle are nearby. Apart from the staff of Carne School the town's residents include Brigadier Havelock and Inspector Rigby of the police force, Mr Cardew, the Methodist Minister, Mr

Mulligan, owner of a furniture removal company, Mr Jardine, a baker
from Carne East, and the ancient night porter at the Sawley Arms. The
train service from London runs via Yeovil and a local bus service is
provided by the Dorset and General Traction Company. Smiley's view of
Carne is soured not just by the bloody murder of Stella Rode which brings
him to the town but by the repeated reminders it provides him of the
continuation of the uglier aspects of the British class system. He is
particularly struck by the antiquated snobbery which pervades the Sawley
Arms and by the enormous gap between the grand public school and the
tawdry state school attended by the local boys. (*MQ*)

Carne School Monastic foundation endowed in the sixteenth century by
King Edward VI in Carne, Dorset – not unlike the public school
Sherborne in its surroundings. The school was obscure until the
nineteenth century but has enjoyed a good reputation since then. The
school crest is a blue dolphin above the motto, *Regem defendere diem
videre* (To Defend the King is to See the Day). Carne prides itself on
maintaining traditional values and in the late 1950s the Master even goes
so far as to revive the seven Canonical Day Hours for the Offices in chapel
– first Prime, then Terce, Sext at midday, and so on. Staff are generally in
accord with the spirit of the place. Charles Hecht is angered by any
questioning of the school's traditional role or of its continued usefulness;
William Trumper, the local curate, is ever ready to justify the use of
private pews. Those such as Simon Snow who would like Carne to be
different soon leave. However, the moral stance adopted by Carne is
called into question by the treatment of Terence Fielding, who, as the
result of a wartime involvement in a homosexual scandal, has been
employed for over twenty years on annual contracts with no prospect of a
pension. The guilty secret which Carne thus harbours within its ranks for
its own financial advantage results in 1960 in the murders of Stella Rode
and Tim Perkins and the subsequent arrest of Terence Fielding. Besides
Hecht and the mathematics teacher, Snow, the staff of Carne School
includes Felix D'Arcy, the Senior Tutor, who teaches French; Terence
Fielding, the Senior Housemaster; and Stanley Rode who teaches
science. Iredale is Commandant of the Cadets. Numbered amongst its
pupils are 'the young Prince' and Lord Sawley's son as well as the less
illustrious Tim Perkins. (*MQ*)

—, Carol Secretary to Leclerc, the Director of the Department.* Prior
to this appointment Carol works in Vienna. She is a tall, well-dressed
woman who enjoys a tentative physical relationship with Avery. Hers is a
rare voice of common sense amidst the fantasies of the Department.*
(*LW*)

Cases For Chronologies of Fennan, Haydon and Karla Cases, *see* Circus chapter, pages 28–40.

*catch-and-carry job** Espionage enterprise aimed at capturing and turning an enemy agent. (*TT*)

—**, Catherine or 'Cat'** Seventeen-year-old daughter of Jerry Westerby who lives with her mother and step-father, Phillie, a civil servant. Telephone calls and presents of money fail to maintain contact with a father she has not seen for ten years and who thinks that she still collects stamps. (*HS*)

'Caviar' (and 'Whitebait') Code names for material simultaneously distributed on both sides of the Atlantic during Operation Dolphin [CIRCUS INDEX]. (*HS*)

*change nappies** To exercise control over an agent in the field from headquarters. (*HS*)

*charm-school** Department of Sarratt* run by Thatch and devoted to preparing future deep-penetration agents on an individual basis. (*TT*)

Chiu, Jake Hong Kong dealer in real estate who is Luke's landlord and the person appointed to sell High Haven, the former British spy headquarters. He is responsible for leaking the news of the Circus withdrawal from Hong Kong to the local journalists. (*HS*)

Christian Voice Nonconformist newspaper founded as a daily by Lord Landsbury at the beginning of the twentieth century. The paper ceases publication during the Second World War but is revived immediately after by the founder's son, John Landsbury, who appoints Ailsa Brimley as editor. Unipress takes it over in 1957, but, much to the surprise of its staff, it is still continuing publication as a weekly in the 1960s. The *Christian Voice* is located in room 619 on the seventh floor of Unipress House and, in addition to Ailsa Brimley, there is a ginger-haired woman who functions as secretary and sub-editor and relies on paper tissues and strongly-scented face powder to get her through the day's work. (*MQ*)

*chummy** Gambling slang for a gullible type, a 'mug', but as used in an espionage context, the target of an operation. (*HS*)

Churayevs, the Husband-and-wife team of British agents who lead the Contemplate network,* covering Georgia and the Ukraine. They are killed while trying to escape from Sochi, a resort on the Black Sea, in 1974, following the fall of Haydon. Smiley takes their deaths hard. (*HS*)

*CIA bracelets** Cousins* jargon for gold link bracelets worn by agents who plan to use them as currency in the event of being stranded in enemy territory. (*HS*)

*Circus, the** Special department of the British Intelligence Service. *See* Circus chapter, pages 12–49

The Berlin Wall

'A dirty ugly thing of breeze blocks and strands of barbed wire . . . East and West of the Wall lay the unrestored part of Berlin, a half-world of ruin, drawn in two dimensions, crags of war.' (*The Spy Who Came in from the Cold*)

During 1961 and 1962 the Wall, with its deadly pillboxes and watch towers from which searchlights constantly probe, claims no less than two Circus agents – Riemeck and Leamas – and Leamas's girlfriend Liz Gold.

Outdoor Chess Game at The Platform, Berne

'(There) stood Counsellor (Commercial) Anton Grigoriev of the Soviet Embassy in Berne . . . intensely following, through his rimless spectacles, each move the players made . . . He was not a fieldman . . . he had an innocence which could never have survived the infighting of Moscow Centre.' (*Smiley's People*)

One Sunday morning in December 1978 Toby Esterhase and his Circus team close in on the game's enthusiasts and discreetly kidnap Grigoriev. Gentle blackmail persuades him to identify the patient whom he visits in the nearby clinic as Karla's beloved daughter, Tatiana, thereby revealing a chink in the previously invulnerable armour of the head of Moscow Centre.

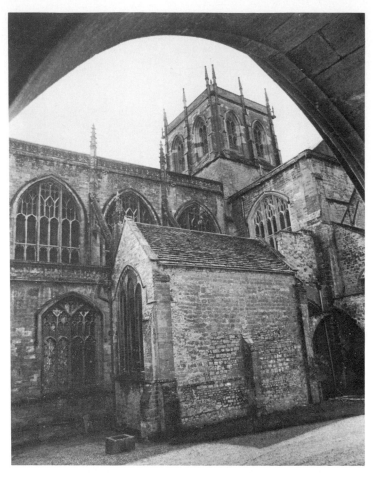

Carne Abbey, Dorset (*above*)

'(Smiley) left the station, with its foretaste of Victorian austerity, and walked along the avenue of bare trees which led towards the great Abbey tower, flat and black against the colourless winter sky . . . Smiley called to a black-coated boy as he ran past: "What's going on?"

"Sext," shouted the boy in reply, and was gone.' (*A Murder of Quality*)

Temporary retirement from the Circus leaves Smiley free in 1960 to become involved in the Rode murder case investigation at Carne, famous, as is Sherborne, for its Abbey and its public school. By digging deep beneath the placid and smug surface of Carne life, Smiley eventually identifies the murderer as the school's Senior Housemaster, Terence Fielding, homosexual brother of the early Circus luminary, Adrian Fielding.

Circus Headquarters, Cambridge Circus, London (*right*)

'. . . eight or nine unequal roads and alleys for no good reason had chosen Cambridge Circus as their meeting point. Between them, the buildings were gimcrack, cheaply fitted out with bits of empire: a Roman bank, a theatre like a vast desecrated mosque.' (*Tinker, Tailor, Soldier, Spy*)

Exactly where the London headquarters (since 1945) stand in Cambridge Circus is uncertain but the tall building on the south-west curve, with its pepper-pot corner rooms reminiscent of Haydon's office, is a likely candidate (see centre building). The famous 'fifth floor' is possibly a misnomer as a *third* is nowhere referred to in the Circus annals and this building has only four storeys above the ground floor.

The Fennan Case: Battersea Bridge, London

'It was in the shadow of the four massive chimneys of Fulham Power Station, perhaps sixty feet from the Cheyne Walk mooring, that Dieter Frey had found a sanctuary.' (*Call for the Dead*)

A long pursuit through fog-enshrouded London streets ends when Inspector Mendel and Smiley corner Elsa Fennan's murderer, Dieter Frey, at his dilapidated houseboat close by Battersea Bridge. Smiley grapples with his former friend and then watches in horror as Frey falls to his death in the black river beneath the Bridge.

*coat trailer Either an agent who plays willing to be recruited by the enemy (*HS*) or one who tempts enemy agents into working against their own country. (*SP*)

Code name Fictional name used in Circus files to conceal the identity of an agent or source. (*HS*)

Collins, Sam After taking an unexpected first at Cambridge, by cheating, according to rumour, Collins joins the Circus in 1953 as Haydon's nominee. His subsequent career is spent almost entirely in South East Asia. Five years in Borneo are followed by six in Burma, five more in Northern Thailand and three in Laos. Throughout this time he operates under cover as a general trader named Mellon. Although Collins develops a reputation as a first-rate operator and is even tipped in the early 1970s as a likely contender for promotion to the fifth floor* – seat of the senior Circus administration – only a little is known of his espionage activities. Key moments in his career include a narrow escape from the authorities in Sarawak, Borneo, two spells of intensive interrogation in Thailand, involvement with Smiley in an operation aimed at capturing a Chinese radio operator, and a skilful piece of tradecraft* in Vientiane, Laos, which uncovers Karla's gold seam* to Nelson Ko. This episode supposedly occurs in 1973 which seems impossible in the light of information below. While stationed in Vientiane Collins also works in a private capacity for the local narcotics bureau and employs Lizzie Worthington briefly as an investigator into narcotics and gold-smuggling activities.

On his return to England in October 1972, Collins is drawn into Operation Testify by Control. Although unaware of the significance of the role assigned to him as weekend duty officer, Collins is nevertheless amongst those dismissed in the aftermath of the scandal caused by Prideaux's capture. After leaving the Circus, Collins works as the manager of a gambling club in London, near Grosvenor Square. The job affords him insufficient stimulation, however, and early in 1975 he uses his knowledge of Lizzie Worthington to gain readmittance to the Circus as part of the team gathered together by Smiley to seek out weak spots in Karla's armour. His rank is assistant co-ordinator and at last he rises to the fifth floor.* Although Collins contributes to Operation Dolphin [CIRCUS INDEX] by using his knowledge of Lizzie's drug-smuggling activities to force her to betray Drake Ko, his real achievement is of a much more sinister kind. While Smiley, Connie Sachs, di Salis and Guillam dedicate themselves to the intelligence task at hand, Collins enters into a conspiracy that finally enables Enderby to replace Smiley as head of the Service. As a reward for his treachery, Collins is appointed Operational Director, a post he still occupies in 1978.

Collins's most characteristic features are his black moustache and the brown cigarettes which he smokes continually. In 1973 when he is about fifty, Collins shows signs of greying. Nevertheless, he still has a youthful air and looks about thirty-five. At this time his manner is friendly and his smile warm. By 1975, however, there is a change in Collins's appearance which reflects a significant shift in his personality. The moustache and the brown cigarettes are still very much in evidence but the once warm smile has become cold and fixed. It seems that a spark of vitality has gone out of the man. Although never an entirely upright character, as evidenced by his affair with a plain girl who has access to the examination papers immediately prior to finals, Collins has always possessed an admirable willingness to take risks and a lack of concern for what might be of advantage to himself. Furthermore, his tendency to exploit women sexually, which reveals itself not only in the steps he takes to ensure a first, but also in his recruitment of Lizzie Worthington as an agent in order to gain sexual access to her, is balanced by his loyalty to men, such as Control and Smiley, whom he admires. By the time he returns to the Circus, however, Collins has become obsessed with personal security and is willing to do anything which will strengthen his own position. The betrayal of Smiley is the first step on a path which terminates in 1978 in the transformation of the once carefree buccaneer into a grovelling sycophant willing to go to any lengths to protect his pension. (*TT; HS; SP*)

'colonel of police' Trained at the Washington International Police Academy and with experience in PARU (Police Aerial Reinforcement Unit) in Laos, the colonel is now working against communist guerillas in North East Thailand. In addition he looks after Drake Ko's business enterprises in the area and provides protection for his friend Ricardo. Although a member of the police force, the colonel is the archetypal fighting man, ever willing to sacrifice life to achieve his ends. His ruthlessness is reflected in his appearance. He is short, strong and dark with an impassive expression, and he wears battle-drill complete with medal ribbons and wings. (*HS*)

'Commercial Boris' *See* Zimin

*Company, the The American Intelligence Service's jargon name for itself. (*HS*) *See* the Cousins*

*conjuring tricks Set of basic espionage techniques. (*CD*)

*conscious To be informed in matters of operational intelligence. (*HS*)

'Control' Control's career with the Circus dates back at least as far as 1938 when he recruits Connie Sachs. However, little is known of his intelligence activities prior to 1960 except that he seems to have been Smiley's supervisor during the 1950s. In 1960 Control succeeds Maston as head of the Circus and during 1961–62 he develops the elaborate Fiedler–Mundt Operation [CIRCUS INDEX] to protect Mundt, his highly-placed source in East German intelligence, from detection. The scheme is successful but costs the lives of the agent Alec Leamas and Liz Gold. Two or three years later Control encourages the Department,* a rival branch of intelligence, to pursue an operation (Mayfly) he knows will end disastrously and thus remove a threat to his own supremacy in the field. After these successes Control enters a period of failure. Despite his sound espionage technique, which is based on the development of basic networks* and persistent, gentle probing for information, operation after operation fails in the late 1960s. Eventually Control realizes that there is a traitor in the ranks of the Circus and struggles throughout 1971 and 1972, despite the handicap of increasing illness, to discover his identity. Alerted to Control's efforts the traitor Haydon entices him into launching Operation Testify. The inevitable failure of this operation forces Control to resign in November 1973 and he dies of a heart attack in December.

There is considerable mystery surrounding Control's origins and even his real name remains a secret. We do know, though, that he is briefly a don at Cambridge during the early 1940s and that later he lives for many years a dull suburban life in Surrey with a wife, Mandy, who thinks that he works for the Coal Board. After her death in 1962 he takes up residence in a flat on the Western bypass, London, with a Mrs Matthews. During this period he adds gardening and golf to cricket as his hobbies. Since Control scorns domesticity, the bourgeoisie and golf, his entire appearance of a personal life is no more than an elaborate piece of cover from which he escapes only on Monday nights when he stays at his club. The fact that George Smiley alone attends his East End cremation shows how little lies beneath the surface of his existence outside of the Circus.

No detailed descriptions of Control are available. It seems that he is shortish and rather overweight until his final illness, and he has a dreary, braying voice which recalls his academic past. Control wears a shabby black jacket over a cardigan, an outfit which seems to express his suburban persona rather than his real self. A feeble smile and diffident air, a tendency to be querulous, and the cultivation of a formal manner which he seems to find distasteful suggests that Control is a weak and even effeminate man. Draughts, telephones, working at night and alterations in routine are all sources of distress to Control and he fortifies himself against the world with endless cups of lemon jasmine tea. All this, however, is no more than a façade and underneath Control is a tough-minded and remorseless man who clearly relishes the uglier aspects of espionage [CIRCUS INDEX]. (*SC; LW; TT; HS*)

*cooks Criminal jargon for narcotics chemists. (*HS*)

'Countess Sylvia' *See* Sylvia, Countess

Cousins, the The Circus jargon name for the American Intelligence Service. Remarkably little information is available on the Cousins (or the Company as they call themselves). Their headquarters are in Langley, Virginia, and they are known to have a secret aviation school in Oklahoma. American intelligence activities in Britain are centred on the Annexe,* a section of the Embassy in Grosvenor Square, London. The quality of the Cousins' field work is considered to be low because of an excessive and always very visible use of electronic equipment. Wilbraham's fears that a large American presence in Hong Kong during Operation Dolphin [CIRCUS INDEX] will soon become obvious and cause a scandal seem justified by the ease with which Westerby spots the Cousins' surveillance vans. The only well-documented intelligence operation involving the Cousins is Dolphin. Their role is to provide support services for George Smiley's attempts to seize Nelson Ko, Karla's mole* in China. However, because of the skill with which Martello, their London station chief, enters into an intrigue with Enderby of the Circus, the Cousins are finally given the first opportunity to interrogate Nelson Ko. Links with British Intelligence remain close after this episode. The Cousins are doubtless deeply involved in the Vietnam War, but information is available only on their activities in the Shans where their agents encourage the hill tribesmen to play a combat role and employ pilots such as Captain Rocky, Tiny Ricardo and Charlie Marshall to sustain the opium trade during the absence on military service of the male population. American Intelligence is also active around the Berlin Wall in 1961 but no details are available. Agents working there include the young agent who waits at the Berlin Wall with Leamas for Riemeck to defect. The Cousins' only recorded success against Moscow Centre occurs in 1955 with the discovery of a Soviet network* in San Francisco.

Identified members of American Intelligence include Marty Martello (their London station chief); Murphy, an assistant to Martello; Mac, a listener;* Pike, a field agent operating in Saigon, South Vietnam, under 'information' cover; an agent working under senior American diplomatic cover in Phnom Penh, Cambodia; Major Masters, who is stationed with the American Air Force in North East Thailand; Culpepper, a Harvard professor and expert on Soviet intelligence who is based at Langley, Virginia; a slim young American who spies on Lizzie Worthington at her Star Heights apartment in Hong Kong; a respectful young American who makes contact with Craw on the Peak in Hong Kong; Ed, who is in charge of the computer at the Annexe;* Marge, Ed's assistant. Max Keller, a journalist, is suspected of working for the Cousins. (*SC; TT; HS; SP*)

*cover Identity assumed by agents to conceal their espionage role. (*HS*)

Crail, Miss — The librarian at the Bayswater Library for Psychic Research. Miss Crail is an extremely rigid person who likes to invent rules. Her manner is aggressive and she conducts long arguments with her mother by telephone. However, when confronted she proves timid and falls back on the authority of a probably fictional superior, Mr Ironside. (*SC*)

*crash Emergency or urgent situation. (*TT*)

Craven, Stella Wife of Villem Craven. Stella is a person of considerable presence both because she is tall, black-haired, beautiful and still and because she has a powerful and courageous personality. Her husband, Villem, who is ten years her junior, is almost as reliant on her as her baby, Beckie. A sick mother in Staines is another who draws on Stella's strength. (*SP*)

Craven, Villem or William Long-distance lorry driver who serves on one occasion as a courier for General Vladimir. Estonian by birth and then an exile in Paris, Villem Craven has lived in England since his childhood. His first home there is a room in Ruislip, Middlesex, where his father dies. Because his father was an intense nationalist, Villem has strong connections with the Estonian community. However, under the influence of his wife, Stella, who insists on calling him William, he begins to identify himself as English, going so far as to watch football on television, and to pursue bourgeois goals. Their rented home is near St Saviour's Church at the end of Battle-of-the-Nile Street in Charlton, London, but he has ambitions to provide Stella and his daughter, Beckie, with a house of their own. Villem's involvement in Vladimir's anti-Soviet espionage activity almost certainly marks only a temporary halt in his drift away from his Estonian connections. Villem's brown and passionate eyes, his intense gaze and his purposeful stride reflect the strength of character and courage that is needed to fulfil Vladimir's instructions. However, he is also immature and too easily influenced by strong personalities such as Vladimir and his own wife, Stella. (*SP*)

Craw, Bill Australian agent who works for the Circus under journalistic cover which he has cultivated so well as to have acquired an almost legendary status equal to that of his fellow Australian journalist, Richard Hughes. It is not clear when his career in espionage begins but Craw is working as a journalist as far back as the 1930s. His first position is tea boy and city editor for Shanghai's English daily. Later Craw covers Chiang Kai-shek's struggles with the communists and the Japanese and the various phases of American intervention in South East Asia. By the 1970s he is working out of Hong Kong. A career stretching over forty or more years is brought to a close in 1974 with the story of the 'withdrawal' of British Intelligence (in the form of the Circus) from Hong Kong which manages to be at once a journalistic triumph and a useful piece of disinformation for the Circus. After this Craw retires to a cottage in the New Territories. However, his espionage activities continue and Craw makes use of sources such as Superintendent Rockhurst and Phoebe Wayfarer to obtain information vital to the development of Operation Dolphin [CIRCUS INDEX].

Not much is known of Craw's private life except that he has accumulated sufficient wives and children to ensure that he enters retirement relatively impoverished. In old age at least he appears to have a fondness for young Asian boys. His other recreations are presiding over the Saturday gatherings of a group of eccentric journalists who call themselves the Shanghai Junior Baptist Conservative Bowling Club and smoking opium. Craw is flamboyant in appearance and manner. A fat, sweat-stained man with a large head, he is typically to be seen wearing a soft straw hat, with Etonian hatband striped dark blue and black, and a beige suit. His speech is punctuated with the Vatican-style courtesies favoured by Australian journalists in the 1930s. Beneath his larger-than-life façade, Craw is essentially a solitary person liable to retreat into himself for months at a time. As his many marriages indicate he does not do well in emotional relationships with others and his real love is for the East and espionage. The deaths of Jerry Westerby and Luke and the betrayal of Smiley at the end of Operation Dolphin [CIRCUS INDEX] bring Craw's incipient acidie to the surface and on his last visit to the Shanghai Bowlers he appears much aged and close to despair. (*HS*)

*crusher A guard. (*HS*)

Culpepper, — Harvard professor and expert on Soviet intelligence based with the Cousins* at Langley, Virginia. He is the author of a private paper on 'the mole principle' and is preferred to Connie Sachs as Nelson Ko's interrogator. (*HS*)

*cut-out Agent who acts as an intermediary between the controller and the operation under his or her direction. (*TT*)

—, Cy The assistant to Sol Eckland in the American Drug Enforcement Administration in South East Asia. Cy has sideburns, wears shoes with a rubbery shine and thick welts and has the devout but defensive look of a missionary. His manner is much smoother than his superior's and he says little during Eckland's aggressive negotiations with Smiley about access to Drake Ko. (*HS*)

Czechoslovakia The involvement of the Circus in Czechoslovakia dates

back at least as far as the Second World War when Jim Prideaux works
with partisan groups there. During the 1960s Roy Bland establishes two
Czech espionage networks,* code names Aggravate and Plato. Prideaux is
also involved in their operation. In December 1972 Control sends
Prideaux to Czechoslovakia (Operation Testify) for a meeting with
General Stevcek who, he is informed, is willing to reveal the identity of
Karla's mole* in British Intelligence. Prideaux flies to Prague from
London via Paris and then travels to Brno on a local train which passes
through Chocen and Svitavy. His assistant Max Habolt enters Czechoslovakia from Austria and crosses the border at Mikulov. He makes contact
with Prideaux in Brno. Prideaux and Habolt drive out of Brno on the
Bilovice road as far as Krtiny and then East on the Racice road where they
meet the Magyar driver who is to take Jim to Stevcek. This rendezvous is
intended to take place at a hunting lodge near Tisnov but when Prideaux
gets there he is ambushed by Soviet troops. He is taken from Czechoslovakia to the Soviet Union, leaving the country via Hradec. Habolt is
able to escape and re-enters Austria on a bus to Freistadt. In December of
1972, during a visit to the Restaurant Sport in Prague, Jerry Westerby
meets Stan's nephew, a young conscript, who tells him that, during recent
manoeuvres around Brno, his company's convoy was sent on a wild goose
chase through Trebic, Znojmo and Breclav to keep them out of the way of
Soviet troops seeking out a British spy. The fact that this incident
occurred on October 20, the day before the date set for Prideaux's meeting
with Stevcek, demonstrates that the British agent was betrayed. For both
Prideaux and Westerby, Czechoslovakia at this time is a depressing place
with too much snow, cancelled trains and few places at which to shop.
However, football games and the occasional free-spirited bar such as the
Restaurant Sport offer relief from the generally oppressive atmosphere
created by the communist regime (*TT*). *See* map on page 77

Danish missionary English-speaking Dane to whom Jerry Westerby
turns for information at the airport in Battambang, Cambodia. He is a tall,
thin man with short yellow hair, spectacles and a six-inch silver cross on
his brown shirt. He seems puzzled at the Cambodian forces' disregard for
human life. (*HS*)

D'Arcy, Dorothy Sister of Felix D'Arcy. She is unmarried and her main
interests are breeding King Charles spaniels and refugee relief work. In
appearance she is bony and energetic with unkempt grey hair and the
arrogant expression of the hunting fraternity. Although something of a
snob, Dorothy D'Arcy nevertheless has a genuine concern for the plight of
refugees and is willing to look for good qualities in the generally despised

outsider, Stella Rode. (*MQ*)

D'Arcy, Felix Senior Tutor and French master at Carne School where he has taught since before the Second World War. D'Arcy is a bachelor who lives with his unmarried sister, Dorothy, at the former rectory of the North Fields Church. He has fine, ginger hair. His face is smooth and unlined, his mouth red and his teeth perfect. He smiles constantly. D'Arcy is a snob and a stickler for protocol who is completely dedicated to Carne. During the War he is involved in the disgraceful manoeuvre by means of which Terence Fielding is forced to accept a career without security at the school. Because he knows that Stella Rode has been blackmailing Fielding, it is almost certain that D'Arcy is aware from the beginning of her murderer's identity. Both of these morally dubious pieces of behaviour are justifiable in D'Arcy's view because they serve the interests of his beloved school. (*MQ*)

*dead Term used to describe a retired agent. (*SP*)

*dead letter box Place used to hide secret messages. (*TT*)

'Deathwish the Hun' Photographer from Cape Town, South Africa. He lives in Hong Kong and lets Jerry Westerby have the use of his flat during his absence in Cambodia. Apart from his animation at the news of the evacuation of High Haven (the Circus headquarters in Hong Kong), Deathwish usually displays no interest in anything beyond photography. The man's character is accurately reflected by his flat which is bare of any furniture except a mattress, a kitchen table and chair, a plate, a girlie calendar, a telephone, an ancient record player, and two opium pipes. (*HS*)

de Jong, — British agent who works under Leamas in Berlin. Riemeck establishes contact with British Intelligence by leaving a secret microfilm in de Jong's car. De Jong is killed, perhaps murdered, in a traffic accident in 1959. (*SC*)

'Delassus, Mr' Cover name used by Zimin (Commercial Boris) when handling the Moscow Centre gold seam* in Vientiane, Laos. (*HS*)

Delaware, Mo Member of London Station* during Alleline's time as head of the Circus. Despite the high position which Mo Delaware occupies within the Circus hierarchy during 1972–73 nothing is known of her career in espionage either before or after these dates. Her sudden rise to prominence seems to owe more to the desire for a token female, a role which this dull, rather masculine woman with her bobbed hair and brown suit just about fills, than to any marked abilities on her part. She is silent during meetings even when subjected to a barrage of sexist comments from Alleline. (*TT*)

Dell, Major — Manager of the Alias Club, a discreet drinking club in a basement near Charing Cross, London. Like the members of his club, who include Wilf Taylor and Bruce Woodford of the Department,* Dell is a relic of the Second World War. His use of his wartime title, his moustache and his tie with its blue angels on a black background all reflect Dell's continued commitment to a role which ceased twenty-five years ago. (*LW*)

*Department, the Branch of British Intelligence concerned with military targets. The Department is of major importance during the Second World War. By the 1960s, however, its role is greatly diminished and most of its functions have been taken over by the Circus. The Department's forgers, Hyde and Fellowby, are now with the Circus, for instance. The decline of the Department is marked by the transference of its headquarters from Baker Street in central London to a dingy house south of the river in Blackfriars Road, by the reduction of its vehicle pool to two vans, and by the nickname 'the Grace and Favour Boys'. The Department's senior staff are Leclerc, the Director; Adrian Haldane, who is in charge of Registry; John Avery, the Director's aide, also known as Special Office; Sandford of Administration; and Bruce Woodford. All but Avery have been with the Department since the war. Support staff include Wilf Taylor, a courier; Gladstone, Haldane's assistant; the technicians McCulloch and Dennison; Berry, a cipher clerk; Miss Courtney of the library; Carol, Leclerc's secretary; and Pine, the porter. The only two field agents identified are Jimmy Gorton in Hamburg and Arthur Fielden in Budapest.

The one activity of any note associated with the Department since the war is Operation Mayfly. In 1964 (or 1965) an East German defector named Fritsche convinces Jimmy Gorton, the Department's agent in Hamburg, that he has evidence of the introduction of Soviet rocketry into the Kalkstadt area of East Germany on September 1 or 2. Impressed by the photographs that Gorton submits, Leclerc commissions Lansen, a commercial pilot on the Department's books as a freelance agent, to take aerial photographs of the area. Lansen completes his mission and hands the film over to Wilf Taylor in Finland. However, Taylor is killed by a car shortly afterwards and the film is lost. A conviction that communist agents are responsible for Taylor's death persuades Leclerc that further action is justified. Therefore, he recruits Fred Leiser, a Department agent during the war, to undertake a mission into East Germany.

Responsibility for organizing this mission (Operation Mayfly) is given to Special Section, which consists of Leclerc, Haldane and Avery. Other wartime members of the Department, Jack Johnson, a wireless expert, and Sandy Lowe, a combat instructor, are recruited to help in the training of Leiser. Training takes place in Oxford and lasts a month. On December 2, Leclerc, Haldane, Avery, Johnson and Leiser travel to Lübeck, on the border between West and East Germany, and on the next day Leiser crosses into the East. He kills a guard at the border, and the East German authorities are therefore immediately alerted to his presence in their country. Nevertheless, he travels by foot, motorcycle and train to Kalkstadt where he broadcasts information back to Lübeck. Because his equipment is out of date and because he forgets to change the crystals, the East Germans quickly identify the source of Leiser's broadcasts. A second call the next night results in his arrest. There are clear indications that Control of the Circus encourages Leclerc's efforts with regard to Operation Mayfly in the hope that a disastrous conclusion will bring about the demise of a rival intelligence unit. Although there is no direct evidence about the fate of the Department, the scandal which is sure to follow Leiser's capture seems likely to be enough to gain Control his objective. (*LW*)

Department for the Protection of the People *See* Abteilung

de Sainte-Yvonne, Comte Henri Jim Prideaux's uncle who teaches his schoolboy nephew at the Lycée Lakanal in Paris to play cricket. (*TT*)

de Silsky, Nick Once a legman* for Haydon's Soviet networks,* de Silsky rises to a position in London Station* in 1972. In both roles he keeps close company with Spike Kaspar, and the two are known as 'the Russians'. De Silsky is forced to retire after Haydon's fall but is briefly resurrected in 1974 along with Bland and Kaspar to help in the attempt to rescue the Churayevs. After this he has no further official contact with the Circus but is recruited by Esterhase to play a hard-man role along with Skordeno in the team gathered together in Berne to assist Smiley in the kidnapping and blackmailing of Grigoriev. In appearance de Silsky is blond and stocky but nothing is known of his personality because he speaks only to Kaspar and maintains a blank facial expression. (*TT; HS; SP*)

*deskman Agent who works at headquarters rather than in the field. (*HS*)

'Detective Chief Superintendent of Police' Officer in charge of the investigation into General Vladimir's murder. The team assisting him includes Constable Hall, Sergeant Pike, Inspector Hallowes and Mr Murgatroyd. The Superintendent is a young giant, turning grey, and his manner combines pomposity with a gentleness that doubtless derives from his devout Christianity. Like his former superior, Mendel, he is a good judge of character and needs only a few minutes' acquaintance to grasp something of Smiley's greatness. (*SP*)

di Salis, Doc — Known as the Mad Jesuit or the Doc, di Salis is a man of many parts. At various times he is a priest, an Orientalist, a scholar and a field agent. His present role is head China-watcher for the Circus. Di Salis's field experience is gained in China during the war when, still a Jesuit, he recruits agents for British Intelligence. After the Japanese invasion he spends time in Changi jail. Di Salis's greatest contribution to the Circus occurs during 1974–75 when he uses his deep understanding of things Chinese to advance Smiley's knowledge of Drake and Nelson Ko. Di Salis is yet another in the cast of misfits and outsiders who are attracted to espionage. He is physically small, with spiky silver hair and his clothes are dirty. Placed next to the large figure of Connie Sachs, he bears a clear resemblance to a monkey. Di Salis has a preference for his own company and in social situations he often appears absurd and can be disruptive. The air of eccentricity which surrounds him is enhanced by his simultaneous interest in ping-pong and the *Meditations* of Thomas Traherne, the seventeenth-century mystic. (*HS*)

Dolphin, Diana Assistant to Phil Porteous in Housekeeping,* the administration department of the Circus, and nicknamed the Dolphin. Wedded in perpetual virginity to the Circus, Diana Dolphin guards her purity within an armour of deodorant and chain-mail handbags. Her only known recreation is bridge. (*TT*)

Dolphin, Operation The most important Circus operation in South East Asia [CIRCUS INDEX]. (*HS*)

Dolphinarium Safe house near Maresfield in Sussex prepared for the interrogation of Nelson Ko. (*HS*)

double-double game The turning of agents against their own side. (*TT*)

*drive, to Technique by means of which one agent, acting as the pursuer, causes the quarry to flee towards a second agent who will be the assassin. (*SP*)

*duck-dive Sudden disappearance. (*HS*)

'dwarf, the' Head of the Asian press bureau which employs Luke. His real name is Michael Hanbury-Steadly-Heamoor. Perhaps to compensate for his smallness, his homosexuality, or his pouchy, disorderly appearance, the dwarf cultivates an argumentative and irritating manner. Although tolerated by his press colleagues, this manner gets him into two brawls within a year with strangers and results in a broken jaw and ribs. The dwarf tries to claim the reward offered for information on the missing journalists, Westerby and Luke. (*HS*)

East German Intelligence Service *See* Abteilung

East German Steel Mission Set up in London by Dieter Frey as a base from which to run his agent Elsa Fennan. (*CD*)

East Germany Although espionage activity is focused on Berlin other parts of East Germany play an important part in two missions. The Department's* poorly judged Operation Mayfly eventually takes Fred Leiser across the East German border at a point near Lübeck. He travels east and then south to the Marienhorst Lake and on to Schwerin. From there he uses motor bike and train to take him via Langdorn to his destination, Kalkstadt, south of Rostock. In the Fiedler–Mundt Operation [CIRCUS INDEX] a few years earlier, in 1962, Alec Leamas travels by car from Berlin to an unidentified farmhouse for interrogation by Jens Fiedler. His answers convince Fiedler of Hans-Dieter Mundt's treachery with the result that Leamas is next taken to Görlitz to be a witness at Mundt's trial. Mundt's surprise witness, Liz Gold, is brought to Görlitz from Leipzig where she has been the guest of the Leipzig–Neuenhagen branch of the East German Communist Party (SED).

Although there is no evidence that his espionage work takes him into East Germany after the partition, George Smiley is a frequent visitor to Dresden prior to its destruction in the Second World War. He loves the place dearly but in 1938 he has the unpleasant experience of seeing his Jewish student, Dieter Frey, imprisoned there. All parts of modern East Germany seem to be equally bleak. For Leiser the northern regions are dark and lifeless; the people he meets are either listless or scared. The southern countryside encountered by Leamas is colourless and empty. Buildings, whether they be workers' flats in Kalkstadt, the Peace Hall in Leipzig or the courtroom in Görlitz, are seedy and decaying. (*SC; LW*)

Ebert, Frau Secretary for the Ward Branch of the East German Communist Party in Leipzig–Hohengrün. Liz Gold stays in her house during her visit to Leipzig. Frau Ebert is married to a man who manages a gravel quarry and has several children with an ideologically unsound interest in chocolate. Though small in stature and grey in appearance, she has great energy for discussing political topics. Despite her awareness of the lack of grass-roots enthusiasm for communism and her obvious fear of the authorities, she seems totally loyal to the Party. (*SC*)

Eckland, Sol Senior member of the American Drug Enforcement Administration in South East Asia in succession to Ed Ristow. His heavily-lined complexion, iron-grey crew-cut and stocky build give Eckland an experienced look and he speaks to Smiley with a blunt rudeness when negotiating about the right to investigate Drake Ko. For Guillam, however, Eckland has a redeeming shyness. (*HS*)

Ellis, Jim Jim Prideaux's workname*. Reports of his capture in Czechoslovakia during Operation Testify refer to him under this name. (*TT*)

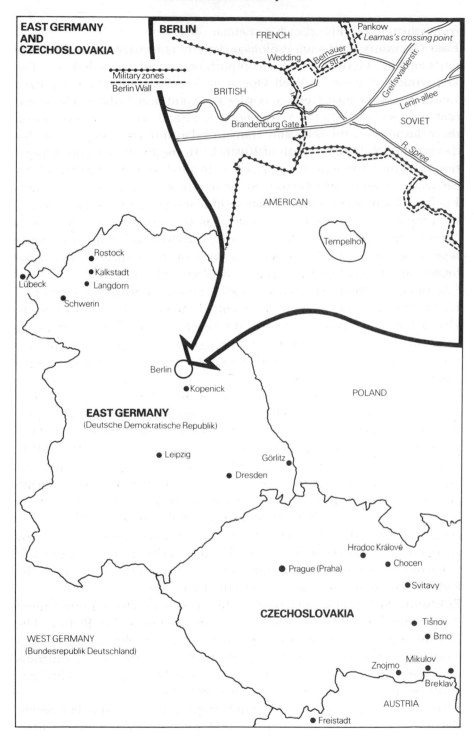

EAST GERMANY
AND
CZECHOSLOVAKIA

BERLIN

FRENCH

Pankow
✗ Leamas's crossing point

••••••• Military zones
– – – Berlin Wall

Wedding

Bernauer Str.

Greifswalderstr.

BRITISH

Lenin-allee

Brandenburg Gate

SOVIET

R. Spree

AMERICAN

Tempelhof

Rostock
Kalkstadt
Lübeck
Langdorn
Schwerin

Berlin
Kopenick

POLAND

EAST GERMANY
(Deutsche Demokratische Republik)

Leipzig
Görlitz
Dresden

Hradoc Králové
Prague (Praha)
Chocen
Svitavy

CZECHOSLOVAKIA

Tišnov
Brno

WEST GERMANY
(Bundesrepublik Deutschland)

Znojmo
Mikulov
Breklav

AUSTRIA

Freistadt

—, **Elvira** Wife of Mikhel and mistress of General Vladimir. Although she has lived with Mikhel for many years, both in and out of wedlock, Elvira's intense reaction to Vladimir's death indicates that her real affections lie elsewhere. A woman over forty, Elvira is stout and has dyed blonde hair done up in a bun. She dresses oddly for her age, in a short skirt and ankle socks. (*SP*)

—, **Elvira** An East German married to a co-worker in an optical firm, and the mistress of Karl Riemeck. She makes her escape into the West shortly before Riemeck is shot down, but is murdered by East German agents about a year later. Elvira is blonde, forty and very tough. (*SC*)

Enderby, Sir Saul Prior to becoming head of the Circus in 1975, Enderby is an Ambassador to Indonesia and the Foreign Office expert on South East Asia. His involvement with the Intelligence Service begins when he is appointed to act as linkman between the Circus and the Foreign Office during Operation Dolphin [CIRCUS INDEX]. A willingness to enter into under-the-table agreements with the American Intelligence Service – the Cousins* – rather than espionage credentials wins Enderby his position as head of the Circus. Between 1975 and 1978 Enderby achieves little success in the espionage field but puts considerable energy into fostering a closer relationship with the Cousins.* Karla's defection in 1978 owes nothing to him.

By 1975 Enderby is on his third wife, an American. He has a number of children who are educated at the French Lycée in South Kensington, London. His leisure pursuits include fishing on his stretch of water in Scotland and playing backgammon, which he does in part at Sam Collins's West End club near Grosvenor Square. With his silk handkerchief and elegant stance, Enderby seems more fitted for the member's enclosure at Ascot than the seamy world of espionage. However, his polish is superficial, and he is in fact a thick-skinned man who cultivates an appearance of stupidity that may have more reality to it than he would like to think. Enderby's lack of sensitivity reveals itself in the way in which he mangles the English language. (*HS; SP*)

Esterhase, Toby At the time Smiley recruits him for the Circus Esterhase is a starving student living in the ruins of a museum in Vienna. His origins, however, are Hungarian. By 1965 when he works with Peter Guillam in Berne in an operation against two Belgian arms dealers, Esterhase has established himself as a watcher* and is beginning to create a reputation for listening.* These skills eventually win him the position of head lamplighter.* In 1971 Esterhase assists Bland in an attempt to salvage a dying network.* He then becomes deeply involved in the collection of Operation Witchcraft [CIRCUS INDEX] material and with

Alleline's accession to power at the end of 1972, Esterhase rises to the position of third in command of London Station* and is mentioned in the New Year's Honours List. Because he is of help to Smiley in the later stages of his investigation into the identity of the mole* Gerald, Esterhase survives the purge that follows the exposure of Haydon's treachery. He is now, however, no more than an ordinary lamplighter* again and he is prominent during Operation Dolphin [CIRCUS INDEX] only when he tapes Connie Sachs and di Salis's interview with Hibbert. The revival of the lamplighters* under Enderby in 1975 is doubtless accompanied by an improvement in Esterhase's professional fortunes, but all that is known of this stage of his career is that he services Circus networks* including the Riga Group of the Baltic Independence Movement led by General Vladimir in Paris.

The termination of lamplighter* activities by a Labour Government unsympathetic to the Circus forces Esterhase into retirement. However, in October 1978, some six months after opening an unsuccessful art gallery in Bond Street, London, under the name Mr Benati, Esterhase is called back to organize the surveillance and kidnapping aspects of the blackmailing of Grigoriev. During his career in espionage Esterhase works under a number of different names. For his dealings with the Riga Group he is called Hector and while in Berne in 1978 he is addressed variously as Jacobi, Anselm and Kurt Siebel.

Little is known of Esterhase's personal life. Of his relatives only one, an uncle who is curator of the ruined museum in Vienna, has been identified. In 1973 he is married to a woman named Mara but it seems that she is one of a number of wives and not necessarily the mother of his two children, a son at Westminster School and a daughter studying medicine. Esterhase's interest in art clearly predates his Mr Benati period. A questionable seventeenth-century Italian painting of the Magi is, for example, to be seen on the walls of his office in 1972. The curator uncle may be the source of Esterhase's knowledge of the subject but the origins of his interest in works of doubtful provenance are not known. For recreation he seems to favour dancing with very young prostitutes, as he does at the Chikito, and taking tea in grand hotels like the Bellevue Palace, both in Berne.

Esterhase's appearance is striking. His hair is white enough to win him the nickname Snow White, he is extremely small, and he stands with the stiff dignity of an ambassador. Other notable features include deep brown eyes, a consistently unfriendly expression, and an odd way with the many languages he speaks. His appearance is of such concern to him that he wears a net over his hair at night and dresses like a male model. One of his most memorable but unsuccessful outfits is the black suit with broad stripe and the large-buckled shoes that he wears for his role as Mr Benati. Beneath this dapper exterior Esterhase is a tough and ruthless character. Not even those with whom he shares the risks of espionage are allowed to draw close and in all relationships he seeks advantage. Generally, the only human qualities Esterhase displays are snobbery and personal vanity, but it does become clear during the final stages of Smiley's pursuit of Karla that he has a real affection for the man who rescued him from poverty in Vienna. (*TT; HS; SP*)

—, **Evdokia** Former secretary and ongoing mistress of Anton Grigoriev. While visiting Evdokia in Moscow Grigoriev confides in her about his recent meeting with Karla. The periodic absence of her husband on military service facilitates Evdokia's affair with Grigoriev. (*SP*)

*fall, the The events precipitated by the revelation of Haydon's treachery. (*HS*)

*fallback Either a cover story (*TT*) or an alternative clandestine meeting place. (*TT*)

*false-flag operation Operation in which agents protect their own country from possible embarrassment by passing themselves off as a member of another Service. (*SP*)

Fanshawe, P. R. de T. Pre-war Oxford tutor and Circus talent spotter, now long dead. A former pupil at Eton and much honoured (OBE and *Légion d'Honneur*), Fanshawe dedicates himself to the preservation of the Empire. To this end he recruits potential spies from the ranks of the Optimates, an upper-class Christ Church club founded by himself. Fanshawe is responsible for directing Haydon and Prideaux towards the Circus. Rumours that he also works for Moscow Centre seem to be untrue. In Smiley's day at Oxford Fanshawe is thin with an eager manner, has flushed cheeks, wears rimless spectacles and carries an umbrella. His sexual preferences are almost certainly homosexual. (*TT*)

Fawley, — Member of the Circus personnel department in 1961. Fawley is a pretentious fool who belongs to several clubs of various kinds, favours representative ties, holds forth on the abilities of sportsmen, and is deeply conscious of his status within the Service. (*SC*)

Fawn, — Before the fall of Haydon, Fawn is a member of the scalp-hunters* and a specialist in assassination. Guillam employs Fawn as Ricki Tarr's guard after his return from Hong Kong in November 1973 and he serves as Smiley's factotum throughout Operation Dolphin [CIRCUS INDEX]. In 1973 Fawn is a small, well-groomed, dark-eyed and soft-spoken man with an obliging manner. His appearance gives little hint of his trade. While working for Smiley he reveals manic traits including self-torture when separated from his beloved chief, a tendency to overreach himself in the performance of any task, and the compulsive squashing of rubber balls during periods of waiting. As the control he has carefully cultivated as a scalphunter* breaks down, so he begins to commit gratuitous acts of violence including a disgusting assault on a would-be thief in Hong Kong and an over-vigorous defence of Smiley from an attack mounted by Jerry Westerby. While it is possible that Fawn is acting on orders when he shoots Westerby (if he is indeed the unnamed killer) this piece of savagery would complete his deterioration into insanity and he is never heard of again. (*TT; HS*)

Feger, Fritz Second man in seniority in the East German DDR Defence Ministry and Alec Leamas's informant from November 1954 to late 1956. He dies in prison. (*SC*)

—, Felicity Bill Haydon's Washington mistress who brings their relationship to a crisis point in 1971 by deciding that she wants a baby. (*TT*)

Felicity, Mother *See* Mother Felicity

'Fellowship, Barbara' *Nom-de-plume* under which Ailsa Brimley writes the advice column in the *Christian Voice*. (*MQ*)

Fennan Case Chronology [CIRCUS INDEX].

Fennan, Elsa Born Elsa Freimann in 1917 in Dresden, she is imprisoned from 1938 to 1945 by the Nazis because she is a Jew. As a result of this experience she is bedridden for three years after the war. Her marriage to Samuel Fennan, with whom she lives in Merridale Lane, Walliston, Surrey, takes place in 1952. In 1955 Elsa Fennan is recruited for the East German Intelligence Service, the Abteilung, by Dieter Frey during a holiday in Garmisch, Switzerland, and steals secrets from her husband, a member of the Foreign Office, until he is murdered in January 1960. Elsa herself is murdered by Dieter Frey in February of the same year. Death spares her almost immediate arrest by George Smiley who is on the verge of solving the Fennan case [CIRCUS INDEX].

Elsa Fennan's appearance is shaped by her wartime experiences. She is frail, looks older than her forty-three years, and has a deeply-worn face. Hair which was once blonde and flowing is now cut short and dyed an ugly yellow. Despite her physical condition Elsa Fennan does not give any impression of weakness. Her expression is fierce and intense and she communicates a sense of endurance and courage. The enormous self-control developed in order to survive the war and the need for concealment created by her role as a spy make it very difficult for us to come to terms with Elsa Fennan's personality or beliefs. She shows little emotion over her husband's death yet their house is organized in a way that suggests intimacy, and we can assume that his loss is deeply felt. The intense fear of a Nazi revival, which she ascribes to Samuel Fennan when accusing him of being a spy, perhaps provides the motive for her own treacherous behaviour. (*CD*)

Fennan, Samuel Arthur   The son of a Jewish banker, Samuel Fennan is born in Germany but flees from the Nazis to England before the war. He is up at Oxford in the 1930s, at which time he temporarily develops Marxist sympathies with the result that in 1936 he joins the Communist Party. Fennan starts his career in the Foreign Office at the German desk but is transferred to the Asian when he expresses a belief in the division of Germany. A few months before his death Fennan begins to work on American material. The suspicion that his wife, Elsa Fennan, whom he married in 1952, is stealing confidential material from him causes Fennan to establish contact with George Smiley. Unfortunately their meeting is observed by his wife's controller, Dieter Frey, and Fennan is murdered on January 3, 1959 (or 1960) by Hans-Dieter Mundt. Fennan has dry, chalky skin and a lined face which makes him seem older than his forty-four years. His profile, however, is youthful and he cuts his hair in an undergraduate style. He has a polished and cultured manner very much at odds with his home environment in Walliston, a lower middle-class area of Surrey. Although clearly serious and rather restrained, Fennan is a kind and popular person and has a wide range of interests including chess, skiing, the works of Brecht, Westerns, and charity work. (*CD*)

Ferguson, —   Former manager of the lamplighters'* transport pool who provides George Smiley with a motorcycle escort during his investigation into Vladimir's death. In his black leather motorcycle gear Ferguson looks like a harbinger of death but in reality he is a good-natured and dutiful man with a keen admiration for Smiley. (*SP*)

*ferret   Person trained to discover electronic listening devices. (*HS*)

Fiedler, Jens   Head of Counter Intelligence and deputy head of Security in the Abteilung. As a child Fiedler, a Jew, is evacuated to Canada but he returns to East Germany in 1946. His training is in law but he pursues a career as an intelligence officer. It is intended that he will replace Hans-Dieter Mundt at the East German Steel Mission in London. However, the Mission is closed after the murder of Samuel Fennan and in late 1959 Fiedler becomes head of Counter Intelligence. Mundt's work as a double agent soon arouses Fiedler's suspicions but he is eventually out-manoeuvred by Control's Fiedler–Mundt Operation [CIRCUS INDEX] and executed for bringing false charges in April 1962. Fiedler is short, slim, neat but slightly animal in appearance. His eyes are brown and bright. He is remorseless and apparently unfeeling but is also serious and honest. By nature a solitary person he avoids cliques and rises in the Abteilung through ability rather than intrigue. Fiedler is a Stalinist with a firm and intelligent belief in communist ideology and a real interest in exploring the philosophical underpinnings of the bourgeois, Christian approach to experience. (*SC*)

Fiedler–Mundt Operation Chronology [CIRCUS INDEX].

Fielding, Adrian French medievalist from Cambridge and an early member of the Circus. Although Fielding rarely leaves his College rooms he travels to Oxford in July 1928 to sit on a committee with Jebedee, Sparke and Steed-Asprey which recruits George Smiley for the Circus. After devoting himself full-time to intelligence during the war, Fielding returns to Cambridge to work on a new thesis on the legendary eighth-century hero, Roland. According to one report Fielding disappears during the war, but it is likely that he is being confused with Jebedee. However, he is definitely dead by 1960. Adrian Fielding is the brother of Terence Fielding. (*CD; MQ*)

Fielding, Terence R. The Senior Housemaster at Carne School. During the Second World War Fielding, along with Felix D'Arcy, virtually runs Carne School and in 1945 he becomes a housemaster but because of his involvement in a homosexual scandal with a young airman he is never granted a permanent position. As a result he has no pension to look forward to and must plan to continue teaching after his retirement in 1960. To this end he secures an appointment at a crammer's in Somerset. Before leaving Carne Fielding murders Stella Rode who is blackmailing him and Tim Perkins who can provide evidence of his guilt. He is arrested for murder after an investigation conducted by George Smiley (who has temporarily left the Circus) at the invitation of his old colleague, Ailsa Brimley, who had been secretary to Adrian Fielding in her Circus days.

Everything about Terence Fielding is large scale. He has a huge physique, an abundance of wild grey hair, a dramatic voice, and he wears a billowing and elaborate gown complete with buttonhole. For him any social occasion demands a performance and he uses a combination of elaborate staging and provocative comments to ensure that his role is a starring one. Because Fielding speaks always for effect he is not an easy man to understand. However, there does seem to be a core of truth in the scorn he expresses both for himself and for Carne School. Fielding's low self-esteem, which compels him to seek escape in play-acting, seems to owe a great deal to his acute sense of how poorly he comes out of any comparison with his richly talented brother, Adrian Fielding, and to the humiliations caused him by his wartime lapse. (*MQ*)

*fieldman Agent who works in enemy territory. (*HS*)

*fifth floor Senior Circus administration [CIRCUS INDEX]. (*SP*)

*finger man Assassin. (*SP*)

*fireman Agent. (*TT*)

*fireproof Invulnerable. (*TT*)

*flash Most urgent grade of cable message from an agent in the field to the Circus. (*TT*)

Fong, Daisy Long-serving assistant to Mr Hibbert at the Lord's Life Mission in Shanghai who eventually abandons Christianity in favour of communism. (*HS*)

*foot-in-the-door operation Situation in which an agent must rely on bluff or force in order to make contact with the target. (*HS*)

*footpad Spy. (*TT*)

*footwork Espionage technique. (*TT*)

Ford, Arthur Grocer in Bayswater, London. His grey overalls, grey trilby hat and cautious, mean, smug attitudes mark Ford as the archetypal *petit bourgeois*. He will not even break a lock to allow Liz Gold access to the sick Alec Leamas until promised compensation for the damage. Although Leamas provokes the quarrel which leaves Ford with a broken jaw it is difficult to be too sympathetic to a man who will not give credit to a customer he has known for some months. (*SC*)

'Forbes-Lisle, Andrew' Cover name used by Peter Guillam during Operation Dolphin [CIRCUS INDEX]. Forbes-Lisle is the Managing Director of Bullion Universal Security Advisers of South Moulton Street, London, a company supposedly planning to employ Lizzie Worthington. Smiley calls on Forbes-Lisle to authorize his interview with Lizzie's father, Humphrey Pelling. His military officer manner clearly impresses Pelling. (*HS*)

*fragged Vietnam War jargon for emotionally fragmented. (*HS*)

Free Baltic Library Bastion of lost hopes, the Library divides its collection into categories made up of the names of countries absorbed into the Soviet Union: Latvia, Lithuania, Estonia. In addition to the books, patrons are provided with chess boards, a samovar and a photocopier. The Library is run by Mikhel and is on the third floor above an antiquarian bookshop. Since it overlooks the forecourt of the British Museum it must be located on, or just off, Great Russell Street, London. (*SP*)

Freimann, Elsa *See* Fennan, Elsa

'Freitag' Nickname given to Hans-Dieter Mundt by Elsa Fennan, from Man Friday in *Robinson Crusoe*. His colleague Dieter Frey is then called Mr Robinson. (*CD*)

Frey, Dieter In 1938 at the age of nineteen Frey is a student at the provincial German University where George Smiley teaches. His outspoken anti-Nazi views ensure that he is arrested when he returns home to Dresden for the vacation. Although his father has already died in a concentration camp, Frey is placed in a general rather than a Jewish prison and is released after three months. During the war Frey is given a clerical position on the railways which allows him ample opportunity to fulfil his simultaneous role as an agent for the Circus working under George Smiley. After the partition in 1946 he returns to Dresden and becomes a member of the Abteilung – East German Intelligence. Frey establishes the East German Steel Mission in London in 1956 to provide him and his colleague Hans-Dieter Mundt with cover while they run the agent, Elsa Fennan, recruited in 1955 in Garmisch, Switzerland. She calls them Mr Robinson and Freitag respectively (from *Robinson Crusoe*). She proves to be a useful source until 1959 (or 1960) when the investigation into the apparent suicide of her husband, Samuel Fennan, causes a chain of events that terminates with her murder by Frey and Frey's death in a struggle with Smiley.

In appearance Frey is a romantic figure, tall, handsome with unruly black hair, and crippled. In his approach to experience he is a total absolutist committed to abstract notions of the general good which make him scornful of individual life. Only in his final moments, when he sacrifices his own life rather than kill his old friend Smiley, does Frey break this pattern. (*CD*)

*frighten the game To alert the target of an operation unintentionally. (*HS*)

Fritsche, — East German defector who persuades Jimmy Gorton (the Department's* agent in Hamburg) that Soviet rocketry has been moved into the Kalkstadt area. He thus provides the motivation for Operation Mayfly. (*CD*)

Frost, J. Deputy Chief Trustee of the South Asian and China Bank in Hong Kong. There is a marked contrast between Frost's respectable position as husband, father and banker, and his private pursuits, which include gambling at the Macao canidrome and Happy Valley Race Track, a mistress in Kowloon, and a liking for nightclubs and brothels such as the Meteor. For some time Frost is able to maintain a balance between the two sides of his personality and within the confines of the bank expresses his anarchistic tendencies only through a lustful attitude to his secretary, Natalie, and through the insulting nickname, Milky Way, by means of which he refers to his superior. His wife's illness, rather fortuitously, leaves him free to become involved in a night of debauchery with Jerry Westerby that makes him vulnerable to blackmail. As a result Frost betrays the bank and gives Westerby access to the trust account held by Drake Ko. For this offence he is brutally tortured and murdered on Ko's orders. Frost is a tubby, small man whose eager expression and sporty green linen suit reflect his longing for excitement. Although hardly the model banker, he is essentially a harmless and likeable person with a considerable zest for life and his peccadilloes scarcely merit the hideous death he experiences. (*HS*)

*funny Police jargon for a member of the Intelligence Service. (*TT*)

Gadfly, Operation This was run by Control probably in the period 1968–71. Little documentation exists regarding Gadfly, perhaps because it was a total failure. Alleline leans heavily on the collapse of the Gadfly despatch system in making his attack on Control's competence. (*TT*)

'Gerald' Code name given by Control to Karla's unidentified mole* in the Circus. (*TT*)

'Gerstmann' Cover name used by Karla in the USA and India in the 1950s. (*TT*)

get into play Department jargon for establishing contact with the target of an operation. (*LGW*)

'Ginger Pig' Nickname given to Oleg Kursky by Connie Sachs. (*SS*)

*give a ticket To kill. (*SC*)

'Glaser, Dr Adolf' Cover name used by Grigoriev for his dealings with Tatiana at the clinic near Berne. (*SP*)

Glaston, Samuel Son of Rufus Glaston, a Lancashire pottery king, and father of Stella Rode. During the Second World War Glaston is a magistrate in the north of England and hears the case in which Terence Fielding is tried for homosexual behaviour. Later he lives in Branxome, near Bournemouth, where he is an important figure in the Tabernacle, a councillor and a member of the Rotary Club. After his wife's death he is cared for by his daughter, Stella, until her marriage. Glaston is an erect man with a strong head who combines a shrewd business sense with firm moral standards. Not even his daughter escapes judgement and he warns her potential husband about her deceitful personality. (*MQ*)

Glikman, Joseph Soviet Jewish music student with a history of dissident behaviour. He spends time in labour camps where he meets Ostrakova. They live together as lovers in Moscow from the time of their release in 1953 until she defects, encouraged by him, in 1956. During this period they exist in one-room poverty because they are not allowed to work. Glikman is the father of Ostrakova's daughter, Alexandra. He dies some time between 1956 and 1978. Ostrakova remembers Glikman as a red-haired man with a ferocious, kindly face. He is an intense talker, passionate about justice and a tireless lover. (*SP*)

Gold, Liz Jewish woman aged twenty-two or twenty-three who divides her time between a job at the Bayswater Library for Psychic Research which pays £6 a week and the Bayswater South Branch of the Communist Party. Her membership of the Party begins in 1954 and, although not possessed of great ideological fervour, she rises to the position of branch secretary. She has a flat at the northern end of Bayswater, London, for which she pays £2.50 a week. In 1961, Liz Gold meets, and falls in love with, Alec Leamas but he terminates their relationship after only a few weeks. An invitation to participate in an exchange between local branches of the Communist Party takes her to Leipzig, East Germany, in April 1962. She is officially the guest of Freda Luman, Secretary of the Leipzig–Neuenhagen Branch, but actually stays with Frau Ebert, Branch Secretary for the Ward Branch of Leipzig–Hohengrün. From there Liz is taken by Holten of the Leipzig District CP to the trial of Hans-Dieter Mundt near Görlitz. Her evidence, as is planned by Mundt and Control, frees Mundt and ruins his accuser, Fiedler. Liz is allowed to escape with Alec Leamas but is shot and killed while crossing the Berlin Wall.

Liz Gold is tall and rather awkward, with a large face that comes near to being pretty. Although closely involved with the Communist Party she is temperamentally at odds with its ideology. For her the individual is all important and she seeks outlets for her warm and loving nature in close relationships with others. Only after her experiences in East Germany does she come to understand her incompatibility with communism. (*SC*)

gold seam Route from bank to bank of laundered funds.

*Golden Oldies Operational directorate of the Circus during Operation Dolphin [CIRCUS INDEX]. (*HS*)

*gorilla Moscow Centre security man. (*TT*)

'Gordon' Cover name used by Peter Guillam during the Hong Kong phase of Operation Dolphin [CIRCUS INDEX]. (*HS*)

Gorton, Jimmy During the war Gorton works in administration with the Department* and takes up his present position after a spell with the Control Commission in Germany. Because of his broken service, Gorton's employment as the Department* agent in Hamburg is on a contract basis. Gorton is responsible for picking up the intelligence report which sets Operation Mayfly in motion, but it seems likely that the faith he puts in material rejected by other intelligence services has more to do with a desire to appear of continuing use than with any rational assessment of its worth. At age fifty-five or fifty-six there would be few further opportunities for him should his position with the Department* be terminated. During the War Gorton has a reputation as a womanizer and includes amongst his conquests Babs Woodford. It is possible that marriage to a German woman may have steadied him down. (*LW*)

'Grace and Favour Boys' Nickname given to the staff of the Department* in the 1960s.

*graded Persil Someone who has been investigated in depth and found to be of no intelligence interest. (*TT*)

Graham, Mrs — Pope Owner of the Hotel Islay, Sussex Gardens, London. According to Mendel, whose long-time informant she is, her real name is simply Graham, Pope being added for grandeur or out of deference to Rome. She is a major's widow and expresses herself in a tired manner intended to emphasize that she is above her present occupation. Despite the superiority of its owner, the Islay, with its restrictions, limited service, clashing wallpapers and poor food is no more than typical of hotels in the Paddington area. (*TT*)

grand slam operation Operation in which numerous watchers are used to keep track of the movements of an enemy agent. (*TT*)

Grant, Captain — Official at the Happy Valley racecourse in Hong Kong. Grant is young, witty, elegant and smokes Turkish cigarettes in a holder. The skullduggery surrounding horse-racing seems to amuse rather than offend him and he maintains an affable manner when confronted with Drake Ko's betting coup. (*HS*)

'Gregory' General Vladimir's workname.* (*SP*)

Grigoriev, Anton After beginning his career as an economics professor Grigoriev moves into the diplomatic service. He holds positions in Moscow, where he works in the Trade Ministry, Bonn, Potsdam, where he is First Secretary (Commercial) to the Soviet Mission for three years, and Berne, again as a Commercial Counsellor. In September 1978 he is recruited by Karla to take responsibility for his insane daughter, Tatiana, who is a patient in a clinic near Berne. Using the cover name Dr Adolf Glaser, Grigoriev manages a bank account in Thun, near Berne, intended to provide funds for Tatiana's care. He also visits her once a week. Because he has no experience of espionage technique, Grigoriev proves an easy target for a blackmail operation mounted by Smiley and Esterhase and provides the final pieces of information needed to secure Karla's defection. As a reward for his betrayal of Karla Grigoriev is allowed to resettle in Australia.

Grigoriev is married and has children who attend the Soviet Mission School in Geneva as weekly boarders. Once he begins to work for Karla, Grigoriev moves out of the embassy ghetto in Muri and takes up residence in the Elfenau. He also buys a second-hand Mercedes. For recreation he plays chess and takes on mistresses. His secretaries in Bonn, Potsdam and Moscow, the last of whom is named Evdokia, and a girl in the Visa Section of the Berne Embassy, known to Esterhase's watchers* as 'little Natasha', all find their way into Grigoriev's bed.

In appearance Grigoriev epitomizes mediocrity. He is rather stout and short, has thick, crinkly grey hair and rimless spectacles, and wears unflattering suits and ill-fitting shoes. His left-handedness is one of his few unusual features. Although pompous in manner, Grigoriev is in fact something of a romantic and has pursued a diplomatic career with its promise of material rewards only to pacify his wife, the terrifying Grigorieva. His affairs provide a last outlet for a romantic spirit which is largely chained up within the institution of marriage. It is perhaps this ability to maintain a dream of love that wins Grigoriev the affection of the watchers* who are inspired to name him Tricky Tony after observing his relationship with 'little Natasha'. (SP)

Grigorieva, — The wife of Anton Grigoriev. Grigorieva is a very large woman with red hair and a scowl who dominates everything around her. She forces her husband into a diplomatic career he does not really want in order to fulfil her desire for foreign clothes, music and privileges, and runs all aspects of embassy life including the kindergarten, indoctrination classes, the ping-pong club and women's badminton. Only machines escape her control; she is unable to ride a bicycle and is an appalling driver. Her intellectual needs are satisfied by the rather light-weight monthly magazine *Schweizer Illustrierte*. (SP)

'Grodescu' Cover name under which Stokovsky operates a photographic business in Paris. Grodescu is a French–Romanian. (TT)

Guillam, Marie-Claire Wife of Peter Guillam. The exact date of their marriage is not known but their relationship begins presumably after his posting to Paris in 1977. She is expecting a baby in March 1979. Marie-Claire is young and rather silly. Her major ambitions are maternal and these embrace Guillam as much as the forthcoming baby – she keeps a stock of invalid foods against the day when he will satisfy her dreams by falling ill. If her notepaper with its grazing bunnies is anything to go by she also has dreadful taste. (SP)

Guillam, Peter A lifetime involvement with the Circus begins for Guillam during the Second World War when he serves with Leamas in Norway and joins Haydon in a parachute drop into Greece. By the 1950s he has developed into an expert on Satellite* (Eastern European countries) espionage and is able to provide Smiley with considerable information on the Abteilung and its methods during the investigation into the murder of Samuel Fennan in 1959 (or 1960). Fennan's murderer, Hans-Dieter Mundt, actually falls into Guillam's hands but, rather than bring him to justice, he turns him into a double agent and then connives in his escape. Some time in 1960 (or 1961) Guillam travels to Ankara but the purpose of this visit to Turkey is not known. In 1961 he also plays a minor role in the Fiedler–Mundt Operation [CIRCUS INDEX] aimed at protecting his agent Mundt.

After 1962 Guillam develops networks* in French North Africa, but these are blown* in 1965. He then returns to England and is sent almost immediately to Berne where he works with Esterhase in an operation directed against two Belgian arms dealers. After this Guillam runs home-based operations including the recruitment of Polish, Soviet and Chinese seamen. Prideaux's capture by Soviet forces in Czechoslovakia during Operation Testify in October 1972 leaves a vacancy as head scalphunter* which Guillam is assigned to fill. After only one year in this position he assists Smiley in the investigations which result in the identification of Bill Haydon as the traitor in the Circus ranks. The reorganization which follows sees Guillam elevated to the fifth floor* for the first time in his career, and he works closely with Smiley throughout Operation Dolphin [CIRCUS INDEX]. However, things turn out poorly for Guillam at the end of the case. He suffers a broken collar-bone as a consequence of a fight with Jerry Westerby and, with Enderby's accession to power, he is exiled once again to Brixton, the scalphunter* headquarters in South London. Two more years as head scalphunter* are followed by a posting to Paris as head (legal) resident* at the Embassy, a position usually reserved for burnt-out agents. Whether this is a fair judgement of Guillam's abilities is question-able in light of the speed, courage and ingenuity he reveals in October 1978 while trying to rescue his wife from what he thinks is a kidnapping attempt. This incident brings him into contact once again with his old chief, Smiley, whom he assists in the concealment of Ostrakova from Soviet assassins. In the course of his career in espionage Guillam uses the cover names Lampton, Will, Lofthouse, Andrew Forbes-Lisle and Gordon.

Guillam's origins shape him for a career in espionage. His father, a French businessman and Arabist, spies for a Circus réseau (network*) during the Second World War and his mother, who is English, works in coding. As a result Guillam develops only a limited life beyond the Circus. Somewhere along the way he manages to become an expert on landscape gardening, but most of his free time is dedicated to his cars, always Porsches, and his girlfriends. The most notable of these are Camilla, a music student with whom he lives for a while at his flat in Eaton Place, London, during 1973, and Molly Meakin, a fellow intelligence officer, with whom he conducts a passionate affair throughout Operation Dolphin [CIRCUS INDEX]. Guillam does not marry until 1978, and then it is to a young French woman called Marie-Claire. They live in an apartment in the Neuilly district of Paris and expect their first child in March 1979.

Guillam is tall, powerful, handsome and graceful and always dresses elegantly. In 1973, for example, he sports a silk umbrella with a stitched leather handle and a gold ring. His most notable feature, however, is his apparent agelessness. In 1962 Liz Gold judges him to be about forty and so does Smiley in 1973. Unfortunately, accompanying this eternal youth is a perpetual immaturity. Guillam's notions of espionage are romantic and chivalric ones and he takes as his model of excellence the apparently heroic figure of Bill Haydon. Experience teaches Guillam little and, although he feels he has grown up after discovering that Haydon is a traitor, there is little evidence that he really changes. During Operation Dolphin [CIRCUS INDEX] he commits himself wholeheartedly to Smiley's cause but reveals throughout a lack of sound judgement and a good deal of impetuosity. His choice of a supremely silly child-bride suggests that in his private life, too, Guillam continues to be motivated by a spirit of chivalry rather than mature judgement. (*CD; SC; TT; HS; SP*)

Habolt, Max Czech agent employed by the Circus as a lamplighter.* Working under the name Rudi Hartmann, Habolt assists Jim Prideaux in Czechoslovakia during Operation Testify. He is dismissed from the Service for his part in this operation and then works in a parking garage in St John's Wood Road, London. Habolt is a fairly complex figure. In appearance he is a dandy. Even at work he wears white overalls with the collar turned up in a rakish way. Underneath are a suit, shirt and tie in carefully matched shades of blue, and zipped flying boots. He also wears a number of rings. Habolt's face is handsome but its heavy lines and still eyes reveal that his personality also has a hard and passionate aspect to it. During his conversation with Smiley about Testify, Habolt reveals himself as an intensely feeling person capable of a rather frightening anger at what he sees as the British betrayal of his native Czechoslovakia. (*TT*)

'Hajeck, Vladimir' Cover name used by Jim Prideaux in Czecho-slovakia during Operation Testify. Hajeck is a Czech photographer resident in Paris. (*TT*)

Haldane, Adrian After taking Greats at Oxford, Haldane pursues a career with the Department* which stretches back at least as far as the Second World War. During the war Haldane uses the workname* Captain Hawkins and works for a time with George Smiley. By the 1960s he is in charge of Registry for the Department* and directs Special Section during Operation Mayfly. Haldane is a bachelor and lives with his sister. Once a cricketer he now fills his leisure time with crosswords and half bottles of burgundy. Haldane's appearance is that of a sick man. He is very thin, continually fidgets with his hands and has a chronic cough. His cultivated voice is used to express complaints and sarcastic comments. Deeply class-conscious, Haldane is particularly scornful of Fred Leiser for his common man's ways and foreigner's uncertainty about the proprieties of English life. Indeed, his attitude to the world in general is scarcely less contemptuous. He distances himself from his colleagues whose dissociation from reality he recognizes, but he lacks the moral energy to intervene when Leclerc's fantasies begin to get out of hand and is supremely indifferent to the sacrifice of Fred Leiser to the pointless Operation Mayfly. (*LW*)

Hall, Constable — Young police officer who vomits and blasphemes at the sight of the murdered Vladimir's shattered face. His blasphemy arouses the ire of his superior, the Detective Chief Superintendent. (*SP*)

Hamburg The scene of several important events in the operation that leads to Karla's defection. Leipzig makes a vital handover to Villem Craven on a steamer on the Aussenalster and Smiley meets Kretzschmar at the Blue Diamond nightclub in the St Pauli district. During this visit Smiley establishes a base at the Four Seasons Hotel in Station Square. Leipzig is murdered at a water camp near to the city. The less successful Operation Mayfly also begins in Hamburg when Fritsche persuades Jimmy Gorton that his information about Soviet weaponry merits investigation. Smiley has spent part of his childhood in Hamburg and he recognizes that what was once a rich and graceful city has been rebuilt after wartime bombing as a characterless conglomeration of high-rise buildings and smoked glass. (*LW; SP*)

Hanbury-Steadly-Heamoor, Michael *See* 'dwarf, the'

*handwriting Agent's individual operational style. (*TT*)

Hankie, Teddy An aged lamplighter* who distinguishes himself by photographing Polyakov (Col. Viktorov) wearing his true military medals at the Cenotaph Remembrance Day service, thus penetrating his cover as that of the son of a transporter. Connie Sachs admits to being very fond of Hankie. (*TT*)

*hardware Electronic equipment. (*HS*)

Harlowe, Mrs — Tim Perkins's cello teacher who lives at Longmeade near Carne School. Although neurotic and insistent on conformity to propriety, Mrs Harlowe is a kind person genuinely concerned for the emotional well-being of her pupils. (*MQ*)

Harriman, Major C. J. Reid- A veterinarian living near Sturminster in Dorset, Harriman tends to Dorothy D'Arcy's dogs and puts down Stella Rode's little mongrel. Although retired from the army, with which he served in the East, Harriman still affects a military style. His shirt and tie are khaki, he wears old Service dress trousers and his wrist-watch is turned inwards. He also plays with his rather foolish moustache in a way typical of senior officers. Not surprisingly, he likes to be called Major. Harriman's further pretension to be a country gentleman is reflected in his tweed jacket with its leather buttons. There is evidence that his business is not successful enough to sustain the way of life to which he aspires. Besides being a snob, Harriman is a bigot with a special prejudice against Roman Catholics. Given his particular combination of qualities it is not surprising that he is rather well liked by the D'Arcys. (*MQ*)

'Hartbeck, Fred' Cover name used by Fred Leiser when operating in East Germany during Operation Mayfly. Hartbeck is an unmarried mechanic from Magdeburg travelling to take up a position at the State Co-operative shipbuilding works in Rostock. (*LW*)

'Hartmann, Rudi' Cover name used by Max Habolt when assisting Prideaux in Czechoslovakia during Operation Testify. Hartmann travels in glass and ovenware. (*TT*)

Havelock, Brigadier — Chief of the Carne Constabulary. Havelock is very much an establishment man with a background of Carne School and the Indian Army. For his services to society he has been awarded the OBE. Now in his last year before retirement Havelock seems far more interested in hunting and his spaniels, which he keeps in his office, than in police work. The running of the station is left largely to Inspector Rigby. Havelock is unprepossessing in appearance, being a tiny man with a heavy yellow moustache and a few thin white hairs stretched across his bald head. His stiff white collar, his blimpish style of speech and his insistence on the value of tradition make him appear comically old-fashioned. Much of Havelock's behaviour during the Rode murder case is very foolish, particularly his insistence that Jane Lyn be arrested. It seems likely that this is the result of excessive concern for the good name of Carne School rather than of any innate stupidity. Presented with the case against Stanley Rode, he is very quick to see the crucial problem concerning the disposal of the murder weapon. (*MQ*)

'Hawkins, Captain' Cover name used by Adrian Haldane during the Second World War. (*LW*)

Haydon, Bill Agent with a lengthy career serving both the Circus and Moscow Centre. His family background and his early achievement make it seem likely that Haydon will achieve greatness. His father is a high-court judge and two of his sisters are married into the aristocracy. Before he turns twenty he begins to develop a reputation as a painter and an explorer, and while at Christ Church, Oxford, he is also known as a right-wing political thinker and a socialite. Membership of the Christ Church

Optimates club provides opportunities for the development of both tendencies, and yet during his undergraduate years Haydon decides to suppress his many talents and possibilities in favour of a career in espionage and in quick succession is recruited by Fanshawe for the Circus and Karla for Moscow Centre. Before leaving Oxford, he directs Prideaux towards the Circus.

The Second World War is one of the busiest periods in Haydon's espionage career. He recruits agents in the Chinese ports of Wenchow and Amoy, runs French fishing smacks out of the Helford estuary in Cornwall, establishes courier lines across southern Europe, and makes a parachute drop into Greece. It is soon after the war is over that Haydon begins to meet his obligations to Moscow Centre. From 1950 to 1956 he passes on information that can be used against the Americans and after Suez secrets of all kinds. He is rewarded for his efforts with Soviet citizenship in 1961 and two medals. Fortunately for the Circus a Middle-Eastern posting from 1961 to 1965 limits Haydon's opportunities for treachery, but from 1965 to 1973 he does enormous damage. As a member of the building committee in 1966 he plants microphones throughout the Circus and as head of personnel he has opportunities to further the careers of incompetent officers, such as Tufty Thesinger, and to hinder those of capable ones, such as Guillam. The passing of secrets is also facilitated during this period by the posting of Polyakov to London to act as Haydon's go-between with Moscow Centre. To keep credibility he sometimes betrays communists such as the Polish diplomat blackmailed by Ricki Tarr on Haydon's tip-off.

In the early 1970s Haydon is travelling back and forth between London and Washington for negotiations with the Americans which he doubtless sabotages. This does not stop him, however, from setting in motion the most ingenious of all his schemes to further the interests of Moscow Centre. By convincing Alleline of the usefulness of cultivating a supposed source in Soviet Intelligence, code name Merlin, Haydon establishes a particularly effective channel through which to filter his Moscow-bound secrets. This is known as Operation Witchcraft [CIRCUS INDEX]. An attempt by Control to uncover the identity of the traitor, whom he calls Gerald, within the ranks of the Circus fails when Haydon entices him into the disastrous Operation Testify. Following Control's retirement in November 1972 Haydon becomes Commander, London Station* and makes more and more use of opportunities provided by Source Merlin; eventually he is close to having access to American secrets. His efforts are rewarded, ironically, with a mention in the New Year's Honours List. Haydon's career of betrayal is finally ended by Smiley in November 1973 and he is murdered by Prideaux at Sarratt* a few days later.

A career in spying does not entirely prevent Haydon from continuing his work as an artist. He judges his creative period to have been completed by the age of seventeen and it can therefore be assumed that the one-man show held in Oxford in 1938 represents him at his best. Nevertheless there are numerous examples of later work. Two pictures are to be found in the Christ Church Common Room, several in the Arnolfini Gallery in Bristol and Miles Sercombe's office, and others on the walls of Haydon's London girlfriend's mews. Judging by the cramped quality of the latter works, Haydon's self-assessment seems to be accurate. Perhaps to escape his failure as an artist, or even his treachery as a spy, Haydon puts consider-able energy into sexual affairs with members of both sexes. Prideaux is rumoured to be his lover at Oxford, and his later lovers include Felicity in Washington, Jan in Kentish Town, London, a sailor in Notting Hill, London, and an assistant barman called Steggie. The most notable of all his sexual conquests, however, is his cousin, Ann Smiley, whom he seduces at least in part to blur Smiley's vision of him and thus of his betrayal of the Circus. For all his artistic leanings and unconventional sexuality Haydon keeps contact with the upper-class world from which he originates and is a member of the Savile Club in London.

Haydon's dress and appearance are somewhat eccentric. The patches on his jacket are sewn on like diamonds rather than squares, he wears his spectacles thrust up on his forehead and his face is dominated by lank grey hair, bright red cheekbones and penetrating pale blue eyes. His smile, however, makes him handsome and young. What is hidden beneath this vivid exterior is difficult to assess. For a number of people Haydon is the reincarnation of a spirit of chivalrous and romantic Englishness thought to have died with Rupert Brooke and T. E. Lawrence. According to this view of Haydon's character, he becomes a traitor out of disappointment at the inability of a shrinking Empire to give him sufficient scope for achievement. In Smiley's opinion, though, there has always been a hollow ring to his more grandiose expressions of nationalistic fervour and, for all his apparently charismatic qualities, Haydon is never quite a leader. Even Karla prefers Haydon to operate as Alleline's second-in-command. To any close observer it is obvious even before his relationship with Karla is discovered that Haydon's real talents lie in the area of deception. This is why he is such a brilliant operator in the field and why he is drawn so readily to the life of the double agent with its opportunities for multiple betrayals. As with Kim Philby, to what extent a childhood spent with a monstrous father is responsible for shaping Haydon in this way will never be known. (*TT; HS*)

Haydon Case Chronology [CIRCUS INDEX].

*head prefect Member of the Cabinet Office who acts as liaison between the Minister and the Intelligence Service. (*TT*)

Heamoor, Michael Hanbury-Steadly- *See* 'dwarf, the'

Hebden, Adrian Workname* used by George Smiley when visiting Sam Collins at his gambling club. (*TT*)

Hecht, Charles A master at Carne School. Hecht is a pipe-smoker with an athletic profile. A former commander of the Carne Cadet Corps, which he inspected on a white horse, Hecht is a great believer in tradition. Since his values are firmer than his intelligence, Hecht is easily goaded into anger by the cleverly directed jibes of Terence Fielding. (*MQ*)

Hecht, Shane The wife of Charles Hecht. Shane is a truly frightening person. In part this is the result of her enormous physique which is topped off by an aged ermine stole and quantities of black hair. But her real force comes from her remorselessly malicious and snobbish tongue. (*MQ*)

'Hector' Cover name used by Toby Esterhase in his dealings with General Vladimir's Riga Group. (*SP*)

*heeltap Procedure by means of which an agent takes a devious route in order to deceive possible tails (followers). (*HS*)

—, Hercule A Vietnamese much liked by Westerby. Because he has made a practice of supplying information about the Vietcong to British journalists he is desperate to escape following the fall of Saigon. (*HS*)

Hibbert, Doris Daughter of the Reverend Hibbert. Although entering middle age Doris Hibbert is unmarried and devotes herself to the care of her aged father. Born in 1934 or 1935, probably in Shanghai, China, Doris accompanies her father on his extensive travels in the service of God. Before the Japanese invasion and after the war, which is spent in a Japanese prison and in England, she lives in Shanghai. Following the Communist take-over in 1949 she returns to England and lives in Durham before moving to the South Coast in 1967 or 1968. During a visit to the family in Durham in 1967, Doris Hibbert's childhood companion Drake Ko asks her to be his mistress. At age forty Doris Hibbert is a dowdy almost silent woman whose appearance is not brightened by her blonde hair and yellow frock. A lifetime of self-restraint and sacrifice has clearly not suited her and she is a bitter and irascible person, equally cynical about the motives of the Ko brothers and the local garage mechanics. (*HS*)

Hibbert, Reverend — Former Baptist missionary to China. Born in Macclesfield, Cheshire, of a Baptist family, Hibbert attends missionary training school at the age of twenty. Four years later, in about 1918, he joins the Lord's Life Mission in Shanghai. Assisted by Daisy Fong and Charlie Wan he takes in and offers schooling to street children. By the

The Haydon Case: Hotel Islay, Paddington

'The Hotel Islay in Sussex Gardens – where Smiley, under the name of Barraclough, had set up his operational headquarters – was perfectly suited to his needs. . . . Lacon stalked in every evening carrying a fat briefcase containing a consignment of papers from his office . . . Next morning on his way to work he reclaimed the papers and returned the books which Smiley had given him to pad out his briefcase.' (*Tinker, Tailor, Soldier, Spy*)

'You'll do it,' asked Lacon, Cabinet Office adviser to the Circus, 'go forwards, go backwards . . . ?' For one whole week of nights in November 1973, in the down-at-heel Hotel Islay's attic room, Smiley studies minutely the top secret files on Witchcraft material, Source Merlin and Operation Testify which Lacon ferries to him, unknown to Percy Alleline and his Circus staff. And there Smiley finds the vital clue which would lead to the identity of the suspected Circus mole, 'Gerald': the existence of a super-secret safe house in Lock Gardens, Camden Town, to serve the interests of – could it be, both Moscow Centre and the Circus?

Hong Kong: Operation Dolphin

'As they (Jerry and Lizzie) sank into the city, the harbour lay like a perfect mirror at the centre of the jewel box . . . To his surprise she reached across and gave his hand a squeeze. Then he remembered Craw. She did that to everyone, he had said . . .'
(*The Honourable Schoolboy*)

The most important Circus operation in South East Asia – Operation Dolphin – takes place in 1975. Its aim is to investigate the information that funds intended for a Soviet mole are being paid through a Hong Kong bank. Jerry Westerby, journalist and Circus Occasional, is briefed to question the lovely Lizzie Worthington about her 'late' boyfriend Ricardo but commits the fatal – for him – error of becoming infatuated with his target.

The Haydon Case: The Lock Gardens Safe House, Camden Town

'The mole comes first, Smiley thought, the mole plays host: that is protocol, part of the pretence that Polyakov is Gerald's agent . . . The front door opened, someone stepped into the house . . . a second taxi pulled up . . . then he heard voices . . .

"What is our cover story in case we are disturbed?" Polyakov asked in good English. "What is our fallback?" A muffled murmur answered each question . . .

"What will you drink?"

"Scotch," said Haydon, "a bloody great big one."' (*Tinker, Tailor, Soldier, Spy*)

Three long signal flashes from Smiley, ensconced in the scullery of the Lock Gardens safe house, alert Guillam, keeping vigil on the Regent's Canal towpath, that the trap set for Soviet agent Polyakov and Circus traitor 'Gerald' is about to be sprung. Circus personnel quickly converge on the house to learn what Smiley has always known: the traitor in their ranks is Bill Haydon.

time the Japanese invade he has forty-four pupils. In 1936 Drake and Nelson Ko come under Hibbert's wing. Hibbert's wife, Liese, a German Lutheran, dies at the time of the Japanese invasion and, following a period of imprisonment, he returns to England with his daughter, Doris Hibbert. In 1945, after working in the North of England and London, Hibbert returns to China and continues to run the Mission until the Communist take-over in 1949. He is reunited with the Ko brothers during this period, but like his assistant, Daisy Fong, Nelson passes him over in favour of new communist loyalties. Returning to England again, Hibbert works in Durham until retiring in 1967 or 1968 to the South Coast.

In January 1975, when he is interviewed by Connie Sachs and Doc di Salis about the Ko brothers, Hibbert shows every sign of his advanced age of eighty-one. His face has passed beyond weathering, his hair is white, and at times he loses touch with the present. Nevertheless, he can still express himself with vigour and wit in his bluff North Country voice and he resists his daughter's attempts to define him as senile. The most significant aspect of Hibbert's otherwise unremarkable appearance is his continued wearing of the dog collar. For all that he may be retired he clearly continues to define himself in terms of the clerical role which has directed his entire life. For Hibbert religious faith is a fairly simple matter involving love and charity. While by no means naive, Hibbert continues in his eighty-second year to look for good in others and to be tolerant of ways of life different from his own. Much as he has suffered at the hands of the communists, for instance, Hibbert is still willing to accept the sincerity of their search for truth. (*HS*)

—, **Hilary** Up until 1975 when she goes berserk in the cipher office, Hilary works for the Circus. After that she becomes the companion and lover of Connie Sachs at her clapboard cabin outside Oxford. Together, they run the Merrilee Boarding Kennels. Hilary is beautiful with grey eyes but is frail and timid. She uses a dated upper-class slang that recalls her débutante origins. Whether the brutality of the espionage world or the expectation that she will make a conventional marriage within her own class is responsible for her breakdown is not clear. However, a love affair with Connie – who calls her Hils – and the remoteness of their home enable her to keep a tenuous hold on sanity. (*SP*)

*hit-and-run job Espionage mission involving particular danger and the use of violence. (*TT*)

Holten, — Member of the Leipzig District Communist Party who takes Liz Gold to Görlitz for her appearance at Mundt's trial. (*SC*)

*honey-trap Enticing of an enemy agent into a sexually-compromising situation for purposes of blackmail. (*TT*)

Hong Kong Two of Smiley's most important conflicts with Karla are played out partly in Hong Kong. In 1973 a routine mission to Hong Kong brings Ricki Tarr into contact with Irina, a Soviet agent, who informs him that Karla has a mole* in the Circus, and in 1974 Smiley initiates Operation Dolphin [CIRCUS INDEX] by uncovering evidence that Drake Ko, a Hong Kong millionaire, is somehow connected with another of Karla's deep penetration agents. Although the Haydon case [CIRCUS INDEX] which results from Tarr's discovery is worked out in London, Operation Dolphin [CIRCUS INDEX] eventually takes Smiley and his colleagues to Hong Kong.

While conducting his investigations in Hong Kong Tarr stays in Kowloon at the Golden Gate Hotel and his targets, Boris and Irina, are at the Alexandra Lodge off Marble Road out on North Point. At night Boris frequents the Cat's Cradle in Kowloon and Angelika's in Wanchai. Tarr takes Irina to the North Shore and to the New Territories. Other meetings with Irina take place at the English Baptist Church. During Operation Dolphin [CIRCUS INDEX] Westerby stays in an apartment on Cloudview Road, North Point, while Drake Ko lives in Headland Road in the area between Repulse Bay and Stanley and Lizzie Worthington at an apartment in the Midlevels. Frost works at a bank located opposite the Chater Gardens. Phoebe Wayfarer lives in the Chinese area half a mile from Central and Pedder. Much of Craw's social life takes place at the Foreign Correspondents' Club on Chater Road near the Hong Kong Club, but he lives out in the New Territories. Collins has an apartment on Bowen Road in the Midlevels for a short time in 1975. When Westerby takes a devious route to Frost's bank on Chater Square he covers a large part of the Central district between Pedder and Jackson Road. He walks via Cartier's, the Mandarin Hotel, and the old Post Office to the Connaught Centre and then retraces his steps noting Jardine's and Swire's as he goes. After reaching his starting point he continues along Chater Road to the Hong Kong Club and finally walks around two sides of the Chater Gardens to the bank. His escape route takes him over much of Hong Kong Island and Kowloon, including Queen's Pier, Aberdeen, Stanley and towards Clear Water Bay. The final encounter with the Ko brothers takes place on Po Toi, the most southerly of the Hong Kong group of islands. Westerby reaches it by boat from Causeway Bay.

Other Hong Kong locations include Des Voeux Road, where Drake Ko lives after moving from Shanghai, and the Ritz ballroom in the King's Road near Causeway Bay where he runs his prostitution racket; High Haven, the abandoned headquarters of British Intelligence on the Peak; the Walled City, where Frost's body is found; Hollywood Road, which is

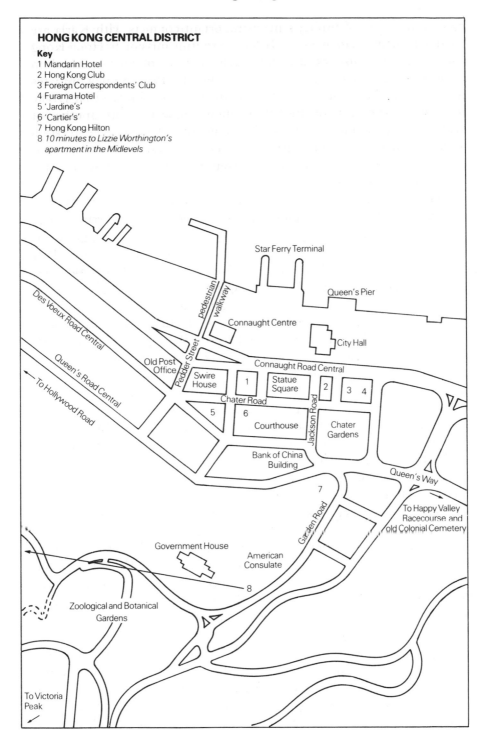

HONG KONG CENTRAL DISTRICT

Key
1 Mandarin Hotel
2 Hong Kong Club
3 Foreign Correspondents' Club
4 Furama Hotel
5 'Jardine's'
6 'Cartier's'
7 Hong Kong Hilton
8 *10 minutes to Lizzie Worthington's
   apartment in the Midlevels*

Star Ferry Terminal

Queen's Pier

Des Voeux Road Central

Queen's Road Central

To Hollywood Road

pedestrian walkway

Connaught Centre

City Hall

Old Post Office

Pedder Street

Connaught Road Central

Swire House

1

Statue Square

2

3   4

Chater Road

5

6

Jackson Road

Courthouse

Chater Gardens

Bank of China Building

Queen's Way

7

Garden Road

To Happy Valley Racecourse and old Colonial Cemetery

Government House

American Consulate

8

Zoological and Botanical Gardens

To Victoria Peak

close to where Ko's fortune-teller lives; the Furama and Hilton Hotels in Chater Road and Garden and Queens Way respectively, which Westerby uses to make phone contact with Craw; the American Consulate, five minutes uphill on Garden Road from the Hilton; Happy Valley Race Track, west of Central district in Wong Nai Chung Road, where Westerby first meets Ko; the Old Colonial Cemetery, just to the southwest of Happy Valley, where Ko's son is buried; Pollock's path on the Peak, where Craw makes contact with an American agent; and Stanley Hospital, where Frost's sick wife is being treated.

The agent trying to operate in Hong Kong finds himself having to deal with two very different worlds. The first is a familiar, dull and European one created by British colonialism. This is the world of aimless cricket

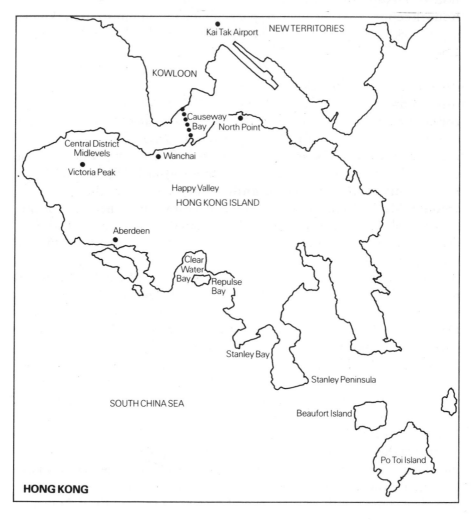

matches, the Hong Kong Club, electric doors, air conditioning, the great trading houses such as Jardine's and Swire's, Henry Moore's 'Oval with Points' and international shops and hotels such as Cartier's and the Hilton. The second is the much more impenetrable world of the Chinese with their complex and confusing financial dealings, crime rings, gambling games, and mass of local customs and activities. Yet much as it makes life difficult for the Westerner it is this latter world that gives Hong Kong its special quality. Far from being merely a bed or a girl, a place that ceases to exist once it has been left, as Luke and Westerby think, Hong Kong is a vital place that glows with life. (*TT; HS*)

*hood A spy. (*HS*)

*house To capture. (*TT*)

housekeeper Staff member responsible for the administration, known as Housekeeping, of the Circus headquarters at Cambridge Circus, London. (*TT*)

*illegal resident *See* below-the-line*

immediate Grade of secret telegram second in urgency to flash. (*TT*)

Indocharter Aviation company based in Vientiane, Laos, for which Charlie Marshall and Tiny Ricardo are pilots. (*HS*)

*inhumane killer Moscow Centre assassination device which can be concealed in a camera or brief-case and fires soft-nosed bullets. (*SP*)

Inter-Ministerial Steering Committee *See* Wise Men, the*

Iredale, Mr — Commandant of the Cadets at Carne School. According to the snobbish Shane Hecht his background is undistinguished and, despite his wife being 'such a nice person', the Iredales are unable to keep their servants. (*MQ*)

'Irina' Moscow Centre agent referred to as Irina by Ricki Tarr. Her real name is not known. Irina's long career as an intelligence officer includes work as a supervisor in the filing department of the Trade Ministry in Dzerzhinsky Square and a field-posting to Hong Kong in 1973 under cover as a textile buyer with a trade delegation. Her skills include a knowledge of English, acquired during a three-year course, and expertise with microdots and radio transmission. During her mission in Hong Kong Irina gives away vital secrets to Ricki Tarr about the existence of a Soviet mole* in the Circus. As punishment for this she is executed at the Lubianka in July 1973.

Irina is the common-law wife of a fellow agent named Boris whom she met during training. By the time they visit Hong Kong together they have become almost completely alienated, but Irina's dissatisfaction with Boris is evident some months earlier when she takes as her lover Brod, known to her as Ivlov, a fellow worker in the filing department and the source of her knowledge about the mole.* Irina is young and plain but has a pretty smile. Her life as a spy has left her with a deep sense of entrapment and she longs to achieve freedom by re-establishing connection with the God she learnt of from her peasant Baptist mother, and with love. Lacking any obvious outlet for her dissatisfactions Irina becomes depressed and drinks too much. Given her state of mind it is not hard for Ricki Tarr to extract secrets from Irina in return for promises of a new life of love and freedom. In the few days before her treachery is discovered Irina is able to enjoy her simultaneous fantasies of becoming a Baptist nun and creating an idyllic family life with Tarr in Scotland. (*TT*)

'Ivlov' Cover name used by Brod, a Moscow Centre agent, while working in London and Moscow. (*TT*)

JPR *See* Ribble, J. P.

'Jacobi' Cover name used by Toby Esterhase during the observation of Grigoriev at the bank in Thun during the Karla case [CIRCUS INDEX]. (*SP*)

—, Jan Girlfriend of Bill Haydon and perhaps the mother of his baby. Jan is a flat-faced girl who lives in some squalor in a mews cottage in Kentish Town, London. Her shaking hands, forgetfulness, rapid changes of mood and the bags under her eyes indicate that she is in a very disturbed emotional state. Haydon is presumably at least partly responsible for this. (*TT*)

jargon terms The intelligence services of Britain, the USA and the Soviet Union use a specialized vocabulary which they occasionally supplement with underworld or police slang. Listed here are those examples of spy jargon defined (and marked with an asterisk) alphabetically within this Who's Who section.

above-the-line	blind eye	car coper
alimony	Bloomsbury Group	catch-and-carry job
angels	blown	(to) change nappies
(the) Annexe	branch lines	charm-school
	British liaison	chummy
(to) baby-sit	(to) brush over the traces	CIA bracelets
back-bearings	(to) burn	(the) Circus
back door	burrower	coat trailer
bearleaders	(to) buy for stock	(the) Company
below-the-line		conjuring tricks
Big Moo	(to) cache	conscious
blind copy	camel	cooks

(the) Cousins
cover
crash
crusher
cut-out

dead
dead letter box
(the) Department
deskman
Dolphinarium
double-double game
(to) drive
duck-dive

fall
fallback
false-flag operation
ferret
fieldman
fifth floor
finger man
fireman
fireproof
flash
foot-in-the-door
    operation
footpad
footwork
fragged
(to) frighten the
    game
funny

(to) get into play
(to) give a ticket
gold seam
Golden Oldies
gorilla
graded Persil
grand slam operation

handwriting
hardware
head prefect
heeltap
hit-and-run job
honey-trap
hood
(to) house
housekeeper
Housekeeping

illegal resident
immediate
inhumane killer

ju ju man

key-holder

lace-curtain job
lamplighters
(to) launder
(the) Laundry
leash dog
(to) leave in
    your socks
legal resident
legman
lifeline
listener
little ship
London Station
long-arm
loser's corner

mailfist job
mainline operation
(to) make a legend
(to) make a pass
meat-and-potatoes
mole

Moscow-gazer
Moscow Rules
Mother

neighbours
network
(the) Nursery
nuts and bolts

Occasionals
Oddbins
operational intelligence

(to) pack your trunk
pavement artist
pax
Peking Tea Club
Pied-Piper appeal
(to) play back
(to) play it long
(to) poodle
postbox job
postman
pug marks
(to) put out smoke
(to) put the bite on

Queen Bee

(to) recycle
reptile fund
resident (legal and illegal)
rumpus room
(a) run
(to) run

safe house/flat
safety devices
safety signals
Sarratt
Satellites, Satellites Four

scalphunters	stinks-and-bangs school	unbutton
secret whisperers	stripe	unpack
sell-and-tell	subscription list	
(to) sell a piece of insurance	(to) sweat	vicar
	(to) swing your legs at	
(to) shake the tree		waitlisted
Shoemaker	(to) take to first base	walk in the park
shopsoiled	talent spotter	(to) watch
sitting-duck position	tiger's claw	(to) watch my back
sound	top table	water games
sound-thief	tradecraft	water school
spook house	tradesman	water-testing
squirt	(to) trail	(the) Wise Men
static post	travelling salesman	workname
(to) steal/steal sound	(to) trawl	wrangler
stick-and-carrot job	(to) turn	

Jebedee, — Smiley's tutor at Oxford and a member of the British Intelligence Service. He lives in Parks Road, Oxford. In 1928 Jebedee is responsible for directing Smiley towards intelligence work. His career ends in 1941 when he disappears after boarding a train at Lille, France, with a young Belgian radio operator. (*CD; MQ*)

'Jefferson, Mr' Cover name used by Polyakov for his visits to the safe house* in Lock Gardens, London. (*TT*)

—, John Assistant to Wilbraham in the Colonial Office. A very young, red-haired man with freckles and a puritanical, blunt manner. He makes a fool of himself twice during Smiley's meeting with the Intelligence Steering Committee. (*HS*)

—, John British diplomat of counsellor rank stationed at the Embassy in Phnom Penh, Cambodia. John is a wiry, stooped man with a moustache, married to a tall and snobbishly self-satisfied woman called Hills. His speech is effusive and rather antiquated in style but he is authoritative and very concerned with protocol. Khmer Rouge shelling does little to disturb the counsellor's sang-froid but there are signs that he is angered at the Americans for the situation they have created in Cambodia. His wife, Hills, is tall, very 'Harrods', boasts of an indifferent collection of Buddhas and enjoys putting her Embassy guests at ease. (*HS*)

Johnson, Jack During the Second World War Johnson works as a trainer in wireless transmission for the Department.* He is first based at Bovington in Dorset with Haldane and then in Oxford. After the war, Johnson runs a radio shop in Clapham Broadway, London, called

Johnson's Fair Deal. He rejoins the Department* briefly to assist in the training of Fred Leiser for Operation Mayfly. During the operation itself Johnson monitors Leiser's radio transmissions from East Germany. There is nothing very remarkable about Jack Johnson. He is short, plain, speaks out of the side of his mouth and wears neat, clean but ordinary clothes. His leisure pursuits include playing bar-billiards and drinking Guinness. In conversation he reveals an obsession with sex but his domesticated behaviour suggests that he does not act out his fantasies. (*LW*)

—, **Joy** Alleline's London mistress. Joy is a pale blonde who sustains herself with 'Je reviens' perfume, sherry, to which she is addicted, and kisses from attractive young men such as Guillam. (*TT*)

*****ju ju man** Intelligence officer responsible for planning rather than carrying out operations. The term is also used more generally to refer to a person with intellectual pretensions. (*TT*)

Kai-Sheng, Yao Name by which Nelson Ko is known in Communist China. (*HS*)

Karden, — Defence counsel for Mundt during his trial for treason. Although now a part of the communist establishment in East Germany Karden was a Nazi during the war and worked at Buchenwald. He is small, about sixty, and wears a black suit and grey tie. His gold-rimmed spectacles and white hair complete his carefully cultivated air of benignity. (*SC*)

'Karla' Information about Karla's origins is limited to two rumours: his father was in Okhrana and Cheka, the pre- and post-revolutionary secret police respectively, and he worked as a kitchen boy on an armoured train against Japanese occupation troops in the East. It is not known when Karla joins the Soviet Intelligence Service but it is thought that he trains under the legendary Berg. His career begins for certain in Spain in 1936 where, posing as a White Russian journalist favourable to Franco, he recruits a network* of German agents which operates under the code name Karla. This name he uses as his own throughout the rest of his career. Karla also visits England in 1936, at which time he recruits Bill Haydon. Other pre-war activities include the recruitment in Japan – where he works under cover as a German journalist called Martin Brandt – of a Japanese defence official. In 1941 Karla visits England again but his purpose is not known. Later in the same year he functions as an intelligence officer under Konev and runs networks* of partisans behind the German lines at Smolensk. Because Karla is able to turn* a radio operator, the Germans shell their own lines at Yelnya.

After the war it seems likely that he helps the Shanghai communist underground rebuild its networks.* In 1948 Karla is caught up in a purge and is first imprisoned and then sent to Siberia. However, the death of Stalin brings with it his reinstatement and in 1955 he establishes a radio link between Rudnev, head of the Thirteenth Directorate, the section of Moscow Centre concerned with illegal networks,* and a Moscow Centre-run spy ring in San Francisco. Out of favour once again despite his success Karla is summoned to Delhi where he is given orders to return home. While awaiting his departure, and using the cover name Gerstmann, he is arrested on orders from British Intelligence and an attempt is made through the medium of George Smiley to persuade him to defect. Smiley's efforts are unsuccessful and Karla returns to Moscow where he outwits Rudnev and takes over his position in the Thirteenth Directorate.

Shortly after this Bill Haydon, already recruited by Karla by 1936, becomes a vital source of information about British and American Intelligence. However, Karla is equally concerned about the possible future threat posed by Communist China and in 1956 he recruits Nelson Ko to work as his mole* in Shanghai. In 1963 Karla establishes a school to train military officers in the skills required to service the network* of deep-penetration agents for which the Thirteenth Directorate is responsible. The graduates of this school include Major Komarov and Colonels Bardin, Stokovsky and Viktorov. Karla's efforts receive a set back in 1966 when Komarov is caught in Tokyo as he takes delivery of intelligence material from the defence official recruited by Karla before the war. However, Bill Haydon proves to be particularly useful after 1965 when he is assisted by Viktorov, then working under the name Polyakov. In the early 1970s Haydon and Karla make a number of clever gambits which give Moscow Centre almost complete access to British Intelligence secrets. It is also likely that Bardin and Stokovsky are servicing moles* in the USA and West Germany respectively. But from 1973 onwards Karla suffers a series of defeats: Haydon is exposed as a traitor; Nelson Ko falls into American hands just as he is becoming useful; and Karla himself is forced to defect by George Smiley's threat to reveal the irregular activities, including the murders of Vladimir and Leipzig, the attempted murder of Ostrakova, and the employment of Kursky, in which he has become involved to protect his insane daughter, Tatiana.

Karla's most important personal involvement is with a young girl he meets during the war while establishing networks* amongst the Balts. She eventually becomes his mistress and is the mother of his daughter, Tatiana. Because she is ideologically unsound, Karla eventually orders her to be killed. The daughter turns out to be as rebellious as her mother, but Karla goes to great lengths to protect her and eventually arranges for her to be treated in a clinic near Berne in Switzerland. During the period between meeting Tatiana's mother and taking her as his mistress, Karla is married to a student from Leningrad who kills herself during his exile in Siberia.

In appearance Karla resembles a priest or a teacher rather than a master spy. He is small and wiry with bright brown eyes and he has white hair and wrinkles as early as 1955. Despite his modest air, Karla has a straight, frosty gaze which reflects both his essential toughness and wisdom. Only his habit of chain-smoking Camel cigarettes suggests that he might be at all vulnerable. For much of his career, George Smiley's analysis of Karla as a single-minded, ruthless and fanatical disciple of communist ideology seems to be completely accurate. However, in 1978 he reveals that, in relation to his daughter at least, he is capable of the deepest emotions. The reality of Karla, therefore, must finally be constructed out of contradictory pictures of him as 'the Sandman' (Vladimir's name for Karla) who kills anyone who gets in his way, and as a fond father. (*TT; HS; SP*)

Karla Case Chronology [CIRCUS INDEX].

Kaspar, Spike A legman* for Haydon's Soviet networks* and a member of London Station.* After Haydon's fall from grace Kaspar is dismissed from the Circus, but makes a brief return along with Bland and de Silsky in 1974 for the attempt to rescue the Churayevs. Kaspar and de Silsky are known as 'the Russians'. Like de Silsky, with whom he always works, Kaspar is blond, squat and taciturn. His personality is impenetrable. (*TT; HS*)

Keller, Max An American wireman who runs a news agency service out of Phnom Penh, Cambodia. Prior to this Keller covers a number of wars including the Congo during the early 1960s where he helps Westerby rescue a child from a burning lorry. Rumour has it that Keller also works for American Intelligence. Keller is broad-shouldered, with grey hair and a grey and pitted face. The fingers of one hand are fused together as a result of burns. A gap in this welded claw proves to be convenient for holding cigarettes. Age and too much war seem to have robbed Keller of his nerve and his sexual confidence. (*HS*)

'Keller's stringer' Unpleasant, grinning and pale young Southerner who is amused by the deaths of Cambodian photographers and by evidence of Keller's loss of nerve. (*HS*)

*key-holder Person who provides a location for a secret meeting. (*SP*)

Kiever, Sam Agent for the Abteilung. Working under cover as the owner of a newspaper article translation service, Kiever takes over from Ashe the task of recruiting Leamas for East German Intelligence. He travels with Leamas to Amsterdam and passes him on to his next contact, Peters. According to Ashe, Kiever has worked as a freelance journalist in Bonn but this is probably untrue. Kiever is small and rather fat. His hair is long, grey and swept back. He wears a double-breasted suit. His accent indicates central European, perhaps German origins. Kiever is a fastidious man who dislikes tawdry night clubs and littered restaurant tables. His expensive flat and rudeness to a waiter indicate that his commitment to communist ideology may not be wholehearted. (*SC*)

'Kirov' Cover name used by Oleg Kursky during his posting to the Soviet Embassy in Paris. (*HS*)

Ko, Drake Born in Swatow in 1925, the child of Chiu Chow boat people. In 1936 Drake Ko, in company with his brother Nelson, comes under the care of the Reverend Hibbert at his Baptist Mission in Shanghai. After the Japanese invasion the Ko brothers are evacuated to Shangjao and then Chunking but on the way to Chunking, Drake Ko is drafted into Chiang Kai-shek's army. Some time during the war Ko meets his long-time henchman, Tiu. In 1945, Drake is reunited with Nelson Ko and returns to Shanghai, where he works in the docks to pay for his brother's education. Stealing helps to supplement his income. In 1951, following the Communist take-over of mainland China and his brother's graduation, Drake Ko moves to Hong Kong and lives with other Shanghainese immigrants on the Des Voeux Road.

Although penniless on arrival he soon lays the foundations of his later fortune through involvement in prostitution at the Ritz ballroom in the King's Road and smuggling oil into China. Ko has become sufficiently respectable by 1966 to be awarded the OBE. In 1967, he reads law at Gray's Inn but is not admitted to the bar. By 1974 he is an extremely wealthy and respected citizen. His house, Seven Gates, is located in a millionaire's ghetto in Headland Road. He owns a fleet of cars, including a Rolls-Royce Phantom, and a yacht named the *Admiral Nelson* and he has a number of racehorses, including Lucky Nelson, which run in his quartered colours of sky-blue and sea-grey. Ko's business interests in South East Asia include nightclubs in Saigon, South Vietnam, the China Airsea company, Indocharter aviation company in Vientiane, Laos, and a tanker fleet in Thailand. In all he is director of over twenty companies. The basis for Ko's respected position within the community is provided by his stewardship of the Royal Hong Kong Jockey Club and his support for charities including a Baptist Church, a Chiu Chow Spirit Temple, and the Drake Ko Free Hospital for Children. For all Ko's aura of respectability it is unlikely that he has strayed very far from his criminal connections as evidenced by his continued employment of his former underworld associate, Tiu. In 1975 Ko becomes an object of interest to both the Circus and the American Drug Enforcement Administration but he is not included amongst those jailed in the wake of Operation Dolphin [CIRCUS INDEX].

Drake Ko's only known blood relation is his brother, Nelson Ko. They remain separate after Ko's departure from Shanghai except for a momentary reunion between Nelson's landing on Po Toi in May 1975 and his capture by British and American Intelligence. Ko is married to a highly-groomed, elderly, kleptomaniac Chinese woman who is probably a former prostitute from the Ritz. His only son, Nelson, dies in 1968 at the age of ten, and is buried in the old Colonial Cemetery near Happy Valley. In 1973 Ko takes as his mistress an English adventuress named Lizzie Worthington, whom he calls Liese Worth. He seems to have a genuine affection for her, not least because she reminds him of his surrogate mother, Liese Hibbert. Ko's hobbies include horse-racing, cruising, collecting jade, and croquet.

In appearance Drake Ko is rather ugly, stooped and thin, with a clean-shaven, lined and dark face which is capable of breaking into a brilliant smile. His clothes are conventional English – grey flannels and black double-breasted blazer, for example – but he tops them off with a jaunty and self-mocking beret. When he speaks English there is a hint of North Country in his accent. Ko is hard and ruthless and is quite willing, even after he becomes a millionaire, to murder those who offend him or to hose down his horse to lengthen its odds. Yet at the same time he has rich human qualities. His love for his brother, Nelson, is so strong that he risks everything to achieve a reunion with him, and he shows almost as much affection for the Hibberts, his son, and Lizzie Worthington. In all his actions Ko takes as his model either the traditions of his own people, the Chiu Chow, or of the Baptist religion and, despite his criminal history, he is a man who has built up a justifiable reputation for keeping his word. (*HS*)

Ko, Nelson Ko Sheng-hsiu, as Nelson Ko is properly named, is the child of Chiu Chow boat people and spends the first years following his birth in 1928 in Swatow. After 1936, however, he and his brother Drake Ko are cared for by the Hibberts at the Lord's Life Mission in Shanghai. During the war Nelson is evacuated to Chunking where he becomes imbued with communist ideology. After his return to Shanghai in 1945 Nelson joins the illegal communist movement and works against KMT fascist elements in the Kiangnan shipyards. He is also active in advocating a union of peasants and students at the University of Communications where he is studying engineering. In the spring of 1949 Nelson Ko is involved in the wrecking of the Lord's Life Mission during a communist uprising. It is possible that he meets Karla during these years.

After his graduation in 1951, Nelson works as a draughtsman in the Kiangnan shipyards. Two years later he is chosen for further training at Leningrad University where he stays until 1956. Some time during his course at Leningrad Nelson is recruited for Soviet Intelligence by Bretlev, a member of the faculty of shipbuilding, and it seems likely that he spends most of 1957 undergoing training as a deep-penetration agent. After this he returns to Shanghai and rises to the position of manager of shipbuilding at Kiangnan. He is also a member of a number of naval planning committees. However, because of his close connections with the Soviet Union, Nelson, by now known as Yao Kai-Sheng, is disgraced in the Cultural Revolution of 1967. It is not until 1973 that he is formally rehabilitated although the need for his skills begins to be acknowledged in 1970. Between 1973 and 1975 Nelson achieves increasingly important positions and provides ever more valuable information to Moscow Centre. At various times during this period he is a member of the Shanghai municipal revolutionary committee; the person responsible for a naval unit of the People's Liberation Army; involved with the Central Committee of the Chinese Communist Party; informal adviser to the Munitions and Ordnance Committee of the Ministry of Defence; and a member of the Peking Tea Club,* a body set up to co-ordinate Chinese Intelligence. In payment for the material provided by Nelson Ko, Moscow Centre deposits large sums of money in a Hong Kong bank account which stands at US $500,000 in late 1974. After an unsuccessful attempt to escape from China by air in 1973, Nelson Ko eventually reaches Po Toi by fishing boat in May 1975 and, after the briefest reunion with his brother, Drake, he is captured by British and American agents. He is then removed to an armed compound in Philadelphia for interrogation.

Nelson Ko is small and stocky and has one arm permanently bent as a result of a childhood accident. At the time of his capture he is wearing a grey kapok coat and a floppy peasant cap. Although he has considerable early experience of personal affection both from the Hibberts and his brother, Drake, Nelson commits himself to ideology rather than people. Whether his decision to defect from China is based on a change of heart is uncertain. (*HS*)

Ko, Sheng-hsiu Chinese name of Nelson Ko. He was later known as Yao Kai-Sheng. (*HS*)

Komarov, Major Mikhail Fedorovich Graduate of Karla's secret training school for spies. Under cover as a Military Attaché at the Soviet Embassy in Tokyo he services a mole* until exposed in 1966. (*TT*)

Konev, — Head of the Thirteenth Directorate branch of Moscow Centre in the Second World War. (*TT*)

Krassky, — Courier for the Soviet Embassy in Berne, Switzerland. Karla uses him to communicate with Grigoriev about Tatiana and it is through him that Smiley sends his blackmail message. Apart from his official duties Krassky is sometimes willing to be the conveyor of goods from Moscow to officials at the Berne Embassy. (*SP*)

Kretzschmar, Claus Close friend of Otto Leipzig and owner of the Blue Diamond nightclub in Hamburg. A Saxon by birth, Kretzschmar engages in low-grade freelance espionage activity in northern Germany after the war in partnership with Leipzig. Partly because Leipzig serves a jail sentence that should have been his, Kretzschmar eventually transcends his underworld origins and achieves relative respectability as the owner of an up-market sex club. Although no longer involved in espionage Kretzschmar helps Leipzig in 1978 to blackmail Oleg Kursky, a Moscow Centre agent. Kretzschmar lives with his wife in a large suburban house with a swimming pool located near Hamburg. His leisure time is taken up with barbecues by the pool. In appearance Kretzschmar is solid and respectable. His suit is dark, his tie pale and he is well-groomed. Although he is about fifty his hair is still blond. Kretzschmar describes himself as a businessman but he is very much motivated by friendship, and grieves deeply at receiving the news of Otto Leipzig's death. (*SP*)

Kretzschmar, Frau — A tall, solidly built and tanned woman who favours for leisure wear a pink two-piece bathing suit with matching diaphanous cloak, gold sandals and a chain around her waist. When sunbathing, her face is obscured by a white plastic nose-protector. She speaks in a playful, motherly voice but is determined to protect her husband, Claus, from invasions on his leisure time. Her conversational style, which is based on bondage metaphors, reinforces the impression created by the waist-chain that Frau Kretzschmar's sexual tastes may not be consistent with her general air of suburban orthodoxy. (*SP*)

'Kursky' Cover name used by Zimin (Commercial Boris) while operating in Vienna. (*HS*)

Kursky, Oleg Supposedly born in Leningrad in October 1929, Kursky begins a long career in intelligence work as an *agent provocateur* at the Tallinn Polytechnical Institute, where he is studying law. There he forms a circle of dissident Estonian dock workers, which includes his friend Otto Leipzig, and then betrays them to the authorities. Nothing is known of his career between this time – approximately 1953 – and 1970 when he becomes a finance officer for Moscow Centre. His job is to uncover irregularities in the accounts of overseas residents* and he achieves his greatest success in 1973 with the discovery of a misuse of funds by Karla's Lisbon resident,* Colonel Orlov. In 1971 it seems likely that Kursky interrupts his regular job to attend a Moscow Centre training course in Kiev. Following the Orlov case Karla recruits Kursky for a special posting to Paris. Working under cover as Kirov, a Second Secretary (Commercial) and as Western European auditor to Moscow Centre's Thirteenth Directorate outstations, Kursky's job is to find cover backgrounds for future agents. Unknown to him his real task is to find a new identity for Karla's daughter, Tatiana. Soon after his posting to Paris on June 1, 1974, Kursky, despite his use of the name Kirov, is identified by General Vladimir of the Riga Group as the former Tallinn Institute *agent provocateur*. Acting on the assumption that he is still involved in intelligence work, Vladimir makes attempts with the assistance of Leipzig to blackmail Kursky in 1974–75 and 1978. The second effort is successful and, following Karla's discovery of his treachery, Kursky is summoned back to Moscow and executed in October 1978.

Kursky is married but his wife stays in Moscow while he is living in Paris. He has no known personal interests other than in prostitutes. Connie Sachs's description of Kursky as the Ginger Pig is totally accurate. He is a big man running to fat; his hair is ginger and his face is notable for its small, dead eyes, its flat nose, weak mouth, and sweatiness. When he eats Kursky reveals his many bad teeth. In addition Kursky emits an extremely unpleasant smell. His sweaty suit, mid-European hairstyle and fidgety behaviour complete a disgusting picture. Kursky's personality is entirely compatible with his appearance since he is at once bully, coward, betrayer, boaster and philistine. (*SP*)

*lace-curtain job Operation involving extremely discreet observation. (*HS*)

'Lachmann, Herr' Cover name used by Smiley when he visits Tatiana at the clinic near Berne during the Karla case [CIRCUS INDEX]. (*SP*)

Lacon, Oliver Member of the Cabinet Office who functions as a senior adviser to various mixed committees and the Circus. Lacon comes to his senior Government position by a completely orthodox route. His family origins place him firmly in the establishment – his father is a dignitary in the Scottish church and his mother a member of the aristocracy – and he is educated at Cambridge where he rows. Although his commitment to the Circus owes something to its usefulness as a personal power base, Lacon seems to be genuinely concerned to protect and improve its position. He acts quickly on receiving convincing evidence in 1973 of the existence of a Soviet mole* in its higher echelons and he provides Smiley with considerable assistance during his efforts to re-establish the Circus after the Haydon affair. Even his efforts to curtail a proper enquiry into Vladimir's murder in 1978 derive from an awareness that this might provide ammunition for an unsympathetic government.

Lacon is married to a woman named Val and they have three children, Charlotte, Jackie and Penny. Charlotte wins a scholarship to Roedean; Jackie is fat and falls off ponies; and Penny, a baby, likes to make naked appearances. Prior to 1978 when Val leaves Lacon for a riding instructor, the family lives in a hideous mansion near Ascot in Berkshire. Afterwards, the daughters are sent to boarding school and Lacon moves into a flat. Lacon's interests include climbing and music and he is a member of the Athenaeum in London. Lacon is very tall and thin with an awkward, boyish style. His youthful face does not fare well as he ages and is subject to rashes. Although often labelled a mere careerist, Lacon is in fact a rather complex person whose self-interest is always modified by Christian ethics. This aspect of his character does not always get the proper credit because it is communicated in a complacent and priggish, public school-prefect manner. Lacon's somewhat babbling, upper-class style of speech often makes him seem stupid but he can make astute comments that reveal a very real intelligence. His greatest weakness lies in the area of personal relations. Although he is genuinely fond of George Smiley he acts towards him in ways that simply cause annoyance and he is completely baffled by female behaviour. The loss of his wife leaves him adrift and heading for a breakdown. (*TT; HS; SP*)

Lacon, Val The wife of Oliver Lacon. Like her husband, Val has upper-class origins and her uncle is a political secretary. At some point in her life she has visited Hong Kong. She marries Lacon very young and bears him three daughters, Charlotte, Jackie and Penny, before deserting him in favour of her riding instructor. Apart from her beauty, which is doe-like and enhanced by long hair, Val Lacon has few redeeming qualities. She is obviously stupid, benignly bigoted and foolishly indulgent towards her children. (*TT; HS*)

Lamb, J. Driver with the Straight and Steady Minicab Service of Islington, London. Lamb has brown Afro hair, manicured white hands, wears a polo-neck sweater, and drives a Ford Cortina at breakneck speed. Although his manner is cheeky he answers Smiley's questions about General Vladimir's trip to Charlton precisely and accurately. (*SP*)

lamplighters Section of the Circus located at Acton, London, which is responsible for providing support services, such as watching, listening,* transport* and safe houses,* for mainline operations* [CIRCUS INDEX]. (*TT*)

'Lampton' Cover name used by Guillam when collecting developed films from Lark the chemist during the Haydon case [CIRCUS INDEX]. (*TT*)

Landsbury, Lord John During the Second World War Lord Landsbury is head of coding for the Circus. Afterwards he revives the *Christian Voice*, a nonconformist newspaper founded by his father. Following the take-over of the paper by Unipress in 1957 Landsbury becomes a farmer in Rhodesia. (*MQ; TT*)

'Lang, Robert' Cover name under which Leamas opens a bank account in Copenhagen during the Fiedler–Mundt Operation [CIRCUS INDEX]. Lang is an electrical engineer from Derby. (*SC*)

Langley, Giles In the late 1930s Langley teaches Bill Haydon modern history. He is still living in Oxford in 1973 although very aged. The passing of the Empire and of men with Haydon's flair obviously bothers him a good deal. Langley's sister runs safe houses* for the Circus. (*TT*)

Langley, Virginia Headquarters of the Cousins* are located here. (*HS*)

Lansen, Captain— Commercial airline pilot with Northern Air Service and freelance agent for the Department,* which commissions Lansen to take photographs of Kalkstadt while flying a party of schoolchildren from Düsseldorf to Finland. He is so alarmed by the dangers involved that he is unlikely to undertake future missions. He is tall and strong with a thick accent, almost an impediment. Fear makes him angry and erratic. (*LW*)

La Pierre, Madame — The concierge of the building where Ostrakova lives in Paris. Although much disliked by her tenant who finds her foolish, goat-like and greedy for money, there is no real evidence of Mme La Pierre's unworthiness. In fact she provides food and fends off visitors during Ostrakova's illness. Mme La Pierre is married to a man whom Ostrakova considers to be a criminal and a troglodyte. He does odd jobs in the building. (*SP*)

'Lapin' Workname* given to Brod during his posting to the Soviet Embassy in London. (*TT*)

launder To prepare clandestine funds for use in open-air channels. The route taken by such funds as they move from bank to bank is known as a gold seam. (*HS*)

Laundry, the The lamplighters' headquarters at Acton, London. (*TT*)

Leamas, Alec As a child Alec Leamas lives in Leiden, Holland, for nine years and acquires a knowledge of Dutch, German and French which brings him to the attention of the Circus while he is serving in the Engineers in 1939. After training at Oxford under Fielding and Steed-Asprey, he is dropped into Holland where he stays from 1941 to 1943. From 1943 to 1945 he operates in Norway. After the war Leamas tries to become involved in his father's machine tool agency in Leiden and spends eighteen months in a travel agency in Bristol. Even though the travel firm fails he rejects an offer to return to the Circus but changes his mind after a year spent on Lundy Island, off the North-West coast of Devon. From 1949 to 1951 Leamas has a desk job with Satellites Four* and is then posted to Berlin as Deputy-Controller of Area. He remains there until 1961 and is head of Berlin command from 1957. By nature Leamas is a fieldman* and he does well in establishing East German networks* until the advent of Mundt in 1960. In March 1961, having lost all his agents, he returns to London. Control then enlists Leamas in the Fiedler–Mundt Operation [CIRCUS INDEX] which is intended to eliminate the threat posed by Mundt.

This Operation involves Leamas's dismissal from the Circus and a long period of personal deterioration aimed at making the Abteilung regard him as a likely intelligence source. During 1961 and early 1962 Leamas moves from the Banking Section* of the Circus to a string of dead-end jobs and then into prison for a violent attack on a local shopkeeper. After his release from prison, Leamas is approached by William Ashe, a representative of East German Intelligence, who passes him on to Sam Kiever. He is taken from London to Holland, where he is interrogated by Peters, and finally to East Germany. The story he offers concerning the fictitious 'Operation Rolling Stone' is plausible enough to convince Fiedler, head of Counter Intelligence for the Abteilung, that Mundt should be brought to trial for treason. At the trial, however, Mundt produces as a surprise witness Leamas's former girlfriend, Liz Gold, and turns the tables on Fiedler. Leamas then realizes that Mundt is indeed Control's agent and that the removal of Fiedler has always been the goal of his mission. Mundt arranges for Leamas to go free and also releases Liz Gold at Leamas's insistence. While they are climbing the Berlin Wall together Liz Gold is shot and Leamas decides to stay with her – thus signing his own death warrant. In the course of his career Leamas uses the cover names Thomas, Robert Lang, Stephen Bennett, Alexander Thwaite, and Amies.

Leamas is divorced and has teenage children. There is no evidence of any other close personal relationships prior to his brief involvement with Liz Gold while working at the Bayswater Library for Psychic Research. He seems to have no recreational interests other than drinking, preferably at the Eight Bells pub in Chelsea, London. Leamas is short but very strong with broad shoulders and stubby hands. He is aged about fifty. His hair is grey and close-cropped. He chooses clothes for purely functional purposes and wears two-piece suits of artificial fibre, button-down shirts and rubber-soled shoes. Even his glasses have steel rims. In Leamas's case the appearance is very much the man. He is direct, cynical, unreflective and not much given to emotion. Discussions of ideology and expressions of love bore him equally and he reads nothing. However, as the constant pressure of espionage work begins to tell on his nerves and as Liz Gold offers him the experience of a caring relationship, so he begins to realize the limitations of his functional approach to experience. Unfortunately the event which completes his disillusionment with the pragmatic ethics of spying – the murder of Liz Gold – is also the cause of his own death. (*SC*)

*leash dog Agent who works under immediate supervision. (*HS*)

*leave in your socks To make a hasty escape. (*TT*)

'Leber' Cover name used by Smiley when checking the Hamburg number listed on Vladimir's telephone bill. (*SP*)

Leclerc, — Director of the Department.* Leclerc's career with the Department stretches back at least as far as the Second World War. At this time he plays an important role in organizing operations against military targets, but since then he has had less and less to do. A trip to America in 1963 (or 1964) is one of his few activities of note. Operation Mayfly which ends disastrously in the capture of the Department's agent, Fred Leiser, is entirely Leclerc's brainchild. However, there is little evidence that he learns from his mistakes because almost immediately afterwards he is involved in a new scheme deriving from a report about troop movements in Hungary.

Not even Leclerc's colleagues know where he lives and his entire personal life is shrouded in mystery. He is a member of one of the larger clubs but feels that its standards have dropped. Leclerc is small, clean-shaven, dark-eyed and unremarkable looking. He dresses with considerable care. In his manner, as in his dress, Leclerc is ever concerned with appearances, and he seeks to impress by cultivating a habit of speech made up almost entirely of oblique allusions. Although he has been Director of the Department* for many years, Leclerc lacks a sense of authority. He is fussy, obsessed with tradition and tiny details of prestige and protocol and, despite a superficially assertive manner, communicates quite clearly an awareness that he is a man excluded from real centres of power. Leclerc's behaviour during and in the aftermath of Operation Mayfly suggests that he has lost even the most tenuous grip on reality. (*LW*)

*legal resident *See* above-the-line*

*legman Agent who carries secret messages between two other agents. (*TT*)

Leipzig, Otto Freelance secret agent and friend of General Vladimir. Because of his Estonian origins, Leipzig takes as the main purpose of his life the overthrow of the Communist government in the USSR. As a young man working as a docker in Tallinn he is involved in an unaligned discussion group which is betrayed by his friend Oleg Kursky. After serving a jail sentence, Leipzig eventually escapes from the Soviet Union with the help of the Riga Group to Schleswig–Holstein. In the years following the war he and his friend, Claus Kretzschmar, make a living selling low-grade and sometimes fictional intelligence to the Americans, French, British and Germans. Even the Soviet Union is allowed to be a customer when the information is inaccurate. Although Leipzig gains a reputation as a fabricator and a confidence man he can always be relied upon to provide material of genuine value against the Soviet Union and he keeps in close contact with his fellow Estonian nationalist, General Vladimir. In 1974 Vladimir enlists Leipzig's help to blackmail his former friend and betrayer, Kursky, who has turned up in Paris under diplomatic cover, using the name Kirov. Leipzig's efforts are brought to a halt by Saul Enderby in May 1975 but in 1978, with the help of Kretzschmar, Leipzig is successful in drawing Kursky into a honey-trap.* The information he acquires leads eventually to the forced defection of Karla but before that happens Leipzig is murdered by Soviet intelligence agents while living on a ruined houseboat, the *Isadora*.

Otto Leipzig has one known relative, an uncle living near Kiel, and one great love affair with a girl in Tallinn who is also betrayed by Kursky and executed. In addition to his espionage and criminal activities, Leipzig, who is incapable of accumulating capital, works at a number of odd jobs including night clerk for P. K. Bergen, Import–Export, of Hamburg. Part of the time he lives near a wharf for cargo ships in an old house stranded in the middle of a container-park and the rest on his houseboat at a nearby holiday water camp. Leipzig is a little man with curved eyebrows, pointed ears, black hair brushed into horns, and a lined face capable of expressing a range of emotions with great intensity. For Ostrakova this face possesses magical qualities and she dubs him 'the magician'. Villem Craven is equally impressed by the violent passion which a man he thinks of as essentially a comedian can communicate in a single glance. The source of Leipzig's powerful feelings is a profound indignation at the offences against humanity committed in the name of communist ideology. While he may cheat and lie to ensure his own economic survival, Leipzig is at core a deeply caring person and he will not yield an inch to the forces of a life-denying social system even when refusing to do so costs him his life. (*SP*)

Leiser, Fred During the Second World War Fred Leiser, a Danzig Pole, is an agent for the Department.* His experiences include capture and escape in Holland. With the return of peace Leiser works for Smethwick's grocers in South Park Gardens near Western Avenue, London, before starting his own garage, the King of Hearts, in the same South Park area. He lives in a flat over the garage. In 1964 (or 1965), when Leiser is a little over forty, he is enlisted for a second time by the Department* to undertake a mission into East Germany under the name Hartbeck. Despite several weeks' training in Oxford, Leiser is ill-equipped for the task set him and is captured in Kalkstadt after killing a young border guard. His fate is unknown but it seems likely that he is executed.

Nothing is known of Leiser's background and he appears to have little in the way of personal relationships except for an involvement with a rather bad-natured woman bank clerk called Betty whom he takes out for dinner and dancing. During training in Oxford he draws close to John Avery and during his mission into East Germany – Operation Mayfly – he becomes briefly involved with a young girl named Anna in Kalkstadt. Leiser is a small, upright man with hairy forearms and a good head of hair cut in a Slavic style. His slightly swaggering manner does not entirely eliminate a certain air of naiveté. He is well groomed and dresses in monogrammed white shirt, gold ring and wrist-watch, tartan tie with gold horse's head and riding-crop tie-pin. His clothes are expensive but flashy. When he travels he wears a camel-hair coat and carries pigskin suitcases of a rather unnatural orange colour. Further gestures towards stylishness are contained within Leiser's habit of drinking White Ladies and eating steak. As his choice of clothes suggests, Leiser is a man who is trying without complete success to fit into a mould to which he does not naturally belong. An exile from his native land, he longs to be accepted by the English as one of them. This he is never quite successful in doing mainly because of an inability to grasp certain nuances of behaviour and language. A final awareness of the illusory nature of what he is seeking drives Leiser to seek comfort in a brief but passionate sexual relationship with the East German girl, Anna. (*LW*)

lifeline System used at the Circus for keeping in touch with retired agents. (*SP*)

Lilley, — Scottish member of naval intelligence who lends his support to Alleline's attempts to establish the credibility of Witchcraft [CIRCUS INDEX]. Control suggests that his judgement is warped by his shared nationality and membership of the Travellers' with Alleline. (*TT*)

listener Member of the Circus staff responsible for electronic surveillance. (*TT*)

'little Natasha' Nickname used by Esterhase's lamplighters* for Grigoriev's mistress who works in the Visa Section of the Soviet Embassy in Berne. It seems likely that she is a spy. (*SP*)

*little ship Chinese Intelligence jargon for a spy. (*HS*)

'Lofthouse' Cover name used by Peter Guillam when contacting Smiley at the Hotel Islay in London during the Haydon case [CIRCUS INDEX]. He is a colleague of Barraclough (Smiley's cover name there) from the finance department. (*TT*)

London For British Intelligence London is truly the centre of the world. Its major institutions are situated there and it is the focal point of many of its most important cases. At the hub of all this activity in London is the headquarters of a special department at Cambridge Circus, known as the Circus. Radiating out from this centre is a network of outstations that covers the entire city and its surrounding counties: the scalphunters* are in Brixton, south of the river, the lamplighters* in Acton, West London, the Circus doctor is in Manchester Square just north of Oxford Street, former agents are paid off in Bloomsbury, the Nursery* at Sarratt* is located outside London in Hertfordshire, between Watford and Rickmansworth, and safe houses (flats and rooms)* exist in St James's, Belgravia, Knightsbridge, Lambeth, near Hampstead Heath, Haverstock Hill in Belsize Park, Lock Gardens (actually St Mark's Crescent in Camden Town), Lexham Gardens in Kensington, and outside London in Suffolk and Sussex. A rival branch of intelligence, the Department,* has its London headquarters in Blackfriars Road, south of Blackfriars Bridge. The American sister Service (the Cousins)* is located in the Annexe* of the Embassy in Grosvenor Square.

A number of major intelligence operations take place in and around London. The Fennan case [CIRCUS INDEX], for instance, starts with a murder in Merridale Lane, Walliston, in Surrey near the Kingston bypass. The investigation which follows takes Smiley and Mendel to Adam Scarr's garage in Prince of Wales Drive, Battersea; to the Repertory Theatre at Weybridge, Surrey; to the East German Steel Mission in Belsize Park; and to the Sheridan Theatre (probably the real Lyric theatre) near Hammersmith Broadway. The final chase which begins at the Sheridan takes a course along the Fulham Palace Road, past Fulham Broadway to the King's Road and finally down to a houseboat on the river near Chelsea's Battersea Bridge at the point where Cheyne Walk meets Lots Road. The struggle which ends in Dieter Frey's death takes place in the fog on Battersea Bridge.

Alec Leamas makes a devious journey during the Fiedler–Mundt Operation [CIRCUS INDEX] to shake off any followers before meeting Control at George Smiley's house in Bywater Street, Chelsea. He starts at the corner of Charing Cross Road and Old Compton Street in Soho, progresses by foot to Fleet Street, jumps on a bus going towards Ludgate

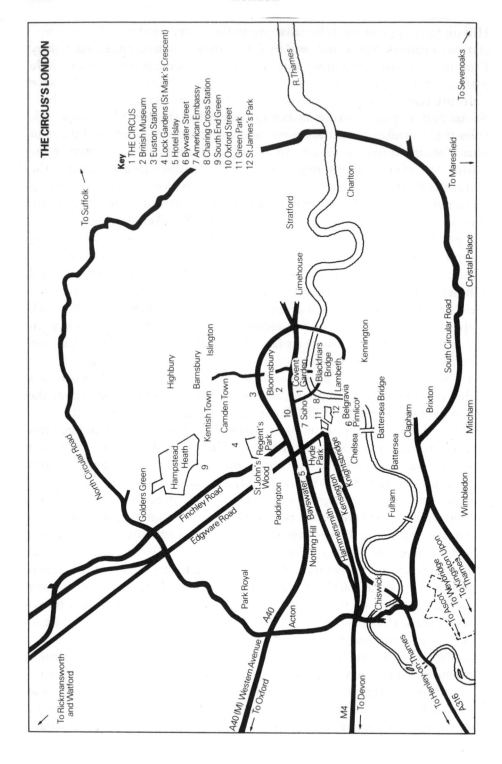

THE CIRCUS'S LONDON

Key
1 THE CIRCUS
2 British Museum
3 Euston Station
4 Lock Gardens (St Mark's Crescent)
5 Hotel Islay
6 Bywater Street
7 American Embassy
8 Charing Cross Station
9 South End Green
10 Oxford Street
11 Green Park
12 St James's Park

Hill on the fringe of the City, changes to the underground and goes one station, changes again and makes for Euston, then doubles back to Charing Cross before ending with a journey by Circus van to Bywater Street, off the King's Road.

In the Karla case [CIRCUS INDEX] when General Vladimir is killed by Soviet agents while walking on Hampstead Heath through the avenue of trees that stretches from the sports field with its tin pavilion to the East Heath Road, Smiley's investigation begins at this spot. From there, during the course of one interminable day, he goes to a safe flat* in Hampstead near the Heath, to Vladimir's flat in Westbourne Terrace, Paddington, back to the Heath, to South End Green to make enquiries, through Central London to Baker Street, north of Oxford Street, to buy a box and wrapping paper for his vital clue, on to the Savoy Hotel on the Strand, where he temporarily checks the parcel before travelling out to Charlton, south of the river to see the Cravens, on to the Free Baltic Library near the British Museum in Bloomsbury to question Mikhel, to the Charing Cross area, back across London to Bayswater to buy photographic material, once more to the Savoy Hotel to retrieve his package, and finally – dead tired – home to Bywater Street where he checks to see that his precautionary door wedges have not been tampered with.

In the pursuit of recreation and safe meeting places spies frequent a wide variety of restaurants, pubs, wine bars and clubs. Amongst the cafés are an Espresso bar near Millbank between Vauxhall and Lambeth Bridge and the Black and White in Fleet Street; the Cadena in Battersea; a Chinese restaurant opposite Limehouse Police Station, not far from the London Docks; an old-fashioned restaurant in Gorringe's department store (now defunct) near Victoria; the Entrechat in Kensington and the classier ones such as Quaglino's near St James's Street; Scott's, now in Mount Street near Grosvenor Square; Chez Victor in Wardour Street, Soho, and the White Tower in Percy Street, just north of the Tottenham Court Road end of Oxford Street.

Favoured drinking haunts include the Clarendon Hotel in Hammersmith; the Prodigal's Calf in Battersea; the Eight Bells in the Cheyne Walk and the Balloon in Lots Road, both in Chelsea; a pub in St John's Wood, a pub in Wardour Street; a wine bar off Charing Cross; a cellar bar and El Vino's in Fleet Street; the Sherlock Holmes in Northumberland Avenue near Charing Cross Station. Clubs range from the traditional gentlemen's clubs such as the Travellers' and the Athenaeum in Pall Mall near St James's Park; the Garrick in Garrick Street, Covent Garden; the Savile in Brook Street near Grosvenor Square; the Junior Carlton now merged with the Carlton itself in St James's, to the private one founded by

Steed-Asprey in Manchester Square, and the Alias, a drinking club near Charing Cross Station run by Major Dell.

When not forced into less salubrious surroundings by operational requirements English secret agents seem to like to eat, drink and relax socially in solid, traditional rather than fashionable or innovatory settings. In choosing a restaurant, for example, the spy will give preference to the faded elegance and cuisine of Scott's or the White Tower over places better loved by the writers of restaurant guides, such as Le Gavroche or the Interlude de Tabaillau. A regard for the traditional also seems to guide the shopping habits of the espionage world. Champagne is bought at Berry Brothers and Rudd in St James's Street near the Park, a necklace at Asprey's in Bond Street and books at Heywood Hill's in Curzon Street, Mayfair. Similarly, banking is done at Blatt and Rodney in the City and hair is cut at Trumper's in Curzon Street.

The major difficulty facing an agent operating in London is not so much its vast area as its social depth. Cases must be conducted within contexts as distinct socially as the Savile Club, the suburbs and Home Counties and Adam Scarr's used car lot-cum-junk yard. Part of George Smiley's greatness as an agent derives from his ability to cope with the full range of London society and ambience. A knowledge of the ticker-tape machine at the Savile Club helps him to trap Bill Haydon; familiarity with lower middle-class *mores* enables him to extract vital information about their daughter, Lizzie Worthington, from the Pellings; and the ability to communicate with an East End lorry driver, Villem Craven, provides clues to the nature of General Vladimir's great secret.

What the spy discovers when he penetrates the city as deeply as does Smiley is that, despite its sometimes glittering surface, London also has its mediocre and rotting places. The very names of the Athenaeum, the London Library, Trumper's and Berry Brothers and Rudd, all in the West End, are redolent with the mystique of tradition and of inherited power. But they provide a thin covering over the city's shoddier streets. Paddington's Westbourne Terrace with its rotting mattresses or Sussex Gardens with its mansions turned into cheap hotels like the Islay serve as reminders of how far certain areas of London have declined since their Victorian heyday. To Smiley, working and walking in this city of alternating grandeur and decay is to experience a sense of confinement and despondency. (*CD; SC; LW; TT; HS; SP*)

*London Station Operational directorate of the Circus during Alleline's time as head. (*TT*)

*long-arm Distant radio transmission. (*HS*)

'Lorimer' Cover name used by George Smiley when lodging with Mrs

Gray in Pimlico, London, prior to leaving for Berne during the Karla case [CIRCUS INDEX]. Lorimer is a retired librarian. (*SP*)

*loser's corner Position occupied by a person under interrogation when unaware of how much the interrogators already know. (*SP*)

—, Lorraine American journalist representing a group of Mid-Western dailies. Lorraine is a tall Californian from Santa Barbara with long, attractive legs. Curiosity and stupidity make her fearless during her first experience of warfare outside Phnom Penh, Cambodia. Although unresponsive to the approaches of Max Keller, Lorraine is quite ready to give herself to Westerby. (*HS*)

Lowe, Sandy Staff sergeant and instructor in unarmed combat during the Second World War, Lowe now teaches boxing at a public school. During the preparation for Operation Mayfly he gives Leiser instruction in fighting with and without a knife. The lessons take place in a gymnasium in the Headington district of Oxford. Lowe is a small Welshman with a wartime reputation for womanizing that wins him the nickname Randy Sandy. In peacetime, however, he has settled down and has a grown-up family. Although his manner is the deferential one of a non-commissioned officer addressing his superiors, Lowe is a demanding and very efficient instructor. (*LW*)

—, Luke American journalist. After reporting the Vietnam War until the American withdrawal, Luke is transferred to Hong Kong where he is employed at the Asian press bureau by 'the dwarf'. During 1975 he takes trips through South East Asia to Phnom Penh in Cambodia, Bangkok in Thailand, and then to Saigon, Hue and Danang to cover the final stages of the Vietcong victory. On his return to Hong Kong in May, he is murdered by Tiu who mistakes him for Westerby. Luke is a twenty-seven-year-old Californian who is tall and gangling in the style of the tennis player which he is. His experiences in Saigon, about which he continues to have nightmares, have left him in an emotionally fragile condition, the main symptoms of which are heavy drinking, self-destructive fighting, and an inability to write. Although he cannot keep his own life in order – even his landlord Jake Chiu throws him out – Luke still manages to scoop his fellow journalists on occasion. It is he who discovers first that the Circus has abandoned their High Haven headquarters and that Frost has been murdered. He is also capable of a considerable degree of loyalty to others. The beating he suffers at the hands of Superintendent Rockhurst is the result of a quixotic attempt to defend the reputation of Ella, a Wanchai bar girl, and he twice assists Westerby's journalistic efforts. On the first occasion he lets him share the Frost murder story and on the second he files for him from Phnom Penh. In return for the second favour Westerby allows Luke the use of his apartment, and as a result is indirectly responsible for his death. (*HS*)

Lusty, Pete At one time a scalphunter,* Lusty serves for a while in the Rhodesian army before resigning in disgust at the killing required of him. In 1978 he is recruited by Esterhase as part of the team charged with preparing for the blackmailing of Grigoriev in Berne. (*SP*)

Lyn, Jane A simple-minded woman who is falsely accused of the murder of Stella Rode. Jane Lyn, or Mad Janie as she is known, lives in the disused King Arthur's Chapel near Pylle in Dorset. She occupies her time with cleaning the Chapel, which she does out of a strong religious conviction, talking to the birds, and selling herbs and charms. She is close to the house at the time of Stella Rode's murder and sees the killer. Because she steals from the dead body and because of her garbled account of events, she is for a while the chief suspect. Jane Lyn has a vacuous face and wears filthy, cast-off clothes which she decorates with evergreen sprigs. When involved in her private religious rituals she daubs her face green and blue. Although her strange appearance and odd ways can make her appear threatening, Jane Lyn is totally harmless. (*MQ*)

'Mac' A listener* who assists Martello in Hong Kong. He lets sexual fantasies distract him from the task at hand. (*HS*)

McCaird, Mrs — The local charwoman who cleans Alec Leamas's Bayswater flat for one week. Her gossiping ensures Leamas's poor reputation in the area and paves the way for his failure to obtain credit at Ford the grocer. (*SC*)

McCraig, Millie Professional eavesdropper for the Circus since 1943. Prior to this Millie McCraig spies for the Circus in Mozambique where she runs Bible Schools and in Hamburg where she is in charge of a seaman's mission. In 1973 she is caretaker of the Witchcraft [CIRCUS INDEX] safe house* at 5, Lock Gardens, Camden Town, and has responsibility for the recording instruments. Because she cooperates in the plan to unmask the mole* Gerald by enticing him to the safe house,* Millie McCraig not only survives the subsequent reorganization of the Circus but is promoted to head listener.* During Operation Dolphin [CIRCUS INDEX] she works in the cellars of the Circus. Millie McCraig is still with the Circus in 1978 and has charge of the safe flat* on the Länggas-strasse in Berne where Smiley interrogates Grigoriev. Millie McCraig is Scottish by birth and has been a widow for an undefined length of time. In appearance she is wiry with wrinkled, shiny skin and hard eyes; she keeps her hair in a bob and wears brown stockings. Although used as a cover for espionage, Millie's mission-ary work seems to be the product of a genuine religious spirit. Her manner is both funereal and censorious, and she is easily angered. (*TT; HS; SP*)

MacFadean, — Elderly Circus janitor who is extremely loyal to Control. In Sam Collins's opinion MacFadean has an inadequate grasp of the subtleties of horse-racing form. (*TT*)

Mackelvore, Steve Long-serving Circus agent who usually works under consular cover. His final postings are Vientiane, Laos, where he operates as the Circus linkman under cover as a Trade Consul, and head resident* at the Paris Embassy, 1973–74. While in Vientiane in 1972 he blunders by assigning Lizzie Worthington to work for Sam Collins. At an earlier stage of his career, during the Cold War, Mackelvore operates under trade cover in Djakarta, Indonesia, where he recruits Ricki Tarr. Although Mackelvore regards the Paris appointment as a dull but comfortable prelude to retirement, it involves him peripherally in two major operations. In 1973 Ricki Tarr forces him at gunpoint to cable the message which flushes Bill Haydon out of cover, and in 1974 Vladimir asks him to initiate an enquiry based on information that Second Secretary (Commercial) – Kirov – is really the spy Oleg Kursky. This unexpected stimulation may explain why Mackelvore dies a little later of a heart attack. Mackelvore is a short, white-haired Yorkshireman with a fatherly manner. Loyalty to the old Circus proves that his heart is in the right place and he has enough spirit even in the twilight of his career to contemplate disarming Ricki Tarr. However, his judgement is not always sound, as he shows in his dealings with Sam Collins and Lizzie Worthington. (*TT; HS; SP*)

'Mad Janie' Name by which Jane Lyn is commonly known. (*MQ*)

'Mad Jesuit, the' Nickname given to Doc di Salis by the Circus staff. (*HS*)

'magician, the' Nickname given to Otto Leipzig by Ostrakova. (*SP*)

Magyar 'driver' The driver in Czechoslovakia who takes Jim Prideaux to his supposed meeting with General Stevcek. In build he is muscular and rigid. His moustache is trimmed in an Edwardian style and he stinks of garlic. He has a taste for dirty stories. It affords Prideaux some satisfaction that he is able to make this unpleasant and almost certainly treacherous man bear the brunt of the first of the ambushes intended for himself. (*TT*)

*mailfist job Operation aimed at assassination. (*TT*)

*mainline operation Major espionage enterprise. (*TT*)

*make a legend To invent a biography, usually for an agent. (*SP*)

*make a pass To approach an enemy agent with the intention of gathering intelligence. (*TT*)

'Malherbe' Cover name used by Wilf Taylor during his mission to Finland. (*LW*)

Maltby, — Pianist, and presumably music teacher, whose employment at Thursgood's school terminates dramatically with his arrest during choir practice. Lacking knowledge of his whereabouts and instructions as to the disposal of his property, Thursgood allows Maltby's mysterious trunk to linger in the school's cellars. (*TT*)

Marcello, Franco Westerby's landlord during his stay in Tuscany. He is the father of Mama Stefano's illegitimate son. Depending on her mood she describes her lover as a cheating pederast or an honest and sophisticated man with an excellent clothes sense. (*HS*)

Markov, General — Soviet military officer, probably airforce, who spends at least some time in Paris. He is the supposed source of Witchcraft [CIRCUS INDEX] report No. 104 which concerns Soviet–French discussions on joint aircraft-production. (*TT*)

'Marlene Dietrich' Nickname given to Maston by the Special Branch police. (*CD*)

Marshall, Charlie Pilot for Indocharter, an aviation company based in Vientiane, Laos, and owned by Drake Ko. Charlie Marshall is the son of a Kuomintang General from the Shans; his mother is Corsican. Prior to his involvement with Indocharter he trains at the CIA secret aviation school in Oklahoma where he meets and befriends Tiny Ricardo. They fly together in the Laos war and take part in the Plain of Jars and Danang operations in 1966. After the war in 1972 he lives with Ricardo and Lizzie Worthington in Vientiane and is involved in many of Ricardo's harebrained enterprises. All significant financial support for their ménage is provided by Charlie's father. Eventually tiring of his son's life of gambling, drinking and opium-smoking, the General, who is a friend of the owner, Drake Ko, gets him a job flying opium for Indocharter to Bangkok in Thailand, and Battambang, Phnom Penh, and Kampong Chan in Cambodia.

Regular work enables Charlie Marshall to put his life in order, so much so that in 1973 Tiu, representing Drake Ko, offers him the job of bringing Nelson Ko out of China. Warned off the enterprise by his father, Charlie passes Tiu on to Ricardo. After Ricardo abandons the rescue mission and absconds with the aircraft and its cargo of opium, Charlie joins Lizzie Worthington in persuading Ko to spare his friend's life. In 1975 Charlie lives in Phnom Penh but is still flying for Indocharter. However, he does so only in the afternoons when he has had time to recover from the effects of his nightly opium-smoking. Charlie's dependency on opium makes him an easy target for Jerry Westerby, who simply has to deprive him of the drug in order to persuade him to reveal Ricardo's whereabouts.

Charlie Marshall's face, with its Chinese eyes and French mouth, reveals his mixed racial origins. At the time Westerby meets him he is extremely emaciated and dresses in an oily, short-sleeved white shirt decorated with plentiful gold stripes on the epaulettes and a mixture of American military and Communist insignia. His outfit is topped off with a large, floppy sailing cap. Charlie speaks Khmer, French and a Chinese-accented English. His English vocabulary is colourful and hyperbolic. Although he purports to hate all mankind Charlie Marshall seems to have strong human feelings including a desperate need for his father's approval, love for Lizzie Worthington, deep friendship for Ricardo, and respect for Westerby's kind treatment of two Chinese peasants. On one occasion he rescues the wounded from Kampong Chan instead of stealing latex for personal profit. His reading of Voltaire may be the source of Charlie's finely developed human qualities. (*HS*)

Martello, Marty The London station chief for the Cousins.* Martello plays a supposedly supportive role in Operation Dolphin [CIRCUS INDEX] but is actually involved in an underhand plot to put Enderby in Smiley's seat as head of the Circus. Little is known of his personal life other than that he was educated at Yale, has children who attend the French Lycée in South Kensington, and enjoys fishing with Enderby in Scotland. Martello is a burly and cheerful-looking man who affects a bluff and solicitous manner. He wears country suits that always seem out of season. A sophistication which Martello maintains with difficulty in London disappears entirely in Hong Kong which is, for a man of his provincial mentality, enemy territory. He reverts to hick American suits and reveals his essential brutality by demanding Westerby's execution. (*HS*)

Martindale, Roddy Old Etonian member of the Foreign Office. During the war Martindale, who has some mathematical ability, is involved in intelligence work and on one occasion assists Lord John Landsbury in a coding operation. His subsequent career is in the Foreign Office but he becomes re-acquainted with the secret world some years later when he serves on a Whitehall working party charged with co-ordinating intelligence. By 1973 he operates entirely on the social side of the Foreign Office and is responsible for entertaining unpopular visiting dignitaries. It is after he is transferred to Enderby's staff that Martindale's status improves. As part of his new job he serves as a Foreign Office representative on the Intelligence Steering Committee known as the Wise Men.* He is thus present on the historic occasion when Smiley applies for funds to develop Operation Dolphin [CIRCUS INDEX]. Enderby's promotion to head of the Circus heralds Martindale's downfall because his blatantly homosexual manner does not match the hustling style which is to be favoured in future relations with the Americans.

Full knowledge of Martindale's personal life would require an exploration of the ways of the homosexual world. His only known friend is the liar Willy Andrewartha and his only known respectable recreation is dining, either at a club – he is a member of the one founded by Steed-Asprey in Manchester Square and of the Garrick – or at a private dinner party which he organizes periodically. Martindale is fat but nimble and has long grey hair delicately perfumed by Trumper's. He wears pale suits and button-holes. His manner is outrageously camp and he makes no attempt to conceal his attraction for butch men such as Fawn. Martindale is an inveterate and usually inaccurate gossip who reveals a mean streak when crossed or bored. Although his non-stop chattering is usually very tedious, he can on occasion come up with cruel but accurate epigrammatic characterizations of people such as Roy Bland, whom he describes as 'the shopsoiled white hope'. (*TT; HS*)

Masters, Major — Paramilitary Cousin* stationed on an air base in North East Thailand. In 1975 Masters provides Westerby with facilities for contacting the Circus after his meeting with Ricardo. Because of carelessness on the part of Masters, Westerby's failure to obey subsequent orders goes unnoticed for several days. On termination of his intelligence career Masters runs a small auto-repair business in Norman, Oklahoma. Masters is a wiry but pale and unhealthy looking man with hollow cheeks and an aggrieved expression around his mouth. He speaks and moves with unusual slowness. At the time of his meeting with Westerby, Masters, a patriot and Southern gentleman, is drunk and embittered at the recent American evacuation of Saigon. He expresses his feelings through a heavily ironic mock-formal manner of speech and through direct attacks on Westerby for being British and a journalist. (*HS*)

Maston, — Former civil servant who is brought into intelligence work during the war because of his bureaucratic abilities. Maston's official title is Minister's Adviser on Intelligence but he is in fact head of the Service. Failure to support Smiley during the Fennan case [CIRCUS INDEX] in 1959 (or 1960) brings his career in intelligence to an end. Maston lives in Henley-on-Thames, has a knighthood and is reputed to be the first man to have played power tennis at Wimbledon (although not with the success of Bill Tilden presumably). He dresses expensively in light suits, silver or grey ties and cream shirts in front of which hangs a monocle. His hair is also a distinguished grey. Maston's manners are as studied as his clothes but he is not entirely successful in creating the desired effect. For Smiley he is a barmaid's idea of a gentleman and for members of the Special Branch he is known as Marlene Dietrich. Maston is a despicable and hypocritical person motivated only by personal ambition. Sycophancy

London: South End Green, North Hampstead

'An overpainted Ford Cortina skidded to a giddy halt outside the cinema . . .

"I'm a private detective," Smiley explained (to the minicab driver) . . . "I would be happy to pay for a little bit of information. You signed a receipt yesterday for thirteen pounds. Do you remember who your fare was?"

"Tall party. Foreign. White moustache and a limp."

". . . And where did you take him, please?"

"Charlton . . . off of Battle-of-the-Nile Street. Ask for a pub called *The Defeated Frog* . . ."' (*Smiley's People*)

During one interminable day Smiley covers the length and breadth of London while investigating Vladimir's murder. He goes straight from his search on Hampstead Heath to South End Green to wait by the marble fountain and filthy telephone boxes for his minicab, the one engaged by Vladimir on the day of his death. The trail leads to the long-distance lorry driver Villem Craven in South East London, the General's courier between London and Hamburg where he collects one of the two 'proofs' about 'the Sandman' (Karla) – the negative Smiley finds only that morning in the discarded packet of Gauloises.

London: Trumper's of Mayfair (*above*)

'(Smiley) set off for Heywood Hill's bookshop in Curzon Street where he occasionally contracted friendly bargains with the proprietor . . . only to walk slap into the arms of Roddy Martindale emerging from Trumper's after his weekly haircut . . . Smiley caught the odour of one of Trumper's most sensitive creations.' (*Tinker, Tailor, Soldier, Spy*)'

To extricate himself from the Foreign Office 'windbag', Smiley weakly agrees to dine that same evening with Martindale in the Manchester Square club to which they both belong and Smiley usually avoids, if only to escape from Roddy's inquisitorial banter.

London: The Travellers' in Pall Mall (*right*)

'"Somehow I can never quite believe in Percy Alleline as Chief, can you . . . George? . . . Poor Percy's such an *obvious* person . . . that heavy good fellowship; how can one take him seriously? One only has to think of him in the old days lolling in the bar of the Travellers', sucking away at that log pipe of his and buying drinks for the moguls."' (*Tinker, Tailor, Soldier, Spy*)

On the whole, Circus spies favour the traditional West End clubs – the Athenaeum, the Garrick and the Savile, besides the Travellers' – but when Steed–Asprey (one of the committee which recruits Smiley in 1928) is expelled from the Junior Carlton for blaspheming within the hearing of a bishop, he founds the private club in Manchester Square where Roddy Martindale of the Foreign Office entertains, or rather bores, Smiley with his malicious gossip about Circus colleagues.

Oxford: Recruiting Ground for Circus Talent

'There are old men who go back to Oxford and find their youth beckoning to them from the stones. Smiley was not one of them . . . Not now. Passing the Bodleian he vaguely thought: I worked there.' (*Tinker, Tailor, Soldier, Spy*)

In 1928 Smiley dreams of a life at Oxford as a fellow of All Souls, devoted to the literary obscurities of 17th-century Germany, but he is lured into the Secret Service instead. Paid off after the war, he returns to Oxford as a don with his beautiful new wife, Ann, but within two years she leaves him and he is back with the Circus. And now, in 1973, he passes the Bodleian Library, one of the oldest in the world, without a pang. He is on his way to tap the encyclopedic memory of Connie Sachs (former queen of research at the Circus), who is working as a don and living in North Oxford. Her long-time suspect, Polyakov, might, Smiley thinks, lead to the identity of the Circus mole, 'Gerald'.

and a preference for Minister's policy over facts are the tools by means of which he seeks to accomplish his goals. (*CD*)

Matthews, Mrs — The widow with whom Control lives in a flat on the Western bypass, London, in the years prior to his death. She is a practical and competent person who finds consolation for Control's death (in 1973) in a cheque from the Circus. Control keeps numerous secrets from her including the fact that his wife died in 1962. (*HS*)

—, Maurice Owner of the Constellation hotel in Vientiane, Laos. Maurice displays little interest in the complex Laotian politics and neither does he put much energy into his business enterprises, if his lack of success with the Löwenbräu concession is anything to go by. He speaks with a stage-French accent. (*HS*)

'Mayfair' Code name given to Karl Riemeck while he is working for the Circus. (*SC*)

Mayfly, Operation Disastrous mission to East Germany to trace Soviet rocketry alleged to be in the Kalkstadt area (*LW*). *See* Department*

'Max' Workname* used by Smiley for his dealings with General Vladimir and the Riga Group. (*SP*)

Meakin, Molly Although only twenty-three, Molly Meakin is regarded as old Circus because her father and brother, Mike, have preceded her into espionage. She is a probationer in Registry in 1973 and is promoted to Vetting Section in the reorganization of 1974. Molly is a competent desk officer and establishes links with American Intelligence in Grosvenor Square that prove useful in identifying Tiny Ricardo. A bright future is promised Molly after Enderby becomes head of the Service in 1975 but nothing is known of her further career. Molly Meakin lives in Highgate, London, and plays squash and swims. She is pretty with a body and knees much admired by Peter Guillam. Her manner is prim and introspective but, having decided to take Guillam as a lover, she reveals an unexpected sexuality. Their affair continues beyond the conclusion of Operation Dolphin in May 1975 but probably ends soon after since he is married to another woman by 1978. (*HS*)

***meat and potatoes** Cousins* jargon for modalities or methods of procedure. (*HS*)

'Mellon' Cover name used by Sam Collins throughout his career in South East Asia. (*HS*)

Mellows, — Head porter at the Circus in 1972. Sam Collins considers him to be lazy and reports his negligence. Mellows's revenge is to report him for drinking on duty. This gives Haydon the chance to get Collins dismissed. (*TT*)

Mencken, — Jerry Westerby's literary agent who goes by the nickname

Ming. Mencken has an extrovert, direct manner and relies on a grey beard to give him a literary air. His background is obscure and he is both a snob and a fool. Mencken met Westerby in a cricketing context and continues to have an interest in the sport. He admires Conrad but condemns Greene, Maugham and Hemingway's journalistic style. (*HS*)

Mendel, Inspector — Member of the Special Branch who works under Ben Sparrow until retiring in 1959 (or 1960). Following his retirement Mendel assists Smiley in the Fennan and Haydon cases [CIRCUS INDEX]. During the Fennan case he interrogates Adam Scarr, makes enquiries at the Weybridge Repertory Theatre in Surrey and is part of the trap set for Dieter Frey at the Sheridan Theatre, Hammersmith. It is Mendel who keeps in touch with Frey as he makes his escape and he is beaten unconscious in the final struggle to capture him. In 1973 Mendel is part of the team gathered together by Smiley to discover the identity of the mole* Gerald. His most important task is to watch the Circus and observe the effects of Tarr's telegram from Paris. He uses the cover name Arthur when making contact with Guillam during this case.

Mendel has Jewish origins and lives in a semi-detached house in Mitcham, Surrey, of which he takes great care. Besides the house, his great passion is bee-keeping. As a young man he boxes middleweight for his Division. Mendel is a thin man with an uncommunicative weasel face and short, spiky grey hair. He speaks out of the corner of his mouth. The battered brief-case used in his police work, his habit of rolling his own cigarettes and a bee-keeping hat which reminds Smiley of a tall mushroom, all suggest an indifference to the impression he makes on others. This characteristic is also evident in Mendel's lack of concern with social niceties and his relaxed attitude to the demands of conversation. Mendel is a straightforward man who believes in humility, common sense, thoroughness and precision and is suspicious of emotional weakness. His career as a policeman has taught him to make simple distinctions between the criminal and the non-criminal. Only reminders of the German persecution of the Jews can stir up deep passions in Mendel. Nevertheless, he is not unfeeling as he demonstrates in his unfailing concern for Smiley. Their friendship, which begins in 1959 (or 1960), is still going strong in 1978 when Mendel several times gives Smiley a meal and a bed during the period of preparation for the blackmailing of Karla. (*CD; MQ; TT; SP*)

'Merlin' Name given to the Source of Operation Witchcraft material [CIRCUS INDEX]. (*TT*)

'Mickey' Thai native who drives Westerby to his meeting with Ricardo. His real name is unpronounceable. Although fat and lazy Mickey turns out to be a capable and cheerful driver whose one major fault is his fondness for repeated playings of the Bee Gees' song, 'The Lights are Always Out in Massachusetts'. (*HS*)

—, Mikhel A Major in the Royal Estonian Cavalry until the Soviet occupation in 1940 and later adjutant to General Vladimir in the Paris Lodge of the Riga Group. In 1978 at the age of about sixty Mikhel runs the Free Baltic Library in, or just off, Great Russell Street opposite the British Museum in London. Mikhel is the recipient of Ostrakova's first letter to Vladimir and it is likely that he betrays his old friend to Karla. Smiley suspects that he has long been a double agent. Mikhel is married to Elvira, formerly his mistress. Apart from his work in the Library he occupies himself with betting on horses and playing chess. Despite his age Mikhel still has the appearance of a cavalry officer. His black jacket, worn like a cloak, and his riding boots are neat and tidy and his body straight and slim. His grey hair and moustache are cut in military style. Although Mikhel's face appears youthful, close examination reveals the crumbling of age and his brown eyes are droopy. Extensive experience of interrogation has enabled Mikhel to develop an impenetrable personality, but we can guess that feelings of jealousy at Vladimir's relationship with his wife Elvira play a part in his betrayal of the General. (*SP*)

'Miller' Surname assumed by General Vladimir after he moves to London. (*SP*)

'Ming' Nickname of Westerby's literary agent, Mencken. (*HS*)

*mole Originally Moscow Centre jargon for foreign nationals recruited in their youth as spies but not activated until many years later when they have penetrated deep into their country's intelligence or governmental structure. (*TT*)

'Mole' Nickname given to Smiley by the Circus staff during the 1950s. (*CD*)

Moscow Centre Only limited information is available on the organization and history of the Soviet Intelligence Service, otherwise known as Moscow Centre. For a fuller picture access must be gained to files held at the Circus, particularly the seven volumes on Karla. Moscow Centre has its headquarters at Dzerzhinsky Square and is also known to have a training school at Kiev. Identified members of Moscow Centre include Bykov, Muranov and Shur, all executed in 1955; Stanley, an assassin who defects in 1963; Avilov, the Hong Kong resident;* Boris and Irina, agents operating under trade cover; an agent working under cover as a Russian Orthodox Archimandrite; Novikov and Trepov, bodyguards.

Within Moscow Centre, the Thirteenth Directorate, sometimes known as the Karla Directorate, forms an élite group which is directly responsible to the Party's Central Committee. The task of the Thirteenth Directorate is to recruit, train and place agents, or moles,* under deep cover in enemy countries. The servicing of the moles* is the responsibility of a Karla representative, usually a military officer attached to an embassy. The Thirteenth Directorate has three or four training establishments including one at Minsk. At one time the master spy Berg may have been head of this branch of Moscow Centre; Konev is head during the Second World War, Rudnev in the years before 1955 and Karla from that date until 1978.

Only a few of the agents trained to service the Thirteenth Directorate's moles* have been identified, and these are Colonel Viktorov, otherwise known as Polyakov, Colonel Bardin (who changes his name to Sokolov and then Rusakov); Colonel Stokovsky, who works under the name Major Grodescu, and Mikhail Fedorovitch Komarov. The rest of the Directorate's staff include Bretlev, a talent spotter, Colonel Orlov of the Embassy in Lisbon; Pudin of the Paris Embassy; Zimin, known to the Circus as Commercial Boris, a paymaster; Brod, workname* Lapin, cover name Ivlov, Polyakov's legman;* Kursky, finance officer; and Milos, an instructor at one of the training schools. It is also possible that Khlebnikov, an academician, recruits for the Thirteenth Directorate during the 1930s.

Details of most of Moscow Centre's activities are lacking but Soviet agents are known to have functioned or to be functioning in the USA, Britain, France, Portugal, Switzerland, West Germany, Sweden, Australia, India, Kenya, Japan, China, Hong Kong, Singapore and Laos. The earliest intelligence initiatives for which information is available occur in the 1930s. At this time agents such as Karla are active in Britain where they recruit deep-penetration agents and in Spain where they help the fight against fascism and do further recruitment of German agents. Moscow Centre is deeply involved in the war effort through the recruitment of agents behind enemy lines and the use of misleading radio transmissions. Karla distinguishes himself in these activities. With the defeat of fascism, Moscow Centre turns its attention to reviving the Shanghai communist underground with the ultimate intention of overturning the regime of Chiang Kai-shek.

The late 1940s are also a time of conflict within Moscow Centre and Karla is amongst those imprisoned in Siberia for belonging to the wrong faction. Internal warfare flares up again in 1955 and results in a number of executions and defections. Karla's brilliant outmanoeuvring of Rudnev seems to bring peace, although it is clear that his powerful position within Moscow Centre is the cause of considerable jealousy. He is very much disliked, for example, for the warnings he offers about possible future conflict with China. Although he is unable to alert Moscow Centre as a whole to the Chinese threat, Karla takes steps to protect Soviet interests by recruiting a young Chinese engineer, Nelson Ko, as his mole.* It is also during this period that another of Karla's moles,* Bill Haydon, becomes the source of useful information taken from British and American sources. The incompetent aspect of Moscow Centre revealed by its blindness to likely developments in Sino–Soviet relations is also evident in its concern with, and clumsy efforts made to penetrate, the many *émigré* groups located in Paris. Far from jeopardizing Soviet security, such groups cannot even agree on common tactics and any threat they do pose is not likely to be lessened by the employment of people such as Ostrakova, an obvious dissident, as informers.

Moscow Centre appears to enjoy considerable success during the 1960s. Haydon's return from foreign postings provides Karla with enough information to strike a series of damaging blows against the Circus. There is also evidence that a number of other moles* are activated at this time, for a special training school is instituted in 1963 to prepare the military officers responsible for servicing them. Although the relationship between Komarov and his mole,* a senior official in the Japanese defence ministry, is uncovered in 1966, Viktorov (Polyakov) in London, Bardin in New York and Stokovsky in Paris and Bonn operate unhindered throughout the 1960s. Moscow Centre is active on a number of other fronts in Europe and Zimin (Commercial Boris), another graduate of Karla's training school, plays paymaster to an East German *apparat* (organization) in Switzerland for six years besides successfully blackmailing a French senator. Intelligence efforts outside of Europe are rather less successful. Karla's mole* Nelson Ko proves to be of little help following his disgrace during the Cultural Revolution and other attempts to penetrate China all fail. These include a network of listening* posts along the border which produce only military intelligence; negotiations aimed at combining forces with Taiwan and the USA; recruitment amongst overseas Chinese communities; and the blackmail of Peking officials in overseas postings. Hong Kong proves to be equally inhospitable territory and both a spy posing as a Russian Orthodox Archimandrite and the crew of a Soviet freighter are exposed while trying to create networks.*

At the beginning of the 1970s Operation Witchcraft [CIRCUS INDEX] seems certain to give Moscow Centre full access not only to all important British intelligence but also American. However, a series of events, beginning with the identification of Boris as yet another Soviet agent seeking a foothold in Hong Kong, culminates in the termination of Karla's best source, Bill Haydon. This set-back is followed by the passing of Nelson Ko into American hands only shortly after he has become useful to

Karla, and finally to Karla's own forced defection. (*TT; HS; SP*)

*Moscow-gazer Expert on Soviet intelligence. (*HS*)

*Moscow Rules Espionage techniques designed for use by an agent operating in the USSR. (*SP*)

Mostyn, Nigel Circus probationer who works in the Oddbins* department, while awaiting overseas posting. Because no one takes General Vladimir's call to the Circus seriously on October 13, 1978, the inexperienced Mostyn is assigned as his case officer. He is waiting at the safe house* in Hampstead while Vladimir is being murdered on the Heath. Although Mostyn sees this, his first mission, as a total failure he does in fact acquire several pieces of vital information which he passes on to Smiley. Mostyn leaves the Circus a few months later. Mostyn's youth is emphasized by his trousers and hair which are fashionably flared and long respectively. He is earnest in manner and generally shows signs of being too sensitive for the life of a spy. (*SP*)

*Mother Senior Circus secretary. (*TT*)

Mother Felicity Head of the clinic near Berne where Karla's daughter, Tatiana, receives treatment. Mother Felicity is a white Russian and her real name is Nadezhda, which means hope. At one time she is a member of the Russian Orthodox Community in Jerusalem. In appearance and manner Mother Felicity is impressive but disconcerting. Her large frame and her commanding way of speaking German give her an air of dignity but this is undercut by her worldly expression and habit of riding a moped. Although in many ways a pompous and even frightening figure, Mother Felicity is deeply sentimental about her Russian origins, particularly when under the influence of sweet wine. (*SP*)

'Mother Russia' Nickname given to Connie Sachs by her colleagues at the Circus. (*HS*)

Mulligan, Mr — Owner of a furniture removal company in Carne, Dorset. Although there isn't much indication of it in his professional life, Mulligan seems to have a strong commitment to traditional morality. Thus, he exiles his daughter to Leamington Spa for the birth of her illegitimate baby. This guilty secret makes Mulligan susceptible to blackmail by Stella Rode. (*MQ*)

Mundt, Hans-Dieter Born in Leipzig in 1919, Mundt is a member of the Hitler Youth before beginning his career with the Abteilung in 1947. After completing his probationary period he sets up intelligence networks* in Scandinavia, particularly Norway and Sweden, and in Finland. Mundt's next posting is to London in 1956. Working under cover as a member of the East German Steel Mission, Mundt is involved in countersubversion against *émigré* groups as well as being the contact with Dieter

Frey's agent Elsa Fennan, who calls Mundt Freitag (after Man Friday in *Robinson Crusoe*), in the Fennan case [CIRCUS INDEX]. Meetings with Elsa Fennan occur at the Weybridge Repertory Theatre on the first and third Tuesdays of each month. To reach Weybridge in Surrey, Mundt rents a car from Adam Scarr, who calls him Blondie. In 1959 (1960 according to another version of events) Mundt murders Samuel Fennan to prevent him betraying Elsa to George Smiley. Soon afterwards he attacks Smiley brutally and murders Adam Scarr. Mundt's attempts to cover his trail are unsuccessful and he is captured by Peter Guillam.

Because he agrees to betray his own Service to the British Mundt is allowed to escape to Berlin. Information supplied by Control enables Mundt to be extremely effective in the period following his return home and by March 1961 he has destroyed Alec Leamas's East German networks.* Success in the field leads to rapid promotion; early in 1960 Mundt is only head of the Ways and Means Department of the Abteilung but by the end of the year he has become deputy director of Operations (also known as head of Counter Espionage). This means that he is second in command of the Abteilung and effective head of Operations. As such he is of enormous use to British Intelligence. Fiedler's suspicions about Mundt's loyalty force Control to concoct an elaborate plan in 1961 to protect his source. The Fiedler–Mundt Operation [CIRCUS INDEX], as it is called, is successful in that it transfers the label of traitor to Fiedler, but it also causes the deaths of Alec Leamas and the civilian, Liz Gold. Nothing is known of Mundt's activities after 1962.

Apart from the fact that he is unmarried and always drinks coffee there is no information on Mundt's personal life and habits. He is tall, well-built and athletic-looking with short, fair hair and handsome features. His face is hard and clean and he has the cold expression of a born killer. He dresses well; when Smiley encounters Mundt in his Bywater Street home he is wearing a light grey suit, white shirt and silver tie which give him the air of a diplomat. Mundt's personality is psychopathic; he is without humour or the ability to fantasize, and he has no compunction about killing. Only torture, especially of a Jew such as Fiedler, appears capable of arousing feeling in him. In other situations he is entirely a man of fact and action. (*CD; SC*)

Mundy, Ted Police sergeant from Okeford in Dorset who leads Inspector Rigby and George Smiley to Jane Lyn's home in the ruined King Arthur's Chapel at Pylle near Carne. He is a local man who speaks slowly and has an acute sense of the history of the area. (*MQ*)

Murgatroyd, Mr — Police forensic expert who assists the 'Detective Chief Superintendent' at the scene of General Vladimir's murder. He has grey hair and complexion, wears a grey suit and speaks in a grey, funereal voice. Smiley's identity is a complete puzzle to him. (*SP*)

Murphy, — The Cousin* responsible for briefing Martello in both London and Hong Kong during Operation Dolphin [CIRCUS INDEX]. Murphy is fair, almost albino, and wears a white shirt and blue trousers. His manner is quiet, polite, respectful, and without emotion. He communicates information fully and monotonously. (*HS*)

'Murphy' Cover name under which William Ashe holds the lease of his flat in Dolphin Square, Pimlico, London. (*SC*)

—, Nadezhda Real name of Mother Felicity. (*SP*)

'narcotics agent' A certain young and inexperienced member of the American Drug Enforcement Administration. On September 2, 1973, while stationed in South East Asia, this agent is approached by Tiny Ricardo who wants to sell him opium and information. Because of an error in judgement on the part of the agent's superior, Ed Ristow, the offer of information, which concerns Drake Ko's attempt to extricate his brother Nelson from China, is rejected. By 1974 the agent has abandoned drug-enforcement in favour of a hippie commune north of Katmandu, Nepal. (*HS*)

Natasha *See* 'Little Natasha'

*neighbours, the Soviet diplomatic jargon for the Soviet Intelligence Service. (*SP*)

*network Spy ring. (*SP*)

'night porter' Censorious old man employed by the Sawley Arms hotel in Carne, Dorset. Smiley, of whom he clearly disapproves, likens him to Charon of Greek mythology who ferried the dead across the river Styx to Hades. (*MQ*)

—, Norman Young man who represents the entire staff of the Hotel Islay in Sussex Gardens, Paddington, London. Norman does not consider cleaning shoes to be amongst his responsibilities but he is willing to let guests in late at night for a fee. In the execution of his duties he wears a black overcoat onto which his employer, Mrs Pope Graham, has stitched a beige velvet collar. Because he shivers a lot Mrs Pope Graham considers Norman to be sensitive but for Smiley he is a grubby little voyeur. (*TT*)

Nursery, the The training school for spies at Sarratt in Hertfordshire [CIRCUS INDEX]. (*TT*)

*nuts and bolts Department of the Circus charged with providing technical and scientific services for field operations. (*TT*)

'Oates' Cover name used by Smiley for his interview with the Pellings during Operation Dolphin [CIRCUS INDEX]. Oates works for Bullion Universal Security Advisers, a company considering giving employment to Lizzie Worthington. He announces himself with a big green card and uses a desire to be discreet to explain his company's absence from the telephone book. (*HS*)

*Occasionals Group of part-time agents called on by the Circus as the need arises. (*TT*)

*Oddbins Circus department staffed by probationers awaiting overseas postings. (*SP*)

Oklahoma CIA secret aviation school is located here. (*HS*)

Operations *See* individual names: Dolphin; Fiedler–Mundt; Mayfly; Rolling Stone; Testify; Witchcraft. For Chronologies of Fiedler–Mundt and Dolphin Operations, *see* Circus chapter, pages 28–40.

*operational intelligence Usable information. (*SP*)

Oriel, Mrs Ludo Manager of the Weybridge Repertory Theatre, Surrey. She is questioned by Mendel as part of the investigation into the murder of Samuel Fennan. Ludo Oriel is a small, dark woman who tries to disguise the fact that she is entering middle age with excessive make-up. Her mouth is long and she holds her cigarette in the middle of it in such a way as to give her a bad-tempered, impatient look. She dresses in slacks and a heavy, distemper-stained sweater. Perhaps because of the financial difficulties of running an unsuccessful theatre or because of the need to meet the demands of the Surrey bourgeoisie for *Peter Pan* and *Treasure Island*, Ludo Oriel is bitchy, cruel and easily aroused to anger. Her hostility to her apprentice-assistant, Elizabeth Pidgeon, seems to have as much to do with the girl's innocence as her lack of talent. Mendel judges Ludo to be clever. (*CD*)

Orlov, Colonel — Karla's Lisbon Embassy resident* whose misuse of Moscow Centre funds is discovered by Kursky in 1973. (*SP*)

'orphan, the' Young woman and former governess in Florence who becomes Westerby's mistress during his sojourn in Tuscany. The orphan is thin, red-haired and sullen-faced, although she is capable of smiling beautifully, and listens only to classical music. She dresses in a shapeless brown dress and carries a shoulder bag containing all her possessions. She speaks in a blunt and direct way and is much given to saying 'bloody'. Nothing is known of the orphan's background, which is very much the way she would want it. Initially suspicious, she finally gives herself entirely to Westerby who is fascinated by her butterfly-like weightlessness in love-making. The orphan, who is some twenty-five years younger than Westerby, only demands of him that he be honest, and is devastated when he abandons her to return to the Circus. (*HS*)

Ostrakov, Igor Former captain of infantry in the Red Army who defects to the West in 1950 while stationed in East Berlin. On taking up residence in Paris, Ostrakov, whose mother is Estonian, joins the Baltic Independence groups. However, by 1956 he is disillusioned with all the *émigrés* except for General Vladimir. Ostrakov is dying of cancer by January 1956 but it is unclear exactly how long he survives. Ostrakov's marriage to Maria Ostrakova dates back to September 1, 1948. They are separated by Ostrakov's defection but reunited in Paris shortly before his death. Ostrakov is a fat, bespectacled man who, despite his appearance, communicates a sense of stillness, gravity and dignity. George Smiley reminds Ostrakova of her dead husband. (*SP*)

'Ostrakova, Alexandra' The name under which Karla's daughter Tatiana is registered at the clinic near Berne. The real Alexandra is Maria Ostrakova's daughter by her lover Joseph Glikman. (*SP*)

Ostrakova, Maria Andreyevna Born in Leningrad on May 8, 1927, Maria Ostrakova, née Rogova, now lives in the 15th district of Paris. Her alienation from the Soviet authorities dates from her marriage to Igor Ostrakov on September 1, 1948, in Moscow. For assisting Ostrakov in his defection Ostrakova is imprisoned in a forced labour camp from 1950 to 1953. Shortly before her release she breaks her leg in three places in a coal slip. After returning to Moscow Ostrakova takes as her lover Joseph Glikman, a Jewish music student and dissident, whom she met in the labour camp. Glikman is the father of Ostrakova's daughter, Alexandra, born in the Lying-in Hospital of the October Revolution. Ostrakova and Glikman are part of a political, religious and artistic circle considered anti-social by the authorities. Encouraged by Glikman, Ostrakova takes advantage of permission to visit her husband in Paris and defects in 1956. She also fails to fulfil promises to Soviet authorities to persuade Ostrakov to return to the USSR and to spy on *émigré* groups.

After many uneventful years, during which she works as a checker in a warehouse, Ostrakova is approached in 1978 by Kirov (actually Oleg Kursky) with an offer to effect a reunion with Alexandra. Doubtful of Kirov's claims, Ostrakova contacts General Vladimir, a man much admired by her husband in the 1950s. Her letter to Vladimir is ultimately responsible for the defection of Karla. Ostrakova herself is almost murdered as Karla tries to cover his traces, but she survives the attack made by two Soviet thugs and locks herself in her apartment until rescued by George Smiley. Smiley removes her first to Peter Guillam's apartment in Neuilly and then to a trusted French couple, a retired agent and his wife, at Arras in the Pas-de-Calais. During her lengthy stay here Ostrakova recuperates mentally and physically and declines a marriage invitation from a local retired brigadier.

Ostrakova has a brother Niki, who hangs himself, and a half-sister Valentina, who is married to a car salesman and lives in Lyon in south-east central France. As a child she rides a pony. Her religion is Russian Orthodox and she attends churches in the 15th and 16th districts, including the Church of the Russian Abroad, the Church of the Apparition of the Holy Virgin, and the Church of St Seraphin of Sarov. At age fifty-one Ostrakova is short and stout with a rolling gait. Her chin is pugnacious, but her brown eyes and the set of her mouth suggest humour, an impression which is emphasized by the flopping lock of hair which escapes from the bun in which her grey hair is gathered. She wears a severe black dress with a white lace collar even in hot weather. Around her neck is a large metal cross. She has cracked shoes and a shabby bag. Because of her labour camp injury she sometimes limps. Ostrakova is an emotionally complex person capable at once of deep affection for her husband, lover and child and intense hatred of Soviet authorities. She is also both quick-witted and brave, qualities that enable her to survive Karla's attempts first to exploit and then to destroy her. (*SP*)

Oxford The history of the Circus is inextricably intertwined with Oxford University. Jebedee and Sparke are Oxford dons as well as early members of the Circus and it is here, in 1928, that Smiley is persuaded to exchange a fellowship at All Souls for a career in espionage. During the 1930s Oxford is a recruiting ground for British and Soviet Intelligence; Fanshawe, a tutor, enlists potential spies for the Circus (often from the Christ Church Optimates club he founded), notably Haydon of Christ Church, and Prideaux. Karla persuades Haydon to become a double agent while he is still an undergraduate. Roy Bland is taken on by the Circus during his student days in the late 1950s and uses his subsequent position as a don at St Antony's College as a cover for his intelligence role. Connie Sachs is also a don after her dismissal from the Circus in 1972 and Smiley is a don from 1945 to 1947. Westerby is a student at Oxford before joining the Circus and Harry Slingo's son goes to Wadham College. Visits to Oxford play a part in two of Smiley's major cases. During the investigation into the identity of the mole* Gerald, Smiley visits Connie Sachs, who is living in North Oxford after her forced retirement from the Circus, to gather information on Polyakov. Connie is also the reason for Smiley's second visit which occurs as part of his attempts to establish that 'Alexandra Ostrakova' is in fact Karla's daughter. This visit takes Smiley to her clapboard cabin outside the city.

Preparation for the Department's* disastrous Operation Mayfly is centred on a house in North Oxford. The location is chosen in deference to

wartime practice. Leiser, the agent, is given target practice at the nearby
Abingdon parachute base and unarmed combat-training in a gym in the
Headington district. A house in Fairford, over the Gloucestershire
border, is used for radio transmission work. During their free time Leiser
and the Department* staff stroll on Port Meadow, play bar-billiards at a
pub behind Balliol, and take a long walk down Walton Street to Worcester
College and then back up the Banbury Road. Two of the Department's*
staff are Oxford graduates; Haldane read Greats in Smiley's time and
Avery German and Italian at a College in the Turl (thus Exeter, Jesus or
Lincoln). While a student Avery lived in Chandos Road in North Oxford.

Because they know it almost entirely from their student days, for most
spies Oxford is a place of lost youthful idealism. It is where Prideaux met
his best friend, Haydon, and had the sheer exuberance needed to run laps
of the Parks after a night of drinking. It is where Avery's love for Sarah
blossomed into a marriage full of hope. The disappointments that follow
perhaps explain why later visits to Oxford, such as Smiley makes in 1973,
are unaccompanied by any sense of returning home. (*CD; LW; TT; SP*)

*pack your trunk, to Connie Sachs's jargon for preparing an archive for
posterity. (*HS*)
*pavement artist Spy who specializes in surveillance. (*TT*)
*pax Internal telephone. (*HS*)
Peersen, Inspector — Finnish police officer in charge of the investigation into Wilf Taylor's death. Peersen is short, fat and shaves his neck. He
smokes cigars and speaks English with an American accent. Peersen's
manner is sympathetic and he expresses an admiration for the British.
Nevertheless, he makes it clear to Avery that he sees through his feeble
claims to be Taylor's brother. (*LW*)
*Peking Tea Club Body set up to co-ordinate Chinese Intelligence. (*HS*)
Pelling, 'Cess' Wife of Humphrey Pelling and mother of Lizzie Worthington. The Pellings live at 7, Arcady Mansions in North London where
they have separate rooms. She is a tall woman with a stoop who speaks in a
mannish, distorted voice that is trying to be refined. The way in which she
drags her leg and her stiff right arm suggests that Mrs Pelling has had a
stroke. Her clothes, which include flat shoes and a belted masculine-style
pullover, reveal a lack of confidence in her own attractiveness. She
smokes, and reeks of gin. Like her husband, Cess Pelling is extremely
eccentric but she only partly shares his fantasies about their daughter's
achievements. For her, Lizzie's love affairs are romantic yet she has few
illusions about the sleaziness of her daughter's business enterprises. (*HS*)
Pelling, Humphrey Husband of Cess Pelling, who calls him Nunc, and

father of Lizzie Worthington. Humphrey Pelling is retired from the Post Office and occupies his time reading the *Daily Telegraph*. He is a small, bald man who wears a dressing-gown and bedroom slippers even in the daytime. His manner is aggressive and officious and he is clearly imbued with the bureaucratic ethos of his former occupation. At the same time, though, he is a dreamer who fantasizes that Lizzie is engaged in intelligence work of national significance. The style in which Nunc Pelling describes his daughter's adventures suggests that he has read too many 'Bulldog Drummond' stories. (*HS*)

Perkins, Tim Pupil at Carne School who is murdered by Terence Fielding because of his knowledge about the murder of Stella Rode. Perkins is a red-haired boy whose cynical attitude to social-climbing is fully justified by his own familial experience. As the son of an Army officer and a mother much admired by Felix D'Arcy because she is related to the right sort of people, Perkins is placed under considerable pressure to pursue a conventional path through life. However, he lacks the academic ability to gain entry into Sandhurst as his father would wish. His own interests in music – he is an excellent cellist – and acting are scorned by his parents. It is ironic that Perkins is murdered at one of those few moments – wildly riding his bicycle – when he feels free from the pressures of conformity. Although driven by desperation to kill Tim Perkins, Fielding is in love with him and makes him captain of his house to improve the boy's chances of getting into Sandhurst. (*MQ*)

Peters, — Abteilung agent who meets Alec Leamas in Holland during his supposed defection to East Germany. Peters is about fifty-five with a hard, lined, grey face devoid of any expression. His hair is also grey. He is left-handed. Leamas believes that Peters is Russian. During their brief relationship Peters reveals nothing about himself to Leamas. However, Leamas deduces that he has been in prison, perhaps at the beginning of the Revolution, and has been on the run. For Leamas Peters has the strength and confidence associated with a professional. He also suspects that Peters's communism has a firm ideological basis. (*SC*)

Pidgeon, Elizabeth Daughter of a local solicitor who indulges his child's theatrical ambitions by paying for her apprenticeship at the Weybridge Repertory Theatre, Surrey. Besides taking an occasional part, Elizabeth helps seat customers during performances. She is therefore able to supply Mendel with the information needed to identify Elsa Fennan's theatre companion as Hans-Dieter Mundt. Elizabeth Pidgeon is the English-rose type, being tall and quite pretty with frizzy blonde hair, pink cheeks and fat, red hands. Her smile is vapid and she speaks in dated schoolgirl slang. Mendel suspects that she is good at tennis and swimming. Despite her obvious good nature Elizabeth Pidgeon is much hated by the Weybridge Repertory staff who call her the Virgin. She also fails to make a good impression on Peter Guillam for whom she is Moby Dick, the big white man-eating whale. (*CD*)

Pied-Piper appeal Charismatic quality that Thatch of the Sarratt charm-school tries to develop in agents who will be living under cover in enemy territory. (*TT*)

play back To return enemy agents to their own country after they have been turned. (*SP*)

*play it long To act with extreme caution. (*TT*)

'Polly' Name by which his London Embassy colleagues refer to Polyakov. (*TT*)

'Polyakov, Aleksey Aleksandrovich' Cover name of Colonel Gregor Viktorov, veteran of Stalingrad and graduate of Karla's secret training school for spies. According to his British visa application Polyakov is the son of a transporter, born on March 19, 1922 in the Ukraine, is a graduate of Leningrad State University, and is married. There is no guarantee that any of this is true. Polyakov is posted to London in 1965 under cover as a Cultural Attaché with the rank of Second Secretary. His real job is to debrief the mole* Gerald. Because he lives his cover so completely, eagerly promoting cultural events and residing in middle-class respectability at 40, Meadow Close, Highgate in North London, the lamplighters* are unable to come up with any evidence to confirm Connie Sachs's immediate suspicion that he is a spy. Polyakov makes his first slip in 1972 when he gives away his military background by wearing his legitimate medals at the Cenotaph Remembrance Day service. It is Haydon who ensures that Connie's demands for action are ignored. Polyakov is eventually betrayed by his assistant, Brod, who reveals his real role to Irina in Moscow. Irina passes the information on to Tarr in Hong Kong, and thus begins the series of events which ends with the unmasking of Polyakov and Haydon at the Lock Gardens safe house.* Polyakov's Embassy colleagues refer to him as Polly and he is known to the residents of Lock Gardens as Mr Jefferson. Polyakov is nearly six feet tall, heavily built and has green eyes and black hair, with a quiff over his right eye. His voice is beautifully mellow. A self-sufficient manner and upright bearing suggest his military origins. Connie suspects him of lechery. Although jolly and a great joker, Polyakov directs tremendous hatred at everyone connected with the exposure of Haydon's treachery. (*TT*)

*poodle To serve as an administrative assistant. (*HS*)

'Poole' Cover name on the fake passport made for Ricki Tarr in Kuala Lumpur in 1973. (*TT*)

Pope Graham, Mrs *See* Graham, Mrs Pope

Porteous, Phil The head housekeeper* at the Circus; he is also part of London Station* during Alleline's time as chief of the Service. Porteous is a wealthy man with a large suburban house. His appearance is as smooth as his manners which he adapts to the status of the company. With his superiors he practises servility but is smugly patronizing to his inferiors. His sleek façade is not impenetrable, however, and Peter Guillam makes him blush by mimicking his pompous phrasing. (*TT*)

Porton, Clive Scottish solicitor who lives in Hong Kong. His manner is falsely affable and he is well known to be crooked. Jerry Westerby believes that he was involved in illegal dealings involving Macao-based gold. Drink makes him sweaty and voluble. It may also distort his judgement of horses since his selection, Open Space, is well beaten by Drake Ko's Lucky Nelson at Happy Valley races. Porton accepts the loss with poor grace. (*HS*)

*postbox job Assignment involving the collection and delivery of secret messages. (*TT*)

postman Case officer who handles the day-to-day needs and problems of an intelligence network. (*SP*)

Prideaux, Jim Prideaux (pronounced Priddo) is the son of lesser aristocrats involved in European banking. His parents live apart during his childhood. Prideaux is a pupil at the Lycée Lakanal in Paris, a Jesuit day-school in Prague, and goes to Strasbourg for two semesters. While in Paris he is taught to play cricket by his uncle Comte Henri de Sainte-Yvonne. He goes up to Oxford in 1936 and acquires a reputation as an athlete. Amongst his achievements is a cricket blue. Because he lacks contemporaries there from his own schooldays, Prideaux joins many societies including the Populars, a debating club, his college drama society, the philatelic society, the modern languages society, the Union, the historical society, the ethical society and the Rudolph Steiner study group. At a meeting of the Populars, he becomes acquainted with Bill Haydon, who soon draws him to the attention of the tutor Fanshawe, a Circus talent spotter.*

At the outbreak of war Prideaux leaves Oxford to join the Circus. His war record is excellent and includes helping Haydon to establish courier lines across southern Europe. Undercover work also takes him to Czechoslovakia, where he fights alongside the partisans. Prideaux teaches for a while after the war but eventually returns to the Circus. Little is known of his career during the 1950s and 1960s but he has considerable contact with the Czechoslovakian networks* Plato and Aggravate. By 1972 Prideaux is head of the scalphunters,* but his career is suddenly terminated in October of that year. A mission to Brno, Czechoslovakia, to meet, as Control believes, General Stevcek, leads Prideaux into a trap. He is wounded in the right shoulder and taken to the USSR for interrogation. Haydon, who is responsible for betraying his old friend and perhaps even lover, finally secures Prideaux's release and he is flown to Inverness by RAF fighter. During Operation Testify, as the mission is called, Prideaux goes under the cover name Vladimir Hajeck and the workname* Jim Ellis. After a brief stay at Sarratt,* Prideaux is ordered by Esterhase to end all contact with the Circus. Thus, he begins a new career as a supply teacher in preparatory schools. For half a term he works in one in Berkshire and at the end of May 1973 he is taken on at Thursgood's school in Devon, near Taunton, to teach French. The peace of his new life, however, is quickly disturbed by Smiley's investigations into the identity of the mole* Gerald. Finally made to face up to the fact that he was betrayed, Prideaux takes revenge by breaking Haydon's neck at Sarratt.* Because Smiley keeps his suspicions about Haydon's murderer to himself, Prideaux is able to return to Thursgood's and his new life as a teacher.

Jim Prideaux's face is fierce and red, and covered with deep lines. He takes on a much kindlier look when he grins. His moustache is brown. Following his gun-shot wound he has a crooked back which distorts his previously magnificent physique. He speaks in a military voice. Prideaux has a number of interests: walking, sports, even after his injury, cooking spicy food, reading aloud to his pupils, the *Daily Telegraph*, drinking vodka, and his red Alvis. However, his self is rooted in a passionate sense of being English. This is expressed in harangues at his pupils, his taste for the novels of Buchan, Captain ('Biggles') Johns, Jeffrey Farnol and Percy Westerman, and in the spirit of service with which he approaches his career with the Circus. Prideaux's patriotism is both his greatest strength and the source of an intense vulnerability. On the one hand it helps make him into an essentially decent person with an air of gentleness which even the boys at Thursgood's notice, and which expresses itself most obviously in his relationship with the unhappy schoolboy Bill Roach. On the other, it short-circuits his critical faculties and makes him blind to the possibility that an Englishman with Haydon's aristocratic origins could be a traitor. This aspect of Prideaux's personality makes the nickname Rhino particularly suitable. (*TT*)

Public Schools Committee for Refugee Relief The assistant to Jill Dawney at the collecting centre in Kennington, South London, is a very beautiful girl who helps Ailsa Brimley identify the parcel containing the blood-stained clothes worn by Terence Fielding while murdering Stella Rode. A pleasant, talkative girl, she seems harassed by her job but is actually quite efficient. (*MQ*)

*pug marks Evidence in the files of Haydon's interference with information likely to harm the Soviet cause. (*HS*)

Purcell, Molly Circus monitor who is on duty the night Prideaux is captured in Czechoslovakia. She plays bridge with Diana Dolphin. (*TT*)

*put out smoke To act in such a way as to reinforce one's cover. (*HS*)

*put the bite on To blackmail. (*HS*)

Pym, — Lacon's private secretary. He is a man with a plummy voice who is offended by Guillam's use of slang. Guillam finds him very irritating. (*HS*)

*Queen Bee, the Female head of the Registry. (*HS*)

Raglan, Johnnie Former schoolmate of Stanley Rode who is now a waiter at the Dolphin restaurant in Branxome, Hampshire. Raglan is a disreputable character who responds readily to an invitation to abandon his duties and join the Rodes at their table. Stella then encourages him to mock her husband. (*MQ*)

'Randy Sandy' Wartime nickname of Sandy Lowe. (*LW*)

*recycle To return defecting agents to their own country before their disappearance is noticed in order that they might be in a position to provide intelligence for their new masters. (*HS*)

Reid-Harriman, Major C. J. *See* Harriman, Major C. J. Reid-

*reptile fund Secret account provided by the Government to pay for intelligence operations. (*HS*)

*resident *See* above-the-line* (legal resident) and below-the-line* (illegal resident)

'Rhino' Nickname given to Prideaux by the boys at Thursgood's School. (*TT*)

Ribble, J. P. Member of the Foreign Office Research Department who establishes the multiple identity of Source Merlin. (*TT*)

Ricardo, 'Tiny' or 'Ric' After training at the CIA's secret aviation school in Oklahoma, where he meets Charlie Marshall, Ricardo flies secret missions for seven years in Vietnam and two years in Laos. During his service in Laos Ricardo carries cargoes of opium. He also claims to have flown two missions over Yunnan Province in mainland China. The CIA pays him US $4,000 a month for his services. At some point, probably after terminating his contract with the Americans, Ricardo trains pilots for the Cambodian air force. However, he gives up this job when he begins to suspect that he will be murdered to prevent him from collecting his fee. In 1972 Ricardo is living in Vientiane, Laos, with his mistress, Lizzie

Worthington, and Charlie Marshall. Their existence is precarious and they lack any secure source of income except for a monthly allowance from Charlie's father, the General, and, later, Charlie's salary while flying for Indocharter. For a while Lizzie carries opium for Sam Collins. When she loses the job Ricardo beats her up for depriving him of a source of income. While his friends support him Ricardo occupies himself with Lizzie Worthington's political, cultural and sexual education and with a number of unsuccessful business enterprises, including a scheme to sell barrels of Scotch whisky and a vacation development in Bali.

In July 1973 Ricardo agrees to fly a cargo of opium into China for Drake Ko, represented by Tiu, in return for a job with Indocharter at $25,000 a year. While waiting for the mission Ricardo plans to launch an all-Asian football team and begins an affair with Rosie, a girl of fourteen living in Bangkok. Rosie later turns up pregnant at the Mexican Embassy. In August Tiu sends him to the Hotel Rincome in Chiang Mai, Thailand, to await orders. From there he is taken north to his plane, a new Beechcraft, and told he must fly to a spot twenty miles north of Tienpao. Fearful of the consequences of capture by the Communist Chinese Ricardo abandons the mission and spends the next few months on the run in the Beechcraft. His task is made easier by the fact that Tiu reports him dead in a crash at Pailin, near the Thai–Cambodian border, on August 21. During this time Ricardo makes money by selling Ko's opium. One of his sales is to an American narcotics agent on September 2. His accompanying offer of information about the China mission is turned down by the agent's superior, Ed Ristow. Eventually Lizzie Worthington manages to per-suade Drake Ko to spare Ricardo even though his desertion has prevented Nelson Ko's escape from China. Ricardo is then allowed to live secretly with two Thai mistresses in the jungle of North East Thailand. He also flies occasionally with Charlie Marshall, and it is on one of these flights that he is spotted by Jerry Westerby. Westerby encounters Ricardo for a second time at his hideaway in North East Thailand, which he seeks out in an attempt to panic Drake Ko into hastening the rescue of his brother. Ricardo attempts to murder Westerby by placing a hand grenade in his petrol tank. However, like most of Ricardo's schemes, this one fails.

Almost nothing is known of Ricardo's life before his involvement with the CIA other than that he was born in Mexico. He claims to have degrees and to be an expert at tennis, horseback-riding, boxing and shooting. Ricardo is tall and handsome with white teeth, a tanned, muscular body and a hairy chest. He walks with a limp and talks with a Latin–American accent. His conversational style is based on an extraordinary combination of business-school English and extravagantly verbose phrasing. As part of his attempt to conceal his identity after the abortive China mission Ricardo grows a beard. When Westerby first meets him the beard is full and he wears a Fidel Castro hat and rubber-soled flying boots. He wears CIA bracelets* and carries an AK-47 automatic rifle. At the time of his second meeting with Westerby Ricardo has trimmed his beard, wears a sarong, and sports a gold cross on his bare chest. His hair is held at the back by a gold ring. Ricardo's is an erratic and unpredictable personality. He is capable of powerful feelings for very young girls and on one occasion during his service in Vietnam he disobeys orders by landing his helicopter in a bombed village in order to search out the body of his dead girlfriend. For this gesture of devotion he receives seven weeks in solitary confinement. He is also extremely violent and destructive. Lizzie Worthington is permanently scarred by a blow from Ricardo and various Vientiane night spots, including the White Rose and Madame Lulu's, bear the marks of his gun-shooting escapades. This inconsistency is a major symptom of Ricardo's dissociation from reality. Amongst its causes are an excessive ego and the daily consumption of a bottle of Scotch. (*HS*)

Riemeck, Karl During the Second World War Riemeck serves as a corporal in the Medical Corps of the German army and is a prisoner of war in Bideford, Devon, for three years. After the war he returns to East Germany and by 1959 is third man at the Ministry of the Interior and Secretary to the Praesidium for the East German Communist Party (SED). In this year Riemeck begins to sell information to Alec Leamas of British Intelligence. He works under the code name Mayfair. Unknown to Leamas he has in fact been recruited by the traitor Mundt to help gather and pass on information destined for Control. Helped by Mundt Riemeck rises into positions with ever-increasing access to intelligence material. At the end of 1959, for example, he is appointed to the Committee for the Protection of the People, which is particularly concerned with security matters. Riemeck meets Control at least once in 1960 when they dine in the Schürzstrasse. Gradually Riemeck attracts suspicion and in 1961 Mundt, to protect his own position, orders him to be shot on sight. He is killed while trying to cross to the West. Riemeck's mistress, Elvira, makes good her escape but is murdered by Mundt's representatives a year later. Riemeck is married with one daughter named Carla. (*SC*)

Riga Group of Baltic Independence Movement *See* Vladimir, General

Rigby, Inspector Bill Member of the Carne Constabulary, Rigby is in charge of the investigation into Stella Rode's murder. He went to police college with Ben Sparrow and is married to a woman who attends Chapel. Rigby's shortness and strong, broad build is for Smiley that of a Celtic miner. He has dark, sharp eyes and short grey hair which comes to a point in the centre of his forehead. Like his body, Rigby's hands are large and powerful but he speaks with a soft Dorset accent and his movements are quiet. Rigby is a thoroughly solid character combining as he does honesty, directness, extreme competence, rectitude, moderation and conservative taste. Although prevented from fully investigating the Rode murder by his chief's delicacy about the affairs of Carne School, Rigby ensures that justice is done by enlisting Smiley's help. The two men come to admire each other very much as they work together on the case. It is a testament to Stella Rode's powers of deception that even Rigby is convinced of her kind disposition. (*MQ*)

Ristow, Ed Senior member of the American Drug Enforcement Administration until his failure to take up Ricardo's offer of information about Drake Ko (made to one of his narcotics agents) forces him to resign. A subsequent coronary provides a convenient official reason for the termination of Ristow's career. (*HS*)

Roach, Bill Pupil at Thursgood's school, nicknamed Jumbo. Roach is a fat, asthmatic boy made dull and unsociable by distress at his parents' separation. He finds it hard to adapt to boarding school and Thursgood's is his second school that term. At his previous one he pretended to have cerebral-palsy fits. Roach's difficulties are increased by the fact that he has the school's richest father. Roach has few positive childhood experiences, other than the glorious occasion when he helps his father smoke out a wasps' nest, and he does not begin to acquire any sense of self-worth until befriended by Prideaux in 1973. Then he is encouraged to take pride in his outsider's ability to 'watch' and manages to perform well in the Alvis car rally. He is third in the first round and probably first in the second. The accidental discovery that Prideaux possesses a gun overwhelms Roach and he retires to the sanatorium. Even as the burden of knowledge wears him down he is still able to warn Prideaux that a stranger (George Smiley) is asking for him. Prideaux's obvious distress after the murder of Haydon gives Roach a new sense of purpose and in working to restore his friend's peace of mind he brings about his own salvation. (*TT*)

'Robinson, Mr' Nickname (after *Robinson Crusoe*) given to Dieter Frey by Elsa Fennan. (*CD*)

'Rocker, the' Nickname by which Superintendent Rockhurst is generally known. (*HS*)

Rockhurst, Superintendent — Superintendent of the Hong Kong police force known as the Rocker. Prior to Hong Kong Rockhurst sees service in Palestine, Kenya, Malaysia and Fiji. He assists Craw with information on Lizzie Worthington, Sally Cale and Drake Ko during

Operation Dolphin [CIRCUS INDEX]. He is later involved in bringing Lizzie Worthington to trial on charges of opium-smuggling. Rockhurst has a generally cynical attitude, especially to the possibility of doing anything significant to eliminate crime in Hong Kong. His main recreation is attending the Foreign Correspondents' Club where he reads the *South China Morning Post*, orders beer in pidgin English, and has the occasional fight. His is an awesome presence which is subdued only by the company of his wife, a dowdy old scold and former Borneo Bible School teacher. (*HS*)

Rode murder case Stella Rode is murdered late one evening in March 1960 in her own home after returning from a dinner party at Terence Fielding's house. The murder, which is done with a piece of coaxial cable, is brutal and bloody. Stanley Rode discovers the body a few minutes later, having been delayed by the need to retrieve a writing-case left behind at Fielding's. Prior to her death Stella Rode warned both the Reverend Cardew, her local Baptist Minister, and Ailsa Brimley of the *Christian Voice* (to which she subscribes) that her husband wanted to kill her. However, even though the murder weapon is his, the fact that the cable is found ten miles away from the scene of the crime, a distance he could not have covered before coming under constant police surveillance, frees Rode from suspicion. Clues at the scene of the crime point to a man six feet tall wearing size ten and a half Wellington boots, leather gloves and a blue overcoat.

Because the crime involves Carne School, a place which demands special privileges, it is very hard for the police to investigate Stella Rode's murder thoroughly. Therefore, when George Smiley introduces himself to Inspector Rigby as a friend of his colleague Ben Sparrow, the Inspector asks Smiley to assist his efforts by making discreet enquiries. Smiley's initial probing reveals that Felix D'Arcy and Terence Fielding share a mysterious sense of guilt, but his first solid clues are provided by Jane Lyn who was at the scene of the crime and identifies the murderer as the devil flying on silver wings. Because she is wearing a blue coat consistent with the belt left near the body, Jane is arrested for the murder. As neither Rigby nor Smiley believes that she had the strength to commit the crime, Smiley continues his investigation.

Through conversations with Fielding, the D'Arcys, the Hechts, the Snows, Stanley Rode and the Reverend Cardew, Smiley tries to build up a picture of Stella Rode's character. The information he receives is contradictory. Most people describe her as simple, direct, honest and good-natured, yet Cardew refuses to endorse this view. Accounts of the circumstances surrounding the death of Stella's dog also indicate that she is a liar and capable of cruelty. More immediately helpful to Smiley is his deduction, based on the likelihood that Jane Lyn took the blue coat after the murder from a pile of clothes destined for a refugee-relief organization, that the murderer created the parcel found near the body and included within it his own bloody clothing. Ailsa Brimley's enquiries at the parcel's collection depot in Kennington, London, prove Smiley's theory to be correct. That the murder clothes turn out to be waterproof indicates that the killer had planned ahead not only how to dispose of evidence but also how to keep himself clean of blood.

At this time the situation is complicated by the death of a Carne pupil, Tim Perkins, who is apparently killed by crashing from his bicycle. Smiley believes the two deaths are connected and, armed with the knowledge that Perkins had carried Rode's writing-case to Fielding's house on the night of the murder and that he had done surprisingly well in the examination paper contained within the case, he questions Fielding. Fielding responds by claiming that he took Perkins's examination paper from the case to improve on it and that while doing so observed that the case contained the murder weapon and clothes. Thus, he accuses Stanley Rode of the murder. Although a warrant is issued for Rode's arrest Smiley is not convinced of his guilt because it still seems impossible for Rode to have disposed of the weapon. On his return to London Smiley gets a chance to talk to Rode who has contacted Ailsa Brimley. He learns the full truth about Stella Rode's malicious and power-hungry nature and that Stella insisted, against his will, that Rode return immediately to Fielding's house for the case. Rode's revelation that his blood group is different from Stella's removes the slight possibility that he used his own blood to prepare the discovered cable ahead of time. Hand-writing experts confirm that all of Perkins's examination paper is in his own writing and, thus, that he and not Fielding opened the case in order to cheat.

Smiley finally confronts Fielding and explains that on the night of the murder Stella Rode had arranged to meet him to continue her series of exercises in humiliation based on the knowledge that he was found guilty of a homosexual offence during the war. She acquired this information from her father, Samuel Glaston, who was the magistrate at the trial. The writing-case was left behind at Stella's instigation in order to get Stanley Rode out of the house. Tired at being made to grovel and afraid that she would eventually make her knowledge public, Fielding planned to use the occasion to murder Stella. Thus, he stole the cable, dressed in waterproof clothes and used his bicycle to reach the house quickly. He knew that the refugee clothes would be available because, as Rigby has discovered, Miss Truebody had phoned during the day – on Fielding's orders – to request that packing be delayed. Fielding killed Perkins after he realized that he must have looked in Rode's case and therefore knew that it did not contain the murder clothes. Smiley's initial sense of a guilty collusion between Fielding and D'Arcy also proves to be justified because D'Arcy knew of Stella's blackmailing and therefore could guess at the identity of her murderer. (*MQ*)

Rode murder case, chronology of Stella Rode is murdered in 1960 on a Wednesday, the 16th day of the month and shortly before Easter. Easter Sunday fell on April 17 in 1960. Therefore, the murder must have taken place in March. *Whitaker's Almanac* confirms that March 16, 1960 was a Wednesday.

Sunday, February 28, 1960	Dorothy D'Arcy's refugees leave.
Tuesday, March 2 (approx.)	Stella Rode tells Cardew that her husband plans to murder her.
	Mr Harriman puts Stella Rode's dog to sleep.
Wednesday, March 16	
11.15–11.45 p.m.	Stella Rode is murdered.
Thursday, March 17	Ailsa Brimley meets George Smiley to discuss the letter she has received from Stella Rode accusing her husband of murderous intentions.
	George Smiley hears that Stella has been murdered.
Friday, March 18	
7.05 a.m.	Smiley takes the train to Carne.
11.00 a.m. (approx.)	Smiley checks into the Sawley Arms.
11.30 a.m.	Smiley meets Inspector Rigby.
morning	The refugee parcel is posted to London.
7.00 p.m.	Smiley dines with Fielding and D'Arcy.
10.45 p.m.	Smiley walks D'Arcy home.
11.00 p.m. (approx.)	Smiley encounters Jane Lyn at the scene of the murder.
11.30 p.m.	Smiley talks to Rigby at the Sawley Arms.
midnight (approx.)	Smiley and Rigby go to Pylle to question Jane Lyn.
Saturday, March 19	
7.30 a.m.	Smiley is called to Rigby's office and informed that Jane Lyn has been charged with murder.

3.30 p.m.	Smiley attends Stella Rode's funeral.

Sunday, March 20

11.00 a.m.	Smiley interviews Stanley Rode.
late morning	Smiley interviews Samuel Glaston.
early evening	Smiley attends the D'Arcy's sherry party. He talks to Shane Hecht, the D'Arcys and the Snows.
evening	Smiley dines with the Snows at the Sawley Arms.
late evening	Smiley reviews the evidence.

Monday, March 21

noon	Smiley telephones Ailsa Brimley to request that she check on the parcel sent to the Public Schools Committee for Refugee Relief.
afternoon	Smiley interviews Harrimann.
late afternoon	Smiley interviews Cardew.
early evening	Tim Perkins is murdered.

Tuesday, March 22

9.00–10.00 a.m.	Ailsa Brimley checks on the refugee parcel and telephones to tell Smiley what she has discovered.
mid-morning to early afternoon	Smiley visits Rigby and is told that Tim Perkins is dead. Smiley visits Fielding who accuses Stanley Rode of the murder. Smiley returns to police station to pass on the accusation.
1.30 p.m.	Smiley takes the train to London.
5.00 p.m. (approx.)	Smiley meets Stanley Rode in the *Christian Voice* office. Later they have supper at Smiley's house.
evening	Rigby telephones to tell Smiley the results of the handwriting tests.

Thursday, March 24

7.45 p.m.	Fielding dines at Smiley's house and is arrested for the murders of Stella Rode and Tim Perkins. (*MQ*)

Rode, Stanley Usher (junior teacher) at Carne School in Dorset. His subject is science. Stanley Rode is born in Branxome near Bournemouth and goes to the local grammar school. He teaches part-time at his former school while attending University. Rode's family is Chapel and it is through his church affiliation that he meets his future wife, Stella Glaston. After a two-year courtship he marries Stella in 1951 at Branxome Hill Tabernacle. He is a blood donor during his time in Branxome. A few years later Rode answers an advertisement in *The Times* and is offered a position at Carne School. In addition to his science duties Rode plans to take charge of the Cadet Corps. In 1960 his wife is brutally murdered at North Fields, their house, and Rode is briefly suspected of the crime before Smiley identifies Terence Fielding as the real killer.

In appearance Rode is entirely ordinary. His plumpish face lacks any defining quality and there is nothing of note about either his body or his black hair. His slightly vulgar manners and his voice, which strives for refinement, both give away his working-class background. Rode's constant struggle to deny his origins and to make himself acceptable to the Carne establishment irritate both the schoolboy Tim Perkins and George Smiley. On further acquaintance Smiley's feelings are modified. Aspects of his behaviour, it turns out, are a reaction to his wife's hypocrisy rather than products of his own. This is true, for example, of his decision to give up the Chapel in favour of the Church of England after arriving in Carne. Smiley also comes to realize that by cutting himself off from his roots Rode has become completely isolated and is therefore an object of pity rather than scorn. (*MQ*)

Rode, Stella The daughter of Samuel Glaston and wife of Stanley Rode. She is murdered at Carne School by Terence Fielding in 1960. Stella Rode is born near Derby but spends her childhood in Gorse Hill, Branxome near Bournemouth. She is a member of an important nonconformist family who are founder subscribers to the nonconformist paper, the *Christian Voice*. Prior to her marriage in 1951 Stella keeps house for her father. In 1956, after moving to Carne with her husband, Stella takes up refugee work and is very active during International Refugee Year. Three weeks before her death she becomes involved in a dispute about two Hungarian refugees who are staying with Dorothy D'Arcy. Her other interests include a dog, which is put down two weeks before she is murdered because it has bitten a postman, and Jane Lyn, a simple-minded woman, whom she befriends. Stella Rode is active in the Chapel and has very little to do with the Carne School community. She does, however, make friends with a young teacher, Simon Snow, and his wife. When they move into their house she assists the Snows by intervening with the unhelpful removal firm, Mulligan's. Immediately prior to her death Stella predicts to both her Minister, Mr Cardew, and by letter to Barbara

Fellowship (Ailsa Brimley) of the *Christian Voice* that she will soon be murdered by her husband.

In manner Stella Rode is plain, direct and unpretentious. Snobs such as Shane Hecht and the D'Arcys dislike her for her working-class eating habits and dowdy clothes. However, she is admired by both Tim Perkins and the Snows for her honesty. For those who really know Stella, such as her father, her husband and her Minister, she is a total hypocrite. Her plain style and friendliness are instruments in gaining the power over others for which she longs. Mr Glaston judges her to be evil and malicious. She becomes involved in the Chapel at Carne only to irritate people at the school. Her interest in refugee work derives from a desire to outdo Dorothy D'Arcy, and it is she, not the D'Arcys, who is to blame for the problem with the Hungarian refugees. She also collects gossip along with garments for the refugees in the hope that it will be useful to her later. Stella's intervention on behalf of the Snows is motivated by a desire to make use of the power given by her knowledge of Mr Mulligan's daughter's illegitimate baby rather than to be of help. Although she is kind to Jane Lyn, it is likely that she would have eventually turned on her as she did with her dog, the other helpless creature under her control. The dog is in fact destroyed, not because it bit the postman, but because Stanley will not permit Stella to beat it any more. Stanley Rode himself is also victimized throughout their marriage and Stella's claims that he plans to murder her are only a further attempt to cause him pain and embarrassment. Given her history there is a poetic justice about Stella Rode's death because her murderer, Terence Fielding, is a victim of blackmail and humiliation who finally turns on his oppressor. (*MQ*)

Rogova, Maria Maiden name of Maria Andreyevna Ostrakova. (*SP*)

Rolling Stone, Operation Fictitious operation devised by Control for Leamas to divulge to the East Germans when he is under interrogation during the Fiedler–Mundt Operation [CIRCUS INDEX]. (*SC*)

Rudnev, — Head of the Thirteenth Directorate branch of Moscow Centre for some ten years until 1955 when he was outmanoeuvred by Karla. (*TT*)

Rüedi, Dr — Psychiatrist at the clinic near Berne. He talks of the 'divided nature' to his disturbed patient, Karla's daughter Tatiana. (*SP*)

rumpus room Meeting room on the fifth floor of the Circus. (*HS*)

*run To control an agent. (*TT*)

run, a Department jargon for a mission into enemy territory. (*LW*)

'Rusakov' Cover name used by Colonel Bardin during his posting to the Soviet Delegation to the United Nations. (*TT*)

'Russian captain' Officer in charge of the East German army unit in

Rostock which picks up Fred Leiser's radio transmission from Kalkstadt. Assisted by a Vopo sergeant and a corporal named Sommer he traces Leiser to his hiding place near the Friedensplatz. The captain is languid and inefficient. Were it not for the advice of his sergeant he would have little idea about how to capture Leiser. Awareness of his inadequacy makes him clumsy, querulous and irritable. (*LW*)

Sachs, Connie An Oxford don and for many years the Circus expert on Soviet intelligence. Connie Sachs is the daughter and sister of Oxford dons and is brought up at Millponds, a Palladian mansion near Newbury, Berkshire. Control recruits her for the Circus over a bridge game while she is still a débutante. Legend has it that this happened on the night Chamberlain promised 'peace in our time' (September 31, 1938). During the war Connie is officially a Wren (as members of the Women's Royal Naval Service are known) but her real occupation until 1972 is gathering intelligence about the affairs of Moscow Centre. After he has unseated Control in October 1972, Haydon quickly arranges for Connie's dismissal because her general knowledge of the Soviet Union and her specific suspicions about Polyakov's role in London make her a major threat to him.

She returns to Oxford as a don and rents out rooms in her North Oxford house. In November 1973 Smiley visits Connie in pursuit of information about Polyakov. When Smiley becomes head of the Circus in 1974 he recalls Connie under the guise of a Mother* and employs her to search out intelligence suppressed by Haydon. Connie comes up with Sam Collins's report of a secret Soviet bank account in Vientiane, Laos, and thus sets in motion Operation Dolphin [CIRCUS INDEX]. During the Operation itself Connie helps Doc di Salis construct a biography of Nelson Ko and interviews Mr Hibbert about the Ko brothers. After the capture of Nelson in 1975 she expects to be involved in his interrogation, but she is passed over in favour of a Harvard professor named Culpepper. During 1974–75 Connie also supports an operation developed by General Vladimir and Otto Leipzig to blackmail a Soviet diplomat, Kirov (real name Oleg Kursky). Enderby terminates this enterprise in April 1975. Connie Sachs retires after Operation Dolphin [CIRCUS INDEX] and by 1978 is living with a former Circus employee, Hilary, in a clapboard cabin outside Oxford which she calls her *dacha*, where they operate the Merrilee Boarding Kennels. Smiley again visits her, this time in search of information on Kursky and on Karla's daughter. Thus, in what is probably the dying Connie's last contact with espionage, she helps to bring about the defeat of Karla. Her workname* is Constance Salinger and her nickname in the

Circus is Mother Russia.

Connie Sachs is a huge woman with a large head. By 1973 her hair and face are equally white and her body is crippled with arthritis. She has pink eyes, a sagging stomach, and wears a brown blazer-like jacket and trousers elasticated at the waist. During Operation Dolphin [CIRCUS INDEX] she wears a grey caftan, carries a plastic shopping bag and makes a not very successful effort to put on lipstick. Her appearance is less than eccentric only during her interview with Hibbert when her hair is bobbed and she wears a dark brown suit with matching hat and handbag. She speaks in a circuitous, jargon-ridden and sometimes babyish fashion which Guillam finds very annoying. Connie's most notable quality is her memory which contains within it everything she has ever learned about the Soviet Union. It is so excellent because for Connie the world of espionage is much more desirable and alive than the real world. Forced back into civilian life Connie has little to occupy her but *The Times* crossword puzzle, drinking gin and the occasional football game, and all the affection she felt for her colleagues and the targets of her investigations must now be focused on her dogs (first Flush, a mangy grey spaniel, and then a mongrel called Trot) and cats. At the end of Connie's life she finds something like real love with Hilary but news of Smiley's final pursuit of Karla makes her eager to give herself entirely once again to the Circus. (*TT; HS; SP*)

*safe house Secure location for clandestine meetings. Safe houses or flats are specially purchased for this purpose or owned by trusted contacts. (*TT*)

safety devices Department jargon for deliberate mistakes made during a radio transmission to communicate that the message is being sent under duress. (*LW*)

*safety signals System of signs communicated between agents to indicate that it is safe to meet. (*TT*)

—, Sal Archivist at the Circus. She is plump, an expert at judo and runs a youth club in Chiswick, London. Her friendliness towards Guillam survives a cynicism about his claims to spend his weekends visiting aunts in Shropshire. (*TT*)

'Salinger, Constance' Connie Sachs's Circus workname.* (*TT*)

'Sampson' Cover name used by George Smiley when making contact with J. Lamb of the Straight and Steady Minicab Service during the Karla case. (*SP*)

San Francisco A Moscow Centre-run Soviet network* is discovered there in 1955 by the Cousins.* (*TT*)

Sanders, Signora Beth Rich neighbour of Westerby in Tuscany. She is the daughter of a general and lives in a lesbian relationship with a short-haired woman given to wearing chain belts who is known to the locals as the man-child. The Sanders, as she is called, and her friend are successful horse-breeders. She is also an informer for the Circus. Beth is intelligent, quick, frugal and a wit. Mama Stefano finds her almost as useful a source as the Circus does. (*HS*)

Sandford, — Man in charge of Administration for the Department.* He takes over Registry from Haldane during Operation Mayfly. Sandford has a fatherly manner and wears gold-rimmed spectacles. Leclerc objects to his motorbike. (*LW*)

'Sandman, the' Vladimir refers to Karla as our 'Sandman' from the German fairy tale where anyone who comes too close to the Sandman has a way of falling asleep – or in the case of Karla, of getting killed. (*SP*)

*****Sarratt** The location in Hertfordshire and alternative name for the Nursery* where new Circus recruits are trained and agents briefed [CIRCUS INDEX]. (*TT*)

'Sasha' Mother Felicity and Grigoriev's pet name for Tatiana, Karla's daughter at the clinic near Berne. (*SP*)

*****Satellites, Satellites Four** Circus department dealing with planning operations in the Soviet satellite countries [CIRCUS INDEX].

'Savage' Cover name used by George Smiley while waiting in the Clarendon hotel in Hammersmith for a telephone call concerning Elsa Fennan's arrival at the nearby Sheridan Theatre during the Fennan case [CIRCUS INDEX]. (*CD*)

Sawley, Earl of — The owner of Sawley Castle, near Carne in Dorset and a cousin of Ann Smiley. The Earl's family goes back four hundred years. He is divorced from Sarah, Countess of Sawley and has a son at Carne School. At the time of George V's funeral (1936) Lord Sawley is at court. Ann's marriage to Smiley affords this unfeeling man considerable amusement and he travels to his club specially to make witty remarks about it. He is equally entertained by the Smileys' separation. (*CD; MQ*)

Sawley, Sarah, Countess of Divorced wife of the Earl by whom she has at least one son. She is the Patroness of the Public Schools Committee for Refugee Relief, a position which provides her with a cheap flat in Belgravia of considerable use during visits to London. Lady Sawley becomes very angry if parcels intended for the working end of the relief operation arrive at her flat. (*MQ*)

*****scalphunters** Department of the Circus (officially called Travel) located at Brixton, London. It handles operations abroad, including murder and kidnapping, which are too dangerous for the resident* agents [CIRCUS INDEX]. (*TT*)

Scarr, Adam Small-time criminal who operates a used-car business in a scrap yard in Battersea, London. In 1956 Scarr buys an old green MG saloon, licence number TRX 0891, on behalf of Hans-Dieter Mundt, or Blondie as he calls him. From then on he garages the car for Mundt who uses it to travel to his meetings with Elsa Fennan. Mundt drowns Scarr in the Thames near Battersea Bridge in 1959 (or 1960) as part of the attempt to frustrate Smiley's investigation into the murder of Samuel Fennan. However, Scarr has already revealed his connection with Mundt to Inspector Mendel. Scarr lives in a wartime pre-fab on a bomb-site alongside his scrap yard and has a daughter of about twelve. For recreation he favours teenage girls and drinking whisky and ginger wine at his local pub, the Prodigal's Calf. In 1958 he spent ten days in Margate with one of his girlfriends and his current companion is an eighteen-year-old blonde with large breasts, white make-up and a surprised expression. Scarr is extremely fat and dresses with bizarre formality. His filthy black suit and waistcoat are shiny, threadbare and unpressed, his flowered red tie is worn outside his waistcoat and his stiff white collar and cuffs are extremely grimy. Paper-clip cuff links and army boots complete his outfit. Smiley finds Scarr frightening, and his manner is overbearing although he has little substance and is easily subdued by a man of real force such as Mendel. (*CD*)

*secret whisperers Chinese jargon for spies. (*HS*)

sell-and-tell Cousins jargon for information provided in return for a previously negotiated payment. (*HS*)

*sell a piece of insurance To offer an enemy agent the opportunity to defect as an alternative to disgrace or death at home. (*TT*)

Sercombe, Lady Ann *See* Smiley, Lady Ann

Sercombe, Miles Minister with responsibility for intelligence at the time of the Haydon case [CIRCUS INDEX]. The subtleties of the Haydon-inspired Operation Witchcraft are beyond Sercombe and he has little choice but to accept the path of action suggested to him by Smiley and Lacon, whose Minister he is. It is not clear how he fares after the fall of the Heath Government in 1974. Sercombe is a cousin of Lady Ann Smiley and is educated at Eton. Although a young man Sercombe is bald. This gives him an air of maturity that his behaviour does not warrant. What hair he does have is allowed to grow thick at the back and is shaped into horns around his ears. His jowls are dark and slightly misshapen. When speaking he combines an English upper-class drawl with an American misuse of auxiliary verbs. His tone is bullying. Ann has nothing good to say about him. Smiley also finds him both foolish, incoherent and deceitful. Other unpleasant qualities include conceit, excessive concern with status, and rudeness. He is proud to be recognized following a television appearance, insists on driving an over-sized Rolls-Royce, known to his relations as the black bed-pan, and fails to show even common courtesy to his host Mendel, presumably because he is not one of his constituents. (*TT*)

*shake the tree To perform acts which are intended to accelerate an operation with a tight deadline by panicking targets into exposing themselves. (*HS*)

'Shallow Throat' Official spokesman of the Hong Kong government. He is a humourless and uncommunicative man once employed by a Northern Irish daily newspaper. (*HS*)

Shanghai Junior Baptist Conservative Bowling Club Informal club made up of journalists which gathers at the Hong Kong Club on Saturday afternoons. Craw presides and members include Luke, the Canadian cowboy, the dwarf, and Deathwish the Hun. Bowling involves throwing a napkin with the intention of lodging it in a wine-rack. Considerable drinking is an integral part of the game. (*HS*)

Sheridan Theatre, Hammersmith Dieter Frey is lured there by a false message and murders his agent Elsa Fennan during the performance. (*CD*)

*shoemaker Forger.

*shopsoiled Agent whose cover has almost ceased to be effective. (*CD*)

'shop-worn girl' Receptionist at Esterhase's Bond Street gallery. Her main task is to keep creditors at bay. She is an ash blonde with a tired, insolent manner and a drawling voice. For amusement she reads horoscopes. (*SP*)

'Siebel, Kurt' Cover name used by Toby Esterhase while kidnapping Grigoriev during the Karla case. Siebel is the chief investigator of the Bernese Standard Bank of Thun. (*SP*)

Sisters Beatitude and Ursula Nurses at the clinic near Berne where Karla's daughter Tatiana is a patient. (*SP*)

*sitting-duck position Exposed and hence vulnerable position during a fight. (*HS*)

Skordeno, Paul Circus agent with a long and varied career. In 1972 he is head of intelligence operations in Germany and by 1975 he is rumoured to be either Bland's fieldman* on Satellite* networks* or Haydon's assistant as well as part of London Station.* Given his close associations with Alleline's regime, Skordeno's fortunes presumably decline after Smiley becomes head of the Circus. However, in 1978 he is part of the team of pavement artists* gathered together by Esterhase in Berne, Switzerland, to observe Grigoriev. For this operation he works under cover as a Reuters stringer. Skordeno, who is forty in 1973, is thin with pock-marked brown face and long arms. His temperament is vicious as evidenced by his violent conflicts with Guillam during unarmed-combat training at Sarratt.* (*TT; SP*)

Slingo, Harry Formerly one of Esterhase's pavement artists,* Slingo is recalled to duty as part of the team which watches* Grigoriev in Berne, Switzerland. His son is reading Physics at Wadham College, Oxford. (*SP*)

Smiley, Lady Ann The former Lady Ann Sercombe comes from an old family with a political tradition. Her relatives include the Earl of Sawley, Miles Sercombe and Bill Haydon, all cousins, a mad Uncle Fry and Harry, whose relationship is not clear. Ann's childhood is spent at an estate in Cornwall, nicknamed Harry's Cornish heap, and Sawley Castle, near Carne in Dorset. During the war Ann works as Steed-Asprey's secretary and in 1943 meets George Smiley, an agent just returned from an undercover posting in Germany. They marry soon after this. When the war ends Ann accompanies Smiley to Oxford but leaves him two years later for Juan Alvida, a Cuban racing driver. The Smileys are reunited during the 1950s and live at 9, Bywater Street in Chelsea. Ann continues to be unfaithful to her husband and in 1955 (or during the 1960s according to an alternative version of events) has an affair with a twenty-year-old ballet dancer referred to by Guillam as the Welsh Apollo. By 1960 Ann is separated from Smiley again and registers at the luxurious Baur-au-Lac hotel in Zürich as Madame Juan Alvida. How her relationship with Alvida has progressed over the years, or whether she is actually with him on this occasion, is unclear. Smiley visits Ann at the end of the Fennan case but is still living alone when he solves the Rode murder. However, in 1962 (or 1963) Ann goes with Smiley to Lucca, not far from Florence. In 1971, at which time the Smileys are once again together in Bywater Street, Ann begins an affair with Bill Haydon. After Haydon drops her she goes from man to man until, sometime after January 1973, she and Smiley separate. Ann lives in Immingham, Yorkshire, with an out-of-work actor until Smiley travels there to reclaim her in December. The affair with Haydon continues to trouble Smiley and, after trying to make their marriage work, he leaves Ann early in 1974. She takes on more lovers by way of consolation. The Smileys never live together again, although they write and meet from time to time.

At some point Smiley regains possession of the Bywater Street house and Ann's existence becomes peripatetic. In 1975 she is living in Wiltshire and in 1978 partly in Kensington with her friend Hilda and partly at her home in Marazion, Cornwall with Harry and his housekeeper, Mrs Tremedda. Immediately prior to his departure for Berne to blackmail Karla, Smiley visits Ann in Cornwall to make it clear that, contrary to her

Smiley's London Home: 9 Bywater Street, Chelsea

'When he had first come to live here these Georgian cottages had a modest, down-at-heel charm . . . now, steel screens protected their lower windows . . . and one Summer evening (Smiley) returned unexpectedly from Berlin to find Bill Haydon stretched out on the drawing-room floor . . . Ann was sitting across the room from him in her dressing gown, wearing no make-up. There was no scene, everyone behaved with painful naturalness.' (*Tinker, Tailor, Soldier, Spy*)

It is hardly surprising that Smiley comes to look on Bywater Street with distaste more often than not. Ann is increasingly away, God knows where or with whom and now, in 1971, she breaks three of her own rules and takes a lover who is not only of the Circus and of her social set but entertains him at Bywater Street against all agreed territorial decencies.

Ann Smiley's Home Ground: Marazion, Cornwall

> 'The coast footpath led in both directions out of the bay . . . they chose the north shoulder and the wind . . .
>
> "I'm going away for a short time," Smiley said. "There's a job I have to do abroad. I don't think you should go to Bywater Street while I'm away . . ."
>
> "And you've come all this way just to tell me the house is out of bounds? . . . out of bounds for good?" she asked.' (*Smiley's People*)

At moments of crisis in his personal life Smiley likes to take the night sleeper to Penzance where Ann often withdraws to her childhood home to nurse her self-inflicted unhappiness. They separate several times and their last reunion is in 1974. Now, some five years on, Smiley's journey has a special purpose – to tell Ann in effect that he no longer loves her. As they walk along the beach he is scared by his own indifference.

General Vladimir's Flat: 6B Wesbourne Terrace, Paddington

'When Smiley shoved the double doors they swung open too freely . . . there was no
light switch and the stairs grew darker the higher he climbed . . . he stepped inside
and closed the door, waiting for something to hit him on the back of the head but
preferring the thought of a broken skull to having his face shot off . . .' (*Smiley's
People*)

Smiley's thorough search of Vladimir's tiny, damp attic flat fails to uncover either of the
proofs. Yet something troubles him about the single packet missing from a new carton of
Gauloises Caporal, since no cigarettes were found on the body of the General, an habitual
smoker. Smiley leaves the squalid 'resettlement' home of his old friend and colleague
convinced that, although the Circus should have done better by its retired agent, Vladimir
has remained loyal and might still lead him to Karla.

Hampstead Heath – Scene of Vladimir's Murder

'(Smiley) stood at the mouth of the avenue, gazing into the ranks of beech trees as they sank away from him like a retreating army into the mist . . . He continued up the avenue . . . thinking about drawing-pins and chalk and French cigarettes and Moscow Rules, looking for a tin pavilion by a playing field.' (*Smiley's People*)

The search goes on for Vladimir's missing clues concerning 'the Sandman' (Karla). Smiley checks all the Moscow Rules signals and then under the watchful gaze of ladies walking their dogs, schoolboys, Buddhist monks from a local Seminary, he retraces every footstep of Vladimir's last moments, as reconstructed for him by the Police Superintendent at dawn that day. Finally, high up in the forked branch of a tree he catches a glimpse of something blue, a packet of Gauloises Caporal . . .

wishes, their separation is permanent. In the time she has to spare from her lovers, who include an ordinand from Wells Theological College in addition to those already mentioned, Ann listens to classical music, including the works of Sibelius and Mahler, tries to learn German and does parts of crossword puzzles. She also writes notes to herself and Smiley which she sticks into the frame of her mirror.

Ann Smiley is tall, brown-eyed and extraordinarily beautiful with a mischievous, Celtic look about her. Ann is essentially a solipsist who lives for the moment. The distinguished history of the Sercombe family means so little to her that for a time in the 1940s she spells her surname as Sercomb, without the final 'e'. Similarly, while her love for Smiley is genuine, she sees no reason to deny any impulse that might cause him pain. Called on to explain her behaviour she hides behind glib and paradoxical epigrams. People are attracted to her because of her ability to handle them naturally. However, if her habit of assigning each of the neighbours nicknames such as Lady Macbeth and Felix the Cat is anything to go by, the closeness that her manner conveys is not based on any real recognition of their humanity. As she ages and so loses the beauty that has enabled her to have command over so many men, Ann becomes a pitiable and even tragic figure. (*CD; MQ; TT; HS; SP*)

Smiley, George Smiley's origins are obscure. Nothing is known of his parents or of his childhood except that he spends time in Hamburg in Germany, is prepared for confirmation by a retired bishop and attends an unimpressive school. Even his birthdate is uncertain. According to one version of events Smiley goes up to Oxford in 1925 and so was born about 1907 or later; according to another his Oxford career does not begin until 1934, thus reducing his age by about nine years. The earlier date seems the more credible in the light of what is known of Smiley's espionage career in the 1930s. At Oxford, where he attends a college as unimpressive as his school, Smiley is a student of German literature with a particular emphasis on the baroque period. He also has an interest in natural history, and in particular Goethe's writing on the topic. The offer of a fellowship at All Souls after graduation demonstrates the success of his academic endeavours. Before he takes up the fellowship Smiley is encouraged by his tutor Jebedee to attend an interviewing board of the Overseas Committee for Academic Research, made up of the distinguished Oxbridge academics Fielding, Sparke and Steed-Asprey. At his meeting with the board in July 1928 Smiley discovers that he is in fact being diverted from academia into espionage.

Training in South America and central Europe is followed in 1937 by Smiley's first operational posting, a two-year appointment as *englischer*

Dozent (lecturer in English) at a provincial German University. There he lectures on Keats, has his first sexual experiences with some of his students and picks out likely candidates for recruitment as agents. This period also shapes Smiley's hatred of Nazism, the evil of which he experiences in the book-burnings of 1937 and a year later the imprisonment in Dresden of his Jewish pupil, Dieter Frey. The year 1939 finds Smiley in Sweden as the agent for a Swiss small-arms manufacturer. This position enables him to travel for four years back and forth between Switzerland, Germany and Sweden, and to develop an espionage network* in Germany. One of his most successful agents is his former pupil, Dieter Frey. In 1943 Smiley's cover has almost ceased to be effective and he is called back to England. Denied permission to work abroad he marries Lady Ann Sercombe and, at the end of the war, returns to academic life in Oxford. By 1947 Smiley is back with the Circus.

Smiley's role in a post-war Intelligence Service made bureaucratic by its new head, Maston, is not distinguished. Still denied permission to work abroad, Smiley is limited to tasks that can be performed from his desk at Cambridge Circus, the post-war Intelligence headquarters of the Circus in London. These include serving on selection boards (he is involved in the decision to reject Jerry Westerby's application for full-time employment), vetting recruits, including Ricki Tarr, and lecturing at Sarratt* on topics such as 'Problems of Maintaining Courier Lines Inside Enemy Territory'. During 1950–51, Smiley is assigned to Satellites Four* (the department concerned with Iron Curtain countries excluding the Soviet Union), where he works with Peter Guillam, Brian de Grey and Alec Leamas. In 1951 he is transferred to Counter Intelligence and controls General Vladimir during the time that he spies for the Circus in Moscow.

Eventually Smiley is given permission to work abroad again and in 1955 he travels extensively to negotiate with defecting Soviet agents. This phase of Smiley's career is brought to an end by an episode which is to colour and lend direction to the rest of his professional life. A routine visit to India to arrange terms with a Soviet agent using the cover name of Gerstmann brings him face to face with an intractable opponent who not only rejects his advances but, aided by Smiley's weariness and distress over Ann's infidelities, causes him to lose all professional control. This man, he learns later, is Karla, the future head of Moscow Centre's Thirteenth Directorate. By the 1970s he is the major focus of Smiley's intelligence activities. On his return to England, Smiley is sent on three months' leave by Control, who is presumably his supervisor at this time. Another version of these events places them in the 1960s.

By the end of the decade Smiley appears to be a spent force and he earns himself the nickname Mole. Even to his secretary, who loves him, he is no more than 'my darling teddy-bear'. However, the Fennan case [CIRCUS INDEX] in 1960 (1959 in another version) finally gives Smiley the chance to reveal the powers of deduction and skill in interrogation by means of which he will achieve greatness in the 1970s. Convinced that all is not as it seems in the apparent suicide of Samuel Fennan, he rebels against Maston's bureaucratic desire to avoid trouble and resigns so that he can conduct his enquiries in a private capacity assisted only by the retired policeman, Mendel, and his former colleague, Peter Guillam. After surviving Hans-Dieter Mundt's murderous attack Smiley links Fennan's murder to his wife Elsa's involvement in an East German spy ring. Mundt, who is the murderer, escapes, but Smiley traps and kills the leader of the ring, his former student and agent, Dieter Frey. Clearly embarrassed at Smiley's success Maston tries to smooth things over by offering him a new position in the Circus as Director of Satellite* Research. Smiley turns him down.

Later in the same year Smiley is asked by his former Circus colleague, Ailsa Brimley, to visit Carne School in Carne, Dorset, to look into a troubling letter she has received from Stella Rode, the wife of one of the teachers. Before he can set out Smiley learns that Stella's prediction of her own murder has been fulfilled. Smiley's subsequent investigation reveals that the murderer is neither Stanley Rode, as Stella insisted it would be, nor Jane Lyn, as the police believe, but Terence Fielding, the school's senior housemaster. Although on this occasion he exercises them in a private capacity, Smiley reveals very much the same abilities during the Rode murder case as he did in the Fennan case. The solution to the crime it turns out depends not so much on any direct forensic evidence as on knowledge of Stella Rode's character and on establishing a link between Fielding's conviction in the 1940s for homosexuality and Stella Rode.

Smiley is still officially retired in 1961 when Control, now head of the Service, launches the complex Fiedler–Mundt Operation [CIRCUS INDEX] designed to protect Mundt, his mole* in East German Intelligence, from exposure. Nevertheless, not only does Smiley help to brief Alec Leamas but he also puts in an appearance at several crucial stages in the Operation. It is not at all clear how much Smiley understands of Control's intentions. His visit to Liz Gold helps to bait the trap Control is setting for Fiedler. At the same time, though, it would seem that he is genuinely unaware of the use which Control intends to make of Liz herself in the later stages of his scheme.

Following the Fiedler–Mundt Operation Smiley's connection with the Circus is officially re-established. Some time in 1962 (or 1963) he is

responsible for vetting recruits, including probably Roy Bland and Toby
Esterhase. And by 1964 Smiley is occupying the North European desk at
the Circus. In 1964 (or 1965) he plays a fringe role in another of Control's
devious schemes. Motivated entirely by a spirit of inter-departmental
rivalry, Control encourages an almost defunct branch of Intelligence, the
Department,* to send an agent into East Germany. A tense encounter
with Control as this Operation Mayfly draws close to inevitable disaster
makes it obvious that on this occasion Smiley has been unaware of his
superior's intentions. Nevertheless, he remains loyal to Control and
travels out to Lübeck, on the East German frontier, to pass on the order
that the agent, Fred Leiser, be abandoned in enemy territory. Little is
known of Smiley's career during the rest of the 1960s except that in 1966
he buys a report from the Toka (Japanese Intelligence) concerning the
interrogation of a defence official exposed as Karla's mole* in Japan, and
that he works in South East Asia with Collins.

Smiley's career following his return to the Circus does not, then,
immediately fulfil the promise revealed in the Fennan and Rode murder
cases, and his reputation in secret circles is poor. Alec Leamas claims that
he has lost his nerve as a result of the Fennan case and Leclerc passes
around the story that he is past it and drinks too much. A more likely
explanation for Smiley's lack of success is that he is too much the tool of
Control, an overwhelmingly powerful figure who has been his mentor
since the 1940s. Eventually Control's tendency to run operations single-
handedly proves to be his undoing and Smiley is given the opportunity to
reveal his full abilities. The events which are to be so crucial to Smiley's
career take place in the early 1970s. By 1971 Smiley has risen to the fifth
floor* of the Circus but is still very much Control's servant. He acts as a
buffer between Control and his petitioners, he goes to Portugal to cover up
a scandal, and he serves as an intermediary in Control's attempts to seduce
Bland, Esterhase and Haydon away from Percy Alleline and Operation
Witchcraft [CIRCUS INDEX]. The issue which most concerns Control at
this time – identifying the mole* Gerald – he keeps secret from Smiley.
Indeed Smiley is one of his chief suspects and, therefore, rather than
involve him in Operation Testify in October 1972, his last and as it turns
out disastrous attempt to find the traitor, Control sends him on an errand
to Berlin.

The immediate aftermath of Testify is almost as damaging to Smiley's
career as to Control's, for both are forced to resign. However, Control's
demise seems immediately to be liberating for Smiley and, even in the
short period before his dismissal, he formulates the theory that a traitor in
the Circus has been responsible for the failure of Testify. The blossoming

that is promised here takes place fully a year later in November 1973 when Smiley is called out of retirement to hunt down the mole* Gerald. By the end of the month, through a brilliant combination of interrogation, investigation of files and trickery, Smiley has exposed Bill Haydon as Karla's agent. Following his success in the Haydon case [CIRCUS INDEX] Smiley is made head of Intelligence.

The Circus which Smiley takes over is in complete disarray as a result of the Haydon scandal. Networks* are blown, budgets are frozen and the building has been literally torn apart in the search for listening* devices planted by Haydon. Out of this chaos Smiley mounts a most brilliant offensive action. Helped by Doc di Salis and Connie Sachs, he discovers that in 1973 Haydon squashed an investigation into the movement of large sums of money by Moscow Centre into Vientiane, Laos. This leads to Operation Dolphin [CIRCUS INDEX] which climaxes in a journey to Hong Kong and the capture of Nelson Ko, Karla's mole* in Communist China. Unfortunately, while Smiley is outmanoeuvring Karla, a cabal of American and British intelligence officers is plotting against him and at the end of things Nelson Ko is in American hands and Saul Enderby has been appointed head of the Service. Whether Smiley has actually been outwitted remains open to question. Peter Guillam's theory, which is supported by a letter from Smiley to Ann, is that he knew of the plot against him and accepted his own betrayal as the suitable termination of a life of conspiracy. This theory gains weight if we accept, as seems likely, that Smiley authorizes the murder of Westerby, an act for which he must have felt he merited punishment.

Smiley's career is not yet at an end. A case which occupies part of his attention during Operation Dolphin, and in the brief period between his return from Hong Kong in May 1975 and his retirement, resurfaces so dramatically in October 1978 that he is recalled into active service. The brutal murder of Smiley's former agent, General Vladimir, by Soviet agents on Hampstead Heath, London, is a great embarrassment to a Circus operating under a Labour Government committed to *détente*. Therefore, Lacon calls in Smiley to clean up discreetly the loose ends of the case. Upon learning from the Circus probationer Mostyn that Vladimir was engaged, as he had been in 1974–75, in seeking information with which to blackmail Karla, Smiley commits himself to completing the old man's mission. This unexpected opportunity to grapple again with his Black Grail rejuvenates Smiley, who may now be as old as seventy, and he masterminds a brilliant operation for the Karla case [CIRCUS INDEX] which takes him all over London, and then to Hamburg, Paris and Berne, and at last forces Karla to defect. This final triumph – for his career is now surely at an end – brings Smiley little satisfaction because it is based on exploiting the humanity which Karla has at last revealed.

During his life as a spy Smiley uses the cover names Alan Angel, Barraclough, Carmichael, Adrian Hebden, Herr Lachmann, Leber, Lorimer, Max, Oates, Sampson, Savage, and Standfast. Little is known of what official recognition Smiley receives for his achievements except that he is awarded an OBE.

George Smiley's private life is dominated by his relationship with his wife, Ann. There is no evidence that he has any major love affairs prior to meeting her in 1943, and she appears to be the only woman in his life after that date. Unfortunately Smiley is by no means the only man in hers. She leaves him first in 1947 for Juan Alvida, a Cuban racing driver, and is also separated from Smiley in 1960, 1973, and from early 1974 onward. Even when they are together, as in 1955 and 1971, Ann continues to have affairs. For many years Smiley's love for Ann survives her repeated betrayals. At the end of the Fennan case, for example, he flies to Zürich in an attempt to effect a reunion. However, the summer evening in 1971 when Smiley returns home to the house at 9, Bywater Street, which they have shared intermittently since about 1950, and finds his wife with Bill Haydon marks a crucial change in his feelings. To have taken as a lover a man who is friend, colleague and in the same social set is too great a betrayal even for tolerant and long-suffering Smiley. Thus their next reunion at the end of the Haydon case in December 1973 ends early in 1974 when Smiley takes the unprecedented step of leaving Ann. They never live together again and in 1978, just prior to the completion of his quest for Karla, Smiley travels to Cornwall to let Ann know that he no longer loves her.

Outside of Ann, Smiley's major interests are scholarly. Having rejected All Souls and Oxford for the Circus, Smiley devotes himself full-time to his passion for German literature only during 1945 to 1947 when he returns to Oxford, and after his retirement in 1975. Throughout his life he continues to make a study of seventeenth-century writers such as Gryphius, Grimmelshausen, Lohenstein and Olearius. His work on the love-poetry of the bard Opitz takes Smiley to the London Library during 1978. More recent German writers who capture his attention are Hesse and Goethe. Of English authors Smiley reveals a knowledge of the dramatist Webster. He subscribes to *German Life and Letters* and *Philology*.

Whatever leisure Smiley has left over from spying, Ann and German literature he divides up in a number of ways. Although the demands of his job take him into dreadful transport cafés, Indian restaurants and steak houses, he maintains an interest in fine restaurants and is to be found eating on various occasions at Quaglino's, the White Tower, Scott's, and the Entrechat in Kensington. Smiley also dines from time to time at his two clubs, one of which is the private one founded by Steed-Asprey in Manchester Square and the other is near Pall Mall. Sometimes Smiley cooks a meal for friends at his Bywater Street house. Burgundy appears to be his favourite wine although he drinks a white wine, Fendant, in Switzerland. Over the years Smiley has built up an art collection which includes a Watteau sketch, a Dresden group, a Callot, and a tiny van Mieris head in chalk. If only he could afford it he would add a Degas ballerina of doubtful provenance because of its resemblance to Ann. Smiley lacks a natural affinity for music but Ann has taught him to listen to Sibelius and Mahler. Driving (he owns a Ford in 1960) is a source of relaxation in his younger days, but he comes to find it tedious. Smiley takes some pleasure in travel and at various times in his life develops an affection for Cornwall, particularly Hartland Quay, and for Hamburg and Dresden (all before the war), and later on for the Cotswolds and Berne. He has also travelled to Los Angeles. Friendship does not play a major part in Smiley's life but he has long-lasting relationships with both Mendel and Peter Guillam. At one time Smiley places great hopes on his house in Bywater Street but gradually has less and less affection for it and is content to leave its upkeep in the hands of his housekeeper, Mrs Chapel.

In appearance Smiley is so ordinary as to be remarkable and he changes little over thirty years. He enters middle age early and leaves it late. Old age begins to show itself only in 1978 with the appearance of extra chins and a slight deafness. Smiley is small and fat with short legs, plump fingers and blinking eyes. For many years he has a twitch in his eye, a result of his wartime experiences in Germany. His movements are clumsy and he tends to blush. He wears thick spectacles and expensive but poorly-fitting clothes. Typical is the black, porous overcoat with over-long sleeves which fails to afford protection from the wet November night in 1973 when he dines with Martindale. In general he refuses to wear hats because they make him look ridiculous. In overall appearance Smiley reminds people of a frog. His manner is generally quiet, earnest and formal but shyness can make him appear pompous. Powerful feelings, which he usually keeps under control, sometimes assert themselves and then he will tremble violently and become inarticulate. Smiley has a number of fidgety habits, the most famous of which is polishing his spectacles on his tie, yet during interrogations he possesses the ability to remain absolutely still.

Smiley's approach to experience is shaped around attempts to reconcile reason with the demands of feeling. Out of such a reconciliation emerges, in his opinion, an ideal of moderation. Smiley does not always possess such a complex vision. As a young man he is almost entirely lacking in passion and views the world in a detached and academic manner. It is the extreme solitude he experiences working under cover in Nazi Germany that awakens Smiley to the need for emotional release. This need is satisfied by Ann, and it is significant that he proposes to her immediately after ending his career as an undercover agent. Notions of control, reason, restraint are anathema to Ann who is guided entirely by her feelings. And for all the distress she causes Smiley during their long marriage she must be credited for teaching him how to feel and thus to progress towards complete humanity. Although the ability to feel is something Smiley acquires relatively late in life, and although the controlled aspects of his personality are more often in view than the passionate, it would be a mistake to take him as an essentially rational being who struggles for feeling. As his moments of spontaneous passion suggest, the two qualities are always there. Indeed, his feelings are so strong that they sometimes come to the fore in situations where the need for discipline and control are most essential. The discovery of Otto Leipzig's body is, for example, almost too much for Smiley.

A perfect balance of reason and feeling is something Smiley is able to achieve only rarely and then always in his capacity as a spy when he combines logical analysis with the guidance provided by his feelings for other people and his instincts. A case in point is his response to the killing of his former colleague, General Vladimir. Caring for Vladimir commits Smiley to the pursuit of his murderers; instinct tells him that there is something wrong with the loose cigarettes he finds in Vladimir's room; and a logical and meticulous recreation of Vladimir's last moments enables him to discover the whereabouts of the cigarette packet he has sensed contains the information he is seeking. Smiley's tragedy is that such moments of equilibrium are absent from his personal life. Here, he is polarized between the isolated, controlled and ultimately lonely existence of the scholar, who knows of passion only as a literary convention, and a complete surrender to feeling in his relationship to Ann.

A recognition of the close interdependence of feeling and reason in Smiley's concept of the self is also essential for a proper understanding of his value system. Like Ann he takes the present moment and his feelings about it as his only reality. As he says to Guillam, quoting Goethe, 'in the beginning was the deed'. Whereas Ann begins and ends in her own feelings and regards each fresh moment of experience as a new reality that has no reference to anything that has gone before, Smiley is willing to bring his rational faculty into play and to generalize from the particular. Thus, Jackie Lacon's fall from her pony elicits a moment of caring response from Smiley; his reason enables him to transform the emotion into an ethical principle. Smiley is therefore able to show concern, not just when he feels like it and not just for those he knows and loves, but for all people at all times. Given this approach to experience it is not surprising that Smiley sets himself against moral absolutists and enemies of individualism. For him the essential flaw in communism is its rootedness in the notion that the whole is more important than the individual. Closer to home he despises bureaucrats such as Maston, because they put their faith in policy rather than experience, and the Press, advertising and television because they focus on the mass rather than the individual.

The complexity and even opacity which Smiley achieves by his refusal to place the problems of living within the straitjacket of creed or of stereotyped reactions is further intensified by the nature of his occupation. The decision to return to the Circus in 1947 is a logical consequence of the view of experience Smiley has developed through his relationship with Ann. His target is now communism which, in the post-war world, poses the single largest threat to his intense commitment to the individual. The problem for Smiley is that, in pursuit of his goal, he has to do things that are antithetical to it. To ensure Ricki Tarr's continued cooperation he keeps from him a report of the death of his beloved Irina; to get information out of Peter Worthington he raises hopes of a reunion with a wife who has long since left him behind; to capture Nelson Ko he sacrifices Lizzie Worthington and Jerry Westerby; to force Karla to defect he exploits his affection for his daughter Tatiana. The only way for Smiley to reconcile ends with means is to distort the reality of the situation in which he is placed. And this he refuses to do, accepting instead the need to struggle painfully, knowing that there is no hope of resolution, to come to terms with the moral implications of his acts. Smiley's only reward for living so completely is that he remains intensely human. (*CD; MQ; SC; LW; TT; HS; SP*)

'Smirnov' Cover name used by Zimin (Commercial Boris) when operating in Switzerland. (*HS*)

Snow, Ann The wife of Simon Snow, a teacher at Carne School, and a friend of Stella Rode. Her home is in Bread Street, Carne. She is pretty with a square face, upturned nose and slender hands. Although obviously immature, talkative and incapable of dealing with practicalities, she has an agreeable personality and sees through the hypocrisies of Carne School. She is an emotional person easily upset by adversity but responsive to kindness or affection. (*MQ*)

Snow, Simon Teacher of mathematics and science at Carne School. Following the death of Stella Rode he is called on to grade Stanley Rode's examination papers and thus is able to draw attention to the unexpectedly high grade of sixty-one achieved by Tim Perkins, who had earned only fifteen in his elementary science course. Snow is tall, thin and stooped and has long, slender fingers. He is shy and much less talkative than his wife, Ann. Although not as passionate on the subject as his wife, he also despises Carne School and plans to leave after only four 'Halves'. He will take a D.Phil. at Oxford in preparation for a University career. (*MQ*)

'Snow White' Circus janitors' nickname for Toby Esterhase. (TT)

'Sokolov' Cover name used by Colonel Bardin. (*TT*)

Sommer, — Vopo corporal stationed in Rostock. He picks up Leiser's radio transmission from Kalkstadt. (*LW*)

*sound Whitehall jargon for one who favours militaristic policies. (*HS*)

*sound thief Hidden microphone. (*HS*)

South East Asia While Hong Kong is the major focus of Circus activities in South East Asia, British agents do operate throughout the entire region. Sam Collins works at various times in Borneo, Burma, Northern Thailand and Laos; Steve Mackelvore in Djakarta in Indonesia and Vientiane in Laos; and Ricki Tarr, who is born in Penang, Malaya, works in Indonesia, Singapore and Malaysia. Both Westerby, who spends much of his career in South East Asia, and Smiley work on various occasions with Sam Collins. Lizzie Worthington is a British agent briefly in 1972 and works out of Vientiane. The most important Circus operation in the region is Operation Dolphin [CIRCUS INDEX]. Its origins can be traced back to 1973 when Sam Collins discovers a Soviet gold seam* terminating in Vientiane. The Operation itself is focused on Hong Kong but the need to track down Tiny Ricardo and Charlie Marshall takes Westerby to Bangkok in Thailand, Phnom Penh and Battambang in Cambodia, Saigon in South Vietnam, Vientiane and North East Thailand.

Despite the attempts of French colonialists to turn it into a province of their own country and of the American military to bomb it into obliteration, South East Asia retains even in 1975 a remarkable degree of vitality and beauty. Thus, for Westerby, who loves the region, the most powerful image of his long journey through it is not the French architecture he sees everywhere he goes or the Gilbertian war created by the Americans but the sight of leaf-like sampans on the moonlit Mekong River. (*TT; HS*)

Soviet Intelligence Service *See* Moscow Centre

Sparrow, Ben Senior member of the Special Branch police, who worked in intelligence during the war. He assigns Inspector Mendel to the Fennan case [CIRCUS INDEX] in 1960 and, later that same year, provides Smiley

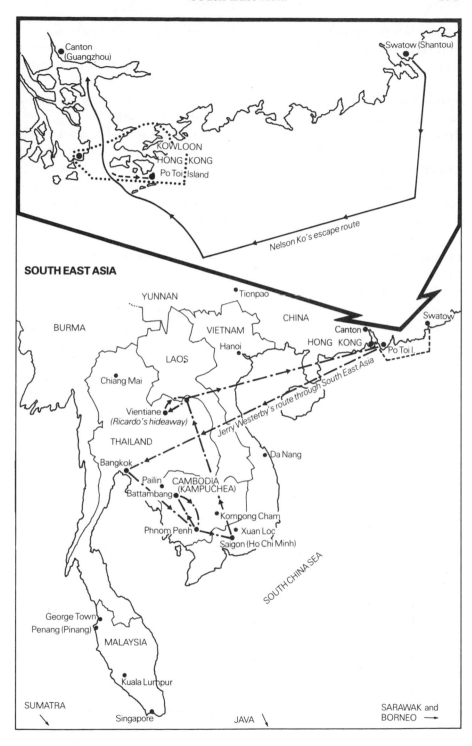

with an introduction to Inspector Rigby of the Carne police as he sets out to investigate the murder of Stella Rode. Sparrow is a great admirer of George Smiley and, according to Rigby, with whom Sparrow attended police college, his judgements are reliable. (*CD; MQ*)

Special Section Part of the Department* responsible for organizing a special mission to East Germany. *See* Department, the*

Spikeley, — A boy in form 5B at Thursgood's school known to his teachers for impertinence and to other boys for courage. He teases Prideaux for his patriotism and imitates his French accent. Prideaux takes revenge by tricking Spikeley into thinking that he has acquired an advance copy of a French test. Their rivalry is, however, essentially friendly as Prideaux reveals by offering Spikeley the opportunity to end his innings during the staff cricket match. (*TT*)

spook house Cousins jargon for a location from which spies operate. (*HS*)

*squirt Radio transmission. (*TT*)

'Staff' Firearms instructor at the Abingdon parachute base near Oxford who helps in Fred Leiser's training for Operation Mayfly. He is a polite, precise man who insists on adherence to correct procedure. Leiser's lack of British propriety clearly offends him. (*LW*)

'Standfast, J.' Cover name used by George Smiley when meeting Control's companion Mrs Matthews after his death. He assumes the same identity for his meeting with Peter Worthington during Operation Dolphin and when visiting Hamburg during the Karla case. Standfast is a stereotypical civil servant who works for the Foreign Office. Smiley eventually rids himself of the identity by posting his Standfast passport to Australia. (*TT; HS; SP*)

—, Stan or Stanislaus Barman at the Restaurant Sport in Prague, Czechoslovakia. He is a football fan whose enthusiasm for Westerby has greatly increased since the time when he brought Holotek, the goalkeeper, to his bar. Westerby admires Stan for remaining a free spirit in a communist country. (*TT*)

'Stan's nephew' Conscripted soldier who meets Westerby in his uncle Stan's bar at the Sport in Prague in December 1972. His information about Soviet troop movements around Brno, which he observed during basic training in October 1972, makes Westerby realize that Prideaux's rendezvous with Stevcek was actually a trap. Stan's nephew is young and has a soldier's pudding-bowl haircut. He is a romantic who has a benevolent view of the whole world because he has fallen in love with a pretty, sexy girl with Garbo eyes. His physically affectionate ways are inoffensive even to the rigidly heterosexual Westerby. Military service does not interest him and he has too little respect for authority to be a good soldier. For him national service is simply a prerequisite for attending university. (*TT*)

'Stanley' Soviet agent who defects to Holland in 1963. The Dutch consider him to be of little intelligence value. However, after being sold to the Circus he reveals a knowledge of Karla's secret training school for spies. Connie Sachs suspects that Stanley's relationship to his instructor, Milos, was homosexual. (*TT*)

*static post Fixed surveillance position. (*HS*)

*steal/steal sound To take photographs or record conversations surreptitiously. (*SP*)

Steed-Asprey, — A don at Magdalen College, Oxford, where he lives in Holywell Street, and a member of British Intelligence. In 1928 Steed-Asprey (who occasionally omits the hyphen) sits with Adrian Fielding, Jebedee and Sparke on the committee which recruits George Smiley. In 1943 he tells Smiley that his career overseas is finished. The bureaucratic orientation of the post-war service does not suit Steed-Asprey and he goes to India in search of a more traditional civilization. Although he approaches espionage with the style of the gentleman amateur and prefers to give orders over port in his College rooms, Steed-Asprey is very much the professional. In later years Smiley frequently bases his technique on lessons taught him by his former colleague.

The intense individuality which marks Steed-Asprey's approach to espionage is also to be found in his club memberships. At one time he belongs to the Junior Carlton but his membership is terminated for blaspheming within the hearing of a bishop. To avoid further clashes with the forces of conformity he founds his own club in a house in Manchester Square run by his former Oxford landlady, Mrs Sturgeon. This club has no rules and will cease with the deaths of its original all-male members, numbering forty, who include Jebedee, Smiley and Martindale. By 1960 it is down to thirty-one members but is still going strong in 1973. Other aspects of Steed-Asprey's personality are revealed by the Dresden china group which he presents to Lady Ann Sercombe, his former secretary, and George Smiley on their marriage. Acquired in Dresden before the war, it is the best of his collection and Smiley later decides that Steed-Asprey parted with it because his knowledge of Ann was such that he anticipated her husband's need for the consolation of the group's sympathetic portrait of female infidelity. Thus, he reveals himself to be both a wise and kind human being. Given this evidence about his humanity it is unlikely that Steed-Asprey lives an isolated existence. Unfortunately we know nothing about his personal life except that he has a brother much less intelligent than himself and a rich relation who gives him the use of the Manchester Square house. (*CD; MQ; TT; HS*)

Stefano, 'Mama' — Postmistress and leading citizen of the Tuscan village nearest to Westerby's farmhouse in Italy. She has an idiot son by Westerby's landlord, Franco Marcello. Mama Stefano is a rugged peasant who wears black and has a fierce manner. She is cunning, greedy, a gossip and generally extremely ungenerous but fairly accurate in her judgements of others. Wealth alone impresses her. (*HS*)

'Steggie' An assistant barman from Chelsea, London, and one of Haydon's lovers. He is young and palely frightful and wears an open shirt which reveals a gold chain worn around his midriff. (*TT*)

*stick-and-carrot job Simultaneous use of bribes and threats to obtain information. (*HS*)

*stinks-and-bangs school Branch of the Circus located in Argyll, Scotland, which is concerned with electronic and chemical devices. (*HS*)

Stevcek, General — Czech general of artillery. Partly because of his expertise in the technology of weaponry and partly because of his pro-Soviet sentiments, Stevcek, although only in his mid-forties by 1973, has won a position close to the top of the Czech military hierarchy. He is fourth in seniority in military intelligence, head of weaponry, a military counsellor to the Praesidium, and occupier of the Anglo–American desk in military intelligence. During his career he has been posted to Warsaw, Moscow (twice), Peking, and Africa (as a military attaché). Because of his intelligence connections and his broad knowledge of Czechoslovakian and Soviet military secrets, Stevcek is a particularly tempting bait for the trap which Karla and Haydon lay for Control in 1972. Having added to Stevcek's biography a period of work in Moscow Centre's England Section and a love affair with a student killed in the Czech uprising of 1968, they convince Control that he has become sufficiently disillusioned with the Soviet Union to be willing to betray the name of Karla's mole* in the Circus. It is while travelling to a supposed meeting with Stevcek at Brno, Czechoslovakia, for Operation Testify that Jim Prideaux is shot and captured, thus causing the scandal which ruins Control. Stevcek's private life seems to include more than one wife and an interest in horses. (*TT*)

Stokovsky, Colonel — Graduate of Karla's secret training school for spies who works in Paris under the cover name Grodescu and passes as a French–Romanian. It is thought that he runs Karla's West German mole* through an affiliate in Bonn. (*TT*)

Strickland, Lauder Member of the Circus who works in Banking* in 1973 and is a fixer in 1978. Strickland is a Scot from Aberdeen. In height he is no more than five feet and he has small, watchful eyes. By 1978 he has grown a reddish-brown moustache, but his clothes consist as ever of an ugly green suit and shoes of brushed pigskin made to look like suede. Strickland is a singularly unpleasant person totally obsessed with his own and other people's status. He is sycophantic towards those above him and has a habit of praising people and things he considers important in order to gain reflected glory. He expresses equal enthusiasm to Peter Guillam about the coffee machine, and Bill Haydon and Diana Dolphin because, like him, they inhabit the fourth floor of the Circus. Those Strickland considers inferior are either patronized, like Guillam, or sneered at, like the retired Smiley. Only with the probationer, Mostyn, does he dare to give full expression to his bullying tendencies. (*TT; SP*)

*stripe Designation given to a message which must be brought urgently to the chief's attention. (*HS*)

Stroll, Mr — Owner of the second-rate supply teaching agency, Medley and Stroll, which sends Prideaux to Thursgood's school. Years of marketing a poor product and a probable involvement with the Circus have made him a master of the lengthy pause and the evasive answer. (*TT*)

Stubbs, — Managing editor of the left-wing group of newspapers which employs Jerry Westerby. Stubbs's jowls and eyelids are heavy and grey and his expression is scowling and resentful. He has a London accent with hints of Fleet Street-Canadian. Incipient ulcers will soon send his career downhill but he survives at least until 1974 by deviousness and by eavesdropping on his correspondents' telephone calls. Westerby finds Stubbs's concern with old expense claims laughable. (*HS*)

Sturgeon, Mrs — Formidable Oxford landlady with a house in Holywell Street. On one occasion she provides a memorable dinner to her lodger, Steed-Asprey, and seven of his friends at a moment's notice. Later in life she runs Steed-Asprey's club in Manchester Square, London. The source of Mrs Sturgeon's power resides in her ability to be at once deeply censorious and completely tolerant. (*CD*)

subscription list Circus and Department jargon for those having access to a secret file. (*SC; LW*)

'Susan' Code name of Phoebe Wayfarer. (*HS*)

Sutherland, Mr — Her Majesty's Consul in Finland. He deals with Wilf Taylor's death. Sutherland is a tall Scot with a thin, stern, red face and a resentful tone of voice. Given his meticulous and precise manner of doing business and his concern with propriety, it is not surprising that Sutherland becomes very irritated by Avery's blundering attempts to pass himself off as Taylor's brother. He lives in a small house which, except for its picture window and potted plants, is very like those to be found in the suburbs of Aberdeen. His wife is middle-aged, much given to dusting. (*LW*)

*sweat To interrogate using some physical force. (*TT*)

*swing your legs at To blackmail. (*TT*)

Sylvia, Countess— French guest at the British Embassy dinner party in Phnom Penh, Cambodia, attended by Jerry Westerby. Once a beautiful woman, the Countess is beginning to show the marks of a life of travel. Her health is also failing although she has recovered from recent heart trouble. It is unclear how she occupies her time but she claims to have diplomas in political science, mechanics and general electricity. When the Embassy comes under Khmer Rouge shellfire, Sylvia reveals her need for the protection of a strong man such as Jerry Westerby. (*HS*)

take to first base Cousins jargon for providing a specimen piece of information in order to confirm the authenticity of the larger body of information which is to follow. (*HS*)

*talent spotter One who picks out potential recruits for a career in espionage. (*HS*)

Tan, Luigi Hong Kong merchant with a reputation for being able to arrange anything. He supplies the boat in which Jerry Westerby and Lizzie Worthington travel to Po Toi. Tan is very small, energetic and proud of his virility. His origins are part-Chinese, part-Portuguese and at one time he worked as a Chinese boxer in Macao booths. He has four sons, some grandchildren and at least one nephew whose mother lives on Lantau, an island off Hong Kong. Lizzie Worthington immediately attracts his interest and he pays court to her by boasting of his sexual potency, his Mercedes complete with stereo and his credit cards. Tan's tiny and crowded shop is located on the other side of Wanchai from Central District. (*HS*)

Tarr, Ricki The scalphunter* who, on a routine mission to Hong Kong in 1973, discovers that there is a mole* in the Circus. He is born in the late 1930s in Penang, Malaya, the son of an Australian solicitor with evangelical tendencies and an actress from Bradford who is also a petty criminal. With the outbreak of war the Tarr family is evacuated to Singapore which is soon invaded by the Japanese. They spend the rest of the war in Changi jail and are unable to return to Penang until 1945. Tarr's failure to take his law studies seriously brings him into conflict with his father and he flees to Borneo. By the time he is eighteen, in the mid-1950s, he is running guns around the Indonesian islands. Disappointed by an unsuccessful involvement with some Belgian gun-runners to whom he loses his girlfriend, Rose, Tarr proves susceptible to Steve Mackelvore's suggestion, made in Djakarta, Indonesia, that he join the Circus as a scalphunter.* Vetting takes place in Djakarta, Singapore and finally at Sarratt* where Smiley is involved. Tarr's first mission sends him back to Malaysia where he rejoins the Belgian gun-runners and Rose, who are supplying arms to the communists. After blowing their contacts he kills four of them and Rose. Tarr is sent next to Kenya to fight the Mau Mau. In 1964, working under Dutch cover, he bungles an attempt to bribe a Brazilian armaments minister but in 1965, acting on a tip from Haydon, he successfully blackmails a Polish diplomat who has become involved with a dancer in Spain. Encouraged by the bonus and commendation he wins for this mission Tarr pressures the diplomat again but the man commits suicide after confessing to his ambassador.

On March 31, 1973 Tarr is sent to Hong Kong under cover as Tony Thomas, an Australian car dealer from Adelaide, to check on a Soviet trade delegate named Boris. Boris proves to be inaccessible but Tarr finds a rich source of intelligence in his common-law wife, Irina. Convinced that Tarr loves her, Irina passes on to him the information that a Moscow Centre deep-penetration agent serviced by Polyakov is operating in the Circus. Made suspicious by the Circus's failure to respond to his cables and by Irina's sudden forced removal to Moscow, Tarr goes underground in Kuala Lumpur, Malaysia, where he has a Eurasian mistress and a daughter, Danny, and acquires a passport in the name of Poole. In November Tarr returns to London secretly via South Africa and Dublin and uses his workname,* Trench, to contact Peter Guillam. The story he has to tell begins the operation which ends in Haydon's exposure as a traitor. During most of the time that Smiley carries out his investigation Tarr is confined to a house in Suffolk near Little Horkseley, Wormingford and Bures Green but he plays a vital role in the final stages of the operation. Armed with the knowledge that the mole* is unaware of Tarr's return to England, Smiley orders Tarr to Paris from where he sends the message which panics Haydon into a crash* meeting with Polyakov at the Lock Gardens safe house.* Despite his enormous contribution to the Haydon case [CIRCUS INDEX], Tarr does not seem to have any further involvement with the Circus.

Ricki Tarr is tall with an aging but immature face and speaks with a colonial accent. Perhaps because of his peculiar childhood and eccentric parents Tarr has never really grown up and he is an incongruous mixture of brutal and romantic qualities. A strong tendency to fantasize, which is equally evident in his projections of a Scottish *ménage à trois* with Irina and his Eurasian mistress and his interest in the football pools, is a further symptom of his immaturity. Peter Guillam dislikes Tarr intensely but he has a boyish quality which is quite appealing and, despite a tendency to overreach himself, he is an intelligent and resourceful agent. (*TT*)

—, **Tatiana** Karla's daughter by a mistress later executed for her anti-Soviet tendencies. Robbed of her mother and unacknowledged by her father, Tatiana develops severe anti-social and schizophrenic tendencies from an early age. While still living in Moscow she commits arson and theft, becomes involved with dissidents and is promiscuous. Despite Karla's interventions she suffers imprisonment and four years of treatment in mental hospitals. At one point Karla enlists a professor from Leningrad University to assist in her political re-education but she merely tries to seduce him. Finally realizing that Tatiana will never be well under the Soviet system of mental-health care Karla arranges for her to be treated in a Swiss clinic near Berne. He chooses this hospital because two of its staff, Dr Rüedi and Mother Felicity, speak Russian. Karla presumably does not want Tatiana to use German, the language she has learnt from her mother. His long-term plan is to find Tatiana a permanent home in the West and to this end he registers her at the clinic as Alexandra Borisovna Ostrakova (the real name of the daughter of Maria Ostrakova, an *emigrée* living in Paris). Karla's attempts to create a new identity for his daughter make him vulnerable to blackmail and are the cause of his eventual downfall.

Tatiana is small and fair-haired with clear, vulnerable eyes and full lips which tremble at the edge. For her meeting with Smiley she wears a long-sleeved green tunic and a cardigan draped over her shoulders. Although Tatiana's mental illness is entirely the result of her family situation and the repressive Soviet system, there seems little likelihood that the Berne hospital will restore her to sanity. What she needs is to be acknowledged as Tatiana, the daughter of Karla, but instead her weekly visitor, Grigoriev (using the cover name Dr Adolf Glaser), insists on reinforcing the fiction that she is Alexandra Ostrakova. His and Mother Felicity's pet name for her is Sasha. Tatiana's acute intelligence enables her to cope with the two identities to some extent, and much of her supposedly mad behaviour is simply rebellion. It seems likely that she will increasingly use complete denial of self as a means of escaping her impossibly dichotomized identity. (*SP*)

Taylor, Wilf Courier with the Department* who is accidentally killed by a car while engaged, under the name of Malherbe, in a rare operational mission to Finland. The loss of the film he had just collected from the pilot Lansen causes Leclerc to conclude that Taylor has been murdered. Taylor's career as a courier goes back as far as the war and has taken him to Berlin, Madrid and Turkey. Taylor is married to Joanie, a gin-drinking woman for whom he has no affection. They live at 34, Roxburgh Gardens in Kennington, London, and have a frail, bespectacled ten-year-old daughter. When Joanie is at work a Mrs Bradley gives the child her dinner. Taylor is involved with another woman who writes him letters. The Taylors' marital problems are made worse by lack of money. He has an overdraft and cherishes the £15 a day operational subsistence. His death leaves his wife without even a pension.

Taylor has collapsed features, pale eyes and a feeble moustache. His expression is one of anxiety. He has a number of irritating gestures designed to foster a military air. Nevertheless, the painful way in which he holds his stiff body has a certain dignity. On the day of his death he is wearing a pebble-weave overcoat and a trilby hat. Taylor is obsessed with denying his essential ordinariness. Faced with his social equals he puts on a drawling voice intended to be distinctive and, much as he hates the mission to Finland, he gains some consolation from the feeling that it makes him into someone special. Even his fantasies are small-scale, as for instance when in his role as Malherbe he assigns himself a rank no higher than major. Taylor's natural home is the Alias Club near Charing Cross, London, run by Major Dell, where a group of people, all equally mediocre, reinforce one another's sense of self-worth. (*LW*)

Testify, Operation Mission to Czechoslovakia by Prideaux to ascertain the name of Karla's mole* at the Circus. He is betrayed by Haydon. (*TT*)

Thatch, — Fanatical type who runs the charm-school* at Sarratt* for training deep-penetration agents. (*TT*)

Thesinger, 'Tufty' Ex-major of the King's African Rifles who is appointed as the Circus Hong Kong resident* by Alleline. Immediately prior to this appointment he operates as a spy in Hong Kong under cover as an importer. He leaves Hong Kong when the residency is closed in 1974. Thesinger is totally incompetent at his job and his crude attempts to gather intelligence are a staple joke at the Foreign Correspondents' Club. Haydon is responsible for Thesinger's unexpected promotion which he encourages as part of his policy of placing candidates unlikely to pose a threat to Moscow Centre in important positions. One of the problems facing Smiley in 1974 concerns a just pension for a man elevated well beyond his level of ability by a traitor. (*TT; HS*)

Thirteenth Directorate *See* Moscow Centre

'Thomas' Cover name used by Alec Leamas while waiting for Riemeck at the Berlin Wall. (*SC*)

'Thomas, Tony' Cover name used by Ricki Tarr during his mission to Hong Kong. (*TT*)

Thruxton, Ben In 1973 a member of the Circus research department. During the Russian Revolution he operated in Moscow under the guise of a Latvian dissident. In old age he is white-haired and very still. (*TT*)

Thursgood, — Headmaster of Thursgood's school which he inherited in 1968 from his father. He has a Cambridge degree and a rather pathetic sense of the dignity of his position. His free time is devoted to his mother, with whom he lives, and his Labrador, Ginnie. Thursgood seems temperamentally unsuited to a position of authority and is easily upset by any disturbance to the rather shaky stability of his school. (*TT*)

Thursgood's school Thursgood's is a minor preparatory school situated in Devon, near Taunton, and commanding fine views of the Quantocks. Its foundation is a recent one, being the creation of the present headmaster's father. The most notable event in the short history of Thursgood's is the elopement in 1968 of Thursgood Sr with the receptionist at the Castle Hotel, Taunton. Rumour has it that funding for the escapade came from the swimming pool appeal fund. Certainly the pool exists as no more than a hole in the ground.

  Academic standards are not high at Thursgood's mainly because of the headmaster's reliance for staff on Mr Stroll of Medley and Stroll, a supply teaching agency of rather doubtful credentials, and because of his willingness to allow half-pay to stand as the equivalent of academic qualifications. More unfortunate results of the Thursgood approach to recruitment include the French teacher, Major Dover, kept on so long beyond retirement that he eventually drops dead at Taunton races, and Mrs Loveday, a part-time substitute divinity teacher, and Mr Maltby, both of whom are removed from the school by the police. Neither could Thursgood's be called a sporting school as evidenced by the eighteen points-to-nil defeat at the hands of the St Ermin's rugby team. The chances for spiritual development possible in the absence of academic and athletic pursuits seem unlikely to be grasped by the elderly vicar, Spargo, known to the boys by the irreverent title, Wells Fargo. Only matron, a warm and insightful person, seems likely to make the Thursgood's experience a profitable one, although Jim Prideaux's decision to remain may well produce an improvement in the teaching of French if not in awareness of the realities of modern life. The staff of Thursgood's includes Miss Aaronson, who teaches violin and scripture, Elwes, Irving and Leonard Marjoribanks. Numbered amongst the pupils are Abercrombie, Aprahamian, Astor, Berger, Best-Ingram, Blakeney, Bradbury, Clements, Coleshaw, Meridew, Prebble, Roach, Spikely, Stephen, Sudeley. Apart from matron the support staff includes Latzy, a displaced Czech, who is the assistant gardener. (*TT*)

'Thwaite, Alexander' Cover name used on the passport supplied to Leamas by the Abteilung for his journey to Holland. Thwaite is a travel agent. (*SC*)

*tiger's claw Self-defence technique involving a blow to the windpipe. (*HS*)

Tiu, — Chief assistant and bodyguard to Drake Ko. Tiu's relationship with Ko begins during the Second World War and continues through Ko's moves to Shanghai and Hong Kong. He is presumably involved in Ko's early prostitution enterprises and is later manager of his companies including China Airsea and Indocharter. In his capacity as Ko's manager Tiu travels annually to Canton, Peking and Shanghai. He is with Ko while he reads law at Gray's Inn, London, in 1967 but the two are separated for at least one five-year period during which Tiu manages Ko's narcotics operation in San Francisco. Tiu plays an important part in Ko's attempts to rescue his brother, Nelson Ko, from Communist China. In 1973 he makes the arrangements for Ricardo's flight into China and in 1974–75 he murders Frost and Luke (in mistake for Westerby) as part of Ko's attempts to frustrate the Circus's investigations into his activities. Tiu accompanies Ko to Po Toi for the reunion with Nelson in May 1975 but, despite carrying an M-16 rifle, he is overpowered and brutally beaten by Westerby. Nothing is known of Tiu's later career but it is possible that he is sacrificed along with Lizzie Worthington in the narcotics trial that follows Operation Dolphin [CIRCUS INDEX].

Tiu is a burly but sleek man with muscular shoulders, chubby hands and fingers always curled in preparation for a fight. His hair is black and greased and his face bland and foreshortened. He could be any age. His favourite suit is electric blue and he wears a gold watch on his right wrist. His choice of soap gives him the aroma of almonds and rosewater. He speaks broken English with a half-American accent. His tastes in food include Kobe beef and raw fish and he drinks Black Label Scotch. Tiu's major strength is his calmness. This makes him both an effective manager and a dangerous opponent. His extreme loyalty to Ko suggests that he possesses some admirable human qualities but he responds to occidentals such as Westerby and Lizzie Worthington with open scorn. (*HS*)

top table The fifth floor of the Circus (*TT*) or the Circus's term for the more prestigious American Intelligence Service (the Cousins).* (*HS*)

*tradecraft Espionage techniques. (*TT*)

*tradesman Person outside of the espionage sphere who can nevertheless be called upon at any time to supply services such as photographic development. (*TT*)

*trail To set up a situation of personal advantage. (*HS*)

travelling salesman Department jargon for an agent. (*LW*)

*trawl To seek out. (*TT*)

'Trench' Ricki Tarr's workname* used to contact Guillam on his return from Kuala Lumpur. (*TT*)

'Tricky Tony' Nickname given to Grigoriev by Esterhase's lamplighters.* (*SP*)

Truebody, Miss — Terence Fielding's housekeeper. She is plump, small and aged about fifty-five. Fielding refers to her as True. It is her telephone call to Stella Rode, made at Fielding's request, which guarantees that he has a place to hide his bloody outer clothes after the murder. (*MQ*)

Trumper, William Formerly a pupil of Carne School in Dorset and now curate at Carne. He is a mild-mannered, long-winded and unintelligent person with an interest in cricket and private pews. He is clearly the Carne type. (*MQ*)

*turn To persuade an enemy agent to betray his or her country. (*TT*)

*unbutton To decode a secret message. (*HS*)

'Under Secretary' The assistant to the Minister with responsibility for the Department.* He is manipulated by Leclerc into recommending funds for Operation Mayfly. The Under Secretary works in an office between Whitehall Gardens and the Thames. He has the manner of a bank manager and is capable of anger and impatience. Mention of the Foreign Office produces a contemptuous response. The Under Secretary has old-fashioned tastes and rejects attempts to modernize his office, a large dark room with rows of books, a gas fire and an oil painting of a sea battle. (*LW*)

*unpack To provide information. (*TT*)

Ursula, Sister Nurse at the clinic near Berne where Karla's daughter, Tatiana, is a patient. (*SP*)

*vicar Controller of an espionage group. (*SP*)

Viktorov, Colonel Gregor Real name of Aleksey Polyakov. (*TT*)

'Virgin, the' Nickname given to Elizabeth Pidgeon by the staff of the Weybridge Repertory Theatre, Surrey. (*CD*)

Vladimir, General Former Circus agent who is murdered by Moscow Centre agents on Hampstead Heath, London, in 1978. Vladimir, or Voldemar as he is christened, is born in Estonia in about 1909. Although his Bolshevik father is murdered by Stalin, Vladimir remains loyal to the Revolution and fights in the Red Army during the Second World War, reaching the rank of general. The purge of Estonia in the years after the war finally disillusions him and he spies for the Circus in Moscow for three years before defecting during a visit to Paris. While in Paris Vladimir joins the Baltic Independence Movement and founds the Riga Group. Those with whom he is involved include Ostrakov, Villem Craven's father and

Mikhel. The Movement eventually fragments into four rival groups – the Riga Group, the Association of Victims of Soviet Imperialism, the Forty-Eight Committee for a Free Latvia, the Tallinn Committee of Freedom – and in-fighting becomes so intense that the French authorities expel Vladimir in December 1975. Prior to his expulsion Vladimir is working with his old friend Otto Leipzig on an investigation of Oleg Kursky, a Moscow Centre agent operating in Paris under diplomatic cover. However, Enderby brings the case to a close in April or May 1975. The Circus has no further use for Vladimir after his move to London and he ekes out an impoverished existence as a translator operating from a tiny flat in Westbourne Terrace, Paddington. He adopts the name Vladimir Miller.

The General keeps in touch with other Estonian exiles living in London, including Mikhel and Jüri. It is through Mikhel in 1978 that Vladimir receives the letter from Ostrakova which initiates his final intelligence efforts. Alerted by Ostrakova's letter to renewed activity on the part of Kursky he concocts, with the help of Otto Leipzig and Claus Kretzschmar, a successful blackmail operation which yields information extremely detrimental to Karla. Leipzig is able to transfer some of his evidence to London via Villem Craven, but Vladimir, operating under the workname* Gregory, is murdered while trying to make contact with Mostyn of the Circus. However, enough hints of what Vladimir was up to reach George Smiley for the operation to continue. The result is Karla's forced defection.

Vladimir is married while living in Tallinn, the capital of Estonia, but leaves his wife behind in Moscow. She dies in a forced-labour camp. During his time in Paris and London he has many mistresses including Mikhel's wife, Elvira. Villem Craven regards Vladimir as his second father and makes him godfather to his daughter, Beckie. In his later years Vladimir rejects Marxism and reverts to the Lutheran religion of his youth. For recreation Vladimir favours chess, vodka and filter-tipped Gauloises Caporals. In old age Vladimir has white hair, cut very short, but still retains his towering and majestic stance. Broad shoulders and a military moustache add to his impressive appearance. On the day of his death Vladimir is not wearing his prized Norfolk jacket. Instead he is dressed in a black beret, black overcoat and North British Century rubber overshoes, and is carrying a heavy cane.

Vladimir is a man of complete integrity, great courage and total commitment to the anti-Soviet cause. Both men and women admire him enormously and few can resist his demands, whether they be political or sexual. Whatever he demands of others, Vladimir expects more of himself and not even a heart attack can diminish the energy with which he responds to Ostrakova's plea for help. (*SP*)

'Vopo sergeant' Member of the unit in Rostock which picks up Fred Leiser's radio transmission. He is an elderly, benevolent-looking man with grey hair and gold spectacles and a calm, authoritative manner. Although officially working under a Russian captain the sergeant masterminds the capture of Fred Leiser. Amongst his virtues is a memory so remarkable that he recognizes Leiser's transmission style from the war. (*LW*)

'waiter in transport café' A tired and indolent boy who has little grasp on the finer points of serving burgundy. Smiley's elaborate good manners afford him a certain secret amusement. (*TT*)

waitlisted Designation in the Circus files for former agents who can be contacted only through the fifth floor. (*SP*)

*walk in the park Clandestine meeting. (*HS*)

—, Walther Resident of the water camp near Hamburg who rows Smiley out to Otto Leipzig's boat, the *Isadora*. Walther is old with brown, deeply wrinkled skin, cracked lips and almond-shaped eyes which shine unnaturally against his dark skin. He wears a jacket made of sailcloth and a black cap with a peak. He smokes constantly, alternating cigarettes and cigars. His presence is powerful and his contemptuous manner threatening. Walther's specific condemnation of Leipzig as scum is a judgement he would probably extend to embrace the rest of the world including himself. (*SP*)

'wardress, the' Commissar of the political prison near Görlitz in East Germany where Liz Gold is held before and after the trial of Hans-Dieter Mundt. She is very big and ugly with a heavy, flabby face and small, crafty eyes. Her hair, which she ties in a bun, is thin. She wears a grey overall with chevrons on the sleeve. Compassion and indeed any emotions other than greed seem to be missing from her personality. The wardress's conversation consists entirely of dogmatic statements of communist ideology and misinformation about life in Britain. Although she thinks of herself as important she is obviously not a party to Mundt's plans regarding Leamas. (*SC*)

*watch To keep an enemy agent under surveillance. (*TT*)

*watch my back Request to a fellow agent to provide protection during a mission. (*TT*)

*water games Training in techniques needed for espionage activities on water. (*HS*)

water school Training establishment on the Helford estuary in Cornwall where water games are conducted. (*HS*)

*water-testing Techniques employed by agents to ensure that they are not under surveillance. (*TT*)

Wayfarer, Phoebe Freelance journalist and Circus agent living in Hong Kong. Phoebe is born in 1941 of an English father, a clerk from Dorking, and a Chinese mother. Her father is killed fighting the Japanese. By the age of fifteen she is trying to support her sick mother and her own schooling by working the dance halls, but is then diverted into espionage by a welfare worker who recruits for the Circus. Operating under cover as a journalist, Phoebe, code name Susan, makes seven missions into mainland China. By 1975 she is providing information on a left-wing group of University students and journalists which she has infiltrated. Its members include Billy Chan, Johnny and Belinda Fong, Billy Lee, and Ellen Tuo. The intelligence she produces is almost completely useless but her controller, Bill Craw, finds her an invaluable if unknowing source of information about Lizzie Worthington during Operation Dolphin [CIRCUS INDEX].

Physically Phoebe is a rather unattractive combination of English and Chinese features. Her face is pale, large and not beautiful. She has a long body and short legs and her hands, which she probably inherits from her father, are ugly and powerful. She wears thick spectacles. For Craw's Sunday visit Phoebe wears a Chinese Communist grey tunic dress and the gold necklace awarded for ten years of service with the Circus. She is an insecure person easily moved to tears. Craw imputes this to the early death of her father and he offers the Circus in general and himself in particular as a paternal substitute. However, it is also clear that the pressures of operating under cover* have contributed to her lack of self-confidence. Attempts at finding security in personal relationships have resulted in nothing better than several unwanted pregnancies and Phoebe copes best through her fantasies. These are sparked off by her bedside picture of the Swiss Alps and by her vicarious involvement in the lives of the Hong Kong millionaires who feature in her gossip columns. A cat, the replacement for two humming-birds which died in quick succession, and neat Scotch are further sources of consolation, as are her fantasies of artistic success. The romantic fictions of that other great dreamer, Lizzie Worthington, evoke a powerful response in Phoebe. (*HS*)

Westerby, the Hon. Clive Gerald (Jerry) Journalist and member of the Circus Occasionals* who dies while engaged in Operation Dolphin [CIRCUS INDEX]. Westerby is the second son of a titled press baron, Sir Samuel Westerby, and is educated at Eton and Oxford. Before going up to Oxford he does wartime military service as an army subaltern and is

recruited as a member of the London Occasionals.* His application for a
full-time position with the Circus is turned down on the grounds that he
needs more experience of the world. After graduation Westerby makes a
career as a foreign correspondent and sports reporter and continues to
work for the Circus on a part-time basis. The operations in which he is
involved include an exchange of packages in Prague, Czechoslovakia, two
undefined missions with Sam Collins in Vientiane, Laos, and the rescue of
a radio operator off a Caspian beach. He is also in the Congo during the
war there in the early 1960s but it isn't known if his activities go beyond the
journalistic. Throughout Westerby's career in the Circus Smiley serves as
his mentor but his official controller is first Bland and then Esterhase. One
of his worknames* is Worrell.

Westerby's career first intersects with the mainstream of Circus history
in December 1972 when, during a stopover in Prague after completing a
routine delivery of a packet in Budapest, he uncovers evidence of
Prideaux's betrayal during Operation Testify. Haydon tries to silence
Westerby by contriving his dismissal from the Service but he is finally able
to tell his story to Smiley in November 1973. In 1974 Westerby at last
plays a central role in a major operation. Impressed by the recent evidence
of his loyalty and limited for choice following the Haydon débâcle, Smiley
calls on Westerby when he needs an agent in Hong Kong to advance
Operation Dolphin [CIRCUS INDEX]. Thus, in October 1974, working
under journalistic cover, Westerby moves into the apartment of Deathwish the Hun, number 7A on the sixteenth floor of a highrise on
Cloudview Road. His first task is to blackmail the banker, Frost, into
revealing information about the secret bank account which has sparked off
the mission. In the second phase of the mission he makes contact with
Lizzie Worthington in Hong Kong and then with Charlie Marshall and
Ricardo by means of a journey which takes him through South East Asia to
Bangkok in Thailand, Phnom Penh and Battambang in Cambodia, back
to Phnom Penh, Saigon in South Vietnam, Vientiane, and North East
Thailand. His intention in each case is to communicate sufficient knowledge of Ko's activities to force him into precipitate action. Westerby's
mission is a success and results in the capture of Nelson Ko as he tries to
enter Hong Kong through Po Toi in May 1975. However, by this time
Westerby has become disillusioned with the operation and is killed,
probably by Fawn, while trying to help the Ko brothers to avoid capture.

Of his many interests outside of spying, the most preoccupying is
women. Westerby has married several. None of his marriages is successful
but one, to a woman now married to a civil servant named Phillie,
produces a daughter Catherine, whom Westerby calls Cat. In 1974 she is

seventeen and Westerby has not seen her for ten years. By way of compensation he sends her money through the Circus bankers, Blatt and Rodney. Other relationships include a brief but intense affair with 'the orphan', some twenty-five years his junior, during the nine months he spends in Italy in a Tuscan farmhouse before being recalled to the Circus in September 1974; a number of purely sexual encounters with his upstairs neighbour in Cloudview Road and some girls in the Mekong village to which he retreats after his meeting with Ricardo; and an overwhelming infatuation with his intelligence target, Lizzie Worthington. It is love for Lizzie more than anything else which persuades Westerby to return to Hong Kong after completing his part of Operation Dolphin [CIRCUS INDEX] and his death occurs while he is trying to bargain with Drake Ko for her freedom. Westerby's other main personal relationships are with his immediate family. His father is a major preoccupation even after his death and he keeps in touch with his stepmother Pet Westerby who lives in Thurloe Square, London. Others in the complex network of Westerby's family are cousin Aldred, who went to jail, and Uncle Paul, who sells ballast. George Smiley is an honorary member of Westerby's family and functions as something close to a surrogate father. Outside of lovers and family Westerby has numerous acquaintances including his literary agent Mencken, his editor Stubbs, fellow journalists Keller, Smoothie Stallwood, Graham, a homosexual Chinese gossip columnist from Hong Kong, and the members of the Shanghai Junior Baptist Conservative Bowling Club, particularly Luke, Hercule, his favourite Vietnamese, and Maurice, the manager of the Constellation hotel in Vientiane.

Journalism, although never as important to Westerby as spying, consumes a fair amount of his energies. His assignments include football games in Czechoslovakia, where he makes the acquaintance of the Prague goalkeeper, Holotek, a story on the West Bromwich Albion centre forward, the war in the Congo and, during his final visit to South East Asia, the war in Cambodia and colour pieces on the fate of the Wanchai bar girls after the American military withdrawal and the sexual deprivation of the Gurkhas. His research into corruption trials, the alleged pregnancy of Miss Hong Kong, and the lives of Hong Kong millionaires fails to produce publishable material.

Westerby's major leisure pursuits are focused on sports. At one time he plays wicket-keeper at County level and keeps up an interest in the fortunes of Lancashire, Kent and Middlesex after his retirement. Probably because of his father's forays into ownership, Westerby also has a good knowledge of horse-racing and brings off a betting coup at Happy

Valley by backing Drake Ko's Lucky Nelson at forty-to-one. During one of his visits to Phnom Penh early in the Cambodian War he water skis on the Mekong River. Despite his father's disapproval Westerby pursues an interest in painting but by 1974 is trying to find an artistic outlet in novel-writing. Recall by the Circus from Tuscany terminates his efforts. When not writing Westerby is a great reader with a particular interest in Conrad (especially when he is in Phnom Penh), Ford Madox Ford, Graham Greene and T. E. Lawrence. A novel which he considers bad, about old Hong Kong, may be James Clavell's *Tai-Pan*. As regards eating and drinking, he particularly favours large pink gins and beer with curry. Among his regular haunts are a ground-floor cellar and El Vino's in Fleet Street, London, a curry house where old Khan makes a special sauce to spice up the hottest curry on the menu, his unnamed club, the Restaurant Sport in Prague, the Constellation in Vientiane, a disco in Kowloon, a club in Hong Kong where the band plays in the Ellington style, a new Japanese restaurant also in Hong Kong, the Foreign Correspondents' Club at the Oriental Hotel in Bangkok, Le Phnom in Phnom Penh, and the Hotel Caravelle in Saigon.

Physically, Westerby is a large, energetic man with an athletic build and a lumbering walk. His sandy hair is flecked with grey, his face is red and he grins a lot. When formally dressed he wears a washable blue-faded suit made by Pontschak Happy House of Bangkok, a cream silk shirt, a Free Foresters' tie, and scruffy buckskin boots. He frequently carries a grey jute book bag. Westerby's is not a complex personality. He is kind, loyal, unreflective, courageous and immature. The Tuscan villagers think of him as a schoolboy. His great ambition is to belong, but this is repeatedly frustrated by the inadequacy of his father, his own many failed marriages and the Circus's refusal to take him on full time. The needs of Operation Dolphin [CIRCUS INDEX] eventually give Westerby the chance for involvement that he has always sought. However, he finds that belonging is more complicated than he had thought and he becomes increasingly disillusioned with the requirement that he sacrifice innocent bystanders. Finally he does the unthinkable and rejects the Circus in favour of an essentially quixotic commitment to the glamorous fantasist Lizzie Worthington. This last attempt to establish a connection results in his death (*TT; HS*). *See* maps of Hong Kong and South East Asia, pages 99, 100 and 171

Westerby, Pet The third wife of Sir Samuel (Sambo) Westerby and therefore stepmother to Jerry Westerby. She lives in a very small converted flat in a house in Thurloe Square, London, crowded with antiques from former homes. Plentiful make-up cannot conceal the fact that she now looks more like a hen than a beauty and this tends to make her bad tempered. She has a booming, theatrical voice which sometimes betrays her North Country origins. Pet sleeps poorly and enjoys drinking *crème de menthe frappée* and talking to Jerry in the middle of the night. Despite his many betrayals she loves Sambo long after his death. (*HS*)

Westerby, Sir Samuel ('Sambo'), later Lord Newspaper tycoon and racehorse owner. Sambo Westerby is the husband of several wives, including Pet Westerby, who is his third, and father of several children. Jerry Westerby is his second legitimate son and he has at least one illegitimate child, Adam. Adam's mother, Mary, lives in Chobham, Surrey. Amongst Sambo's racehorses are Rosalie, stabled at Maisons-Laffitte, and Intruder, stabled in Dublin. Although his company's stock runs into millions of pounds he is bankrupt by the time of his death. He is a fair-haired, domineering and energetic man who repeatedly changes houses and shouts a lot. He has little tolerance for artistic pursuits. (*HS*)

Weybridge Repertory Theatre Elsa Fennan's local theatre in Surrey where she and the East German agent Mundt exchange 'music cases'. (*CD*)

'Whitebait' (and 'Caviar') Code names for material simultaneously distributed on both sides of the Atlantic during Operation Dolphin [CIRCUS INDEX]. (*HS*)

Wilbraham, Chris Leader of the Colonial Office contingent on the Intelligence Steering Committee responsible for Circus activities. He is a school-masterly, thin, fit-looking man with red-veined, weathered cheeks, hairy hands and extremely slow speech. His essential honesty makes him more concerned with the rights of Drake Ko and the governor of Hong Kong than with the implementation of Operation Dolphin [CIRCUS INDEX]. He is easily outwitted by Smiley and Enderby. This lack of worldliness as much as the diminution of the Empire seems likely to limit Wilbraham's progress towards honours. (*HS*)

'Will' Cover name used by Peter Guillam when making contact with Mendel during the Haydon case. (*TT*)

Wiltshire, Andrew English teacher at Peter Worthington's school in Barnsbury, North London. He becomes friendly with the Worthingtons in 1972 and takes yoga classes with Lizzie at the Sobell Sports Centre. On the night that Lizzie leaves Peter, he dines with them at the Knossos, a Kebab house. It seems likely that he is Lizzie's lover. Andrew Wiltshire is a curly-haired Scot with a very physical, extrovert personality. (*HS*)

*****Wise Men, the** Whitehall jargon for an Inter-Ministerial Steering Committee intended to act as a buffer between Cabinet and Intelligence. (*SP*)

Witchcraft, Operation Intelligence material received from Source Merlin [CIRCUS INDEX]. (*TT*)

Woodford, Babs The wife of Bruce Woodford of the Department,* with whom she lives in Wimbledon, London. They have no children and her main hobby is pottery-making although, based on the evidence of the giant initialled and embossed cup and saucer she makes for Bruce, she has little talent for it. She is a thin woman with a cruel look and a hard, artificial laugh. Her usual sarcasm, which she directs at Bruce, Leclerc and the Department,* deteriorates into simple bad temper when she is not drinking. She appears to have been much more lively in the past and to have taken considerable pleasure in sexual promiscuity. Her lovers include Jimmy Gorton. The disappointments of aging and of marriage have a lot to do with her unpleasant disposition. (*LW*)

Woodford, Bruce Member of the Department* whose service dates back to the Second World War. At one time, presumably before the war, he is a teacher. Woodford's main role in Operation Mayfly is to use his wartime contacts at the Alias Club near Charing Cross, London, where he is known as Woodie, to track down Jack Johnson, Fred Leiser and Sandy Lowe. He is athletic, has a big head and heavy shoulders, and smokes a pipe. His suit is green, thick and hairy with brown bone buttons. He has an intimate manner and a dutiful air but is in fact a back-biting complainer who is considered useless even by Leclerc. Like most members of the Department,* Woodford tends to live in the past and feels best in the wartime atmosphere of the Alias Club. His marriage is clearly a disaster and he hides from his wife's constant carping behind the mystique of his job. Although too timid to embark on an affair, Woodford likes to talk about going to bed with Leclerc's secretary, Carol. (*LW*)

*workname Alias used by agents within their own service. (*HS*)

'Worrell' Workname* used by Westerby. His clandestine return to Hong Kong towards the end of Operation Dolphin [CIRCUS INDEX] is made under this name. (*HS*)

'Worth, Liese' Name adopted by Lizzie Worthington on becoming Drake Ko's mistress. (*HS*)

Worthington, Elizabeth Daughter of Nunc and Cess Pelling, wife of Peter Worthington, mistress of Tiny Ricardo and Drake Ko. Lizzie, as she is usually called, is born in the Alexandra Nursing Home in North London in about 1946. She attends a number of schools in accordance with her father's eccentric educational theories and later begins, but does not complete, courses at drama school and secretarial college. The pattern of change established during Lizzie's education continues into her employment and she has six jobs, all in the London area, within eighteen months. None of them advances her parents' ambitions for her to pursue a career in ballet, stage or television. Marriage to Peter Worthington, a schoolteacher in Barnsbury, North London, follows and Lizzie has one child, a boy named Ian. In 1972, possibly spurred on by an affair with Peter's colleague, Andrew Wiltshire, she leaves her husband and takes up a position arranged for her by a woman in Bradford as a nightclub hostess in Bahrein. The job is much less glamorous than claimed and Lizzie moves on to Vientiane in Laos, with two hippies.

In Vientiane Lizzie approaches Steve Mackelvore, the British Trade Consul, for work. Mackelvore, who is really a spy, passes her on to another agent, Sam Collins, or Mellon as he is known in Vientiane. Collins uses Lizzie in drug and bullion investigations. Her secret work brings her into contact with Drake Ko, whom she meets in Hong Kong through Sally Cale, a gold-smuggler, and Ricardo, whose drug dealings she investigates. Lizzie soon becomes Ricardo's mistress and lives with him and his fellow pilot, Charlie Marshall, in a hovel on the edge of the city. Her intelligence activities help for a while to fund Ricardo's many schemes and he beats her up when she is dismissed for incompetence. Lizzie twice tries to kill Ricardo in revenge. Lizzie and Ricardo are involved in selling barrels of Scotch whisky. The appeal of the enterprise seems to reside as much in Lizzie's willingness to make love to many of their fifty-five customers as in the quality of the product. She also earns money by working as a prostitute at the Constellation hotel. In March 1973 Charlie Marshall, who is now a pilot with Indocharter, an aviation company based in Vientiane, gets Lizzie a job as the secretary-receptionist at a salary of $20 a week.

This phase of Lizzie Worthington's life comes to an end later in 1973 when she meets Drake Ko for a second time at the Erawan in Bangkok while trying to save Ricardo from the consequences of abandoning his mission into China. Her willingness to become Ko's mistress is an important part of the deal by means of which Ricardo's life is spared. Ko sets up Lizzie, who is renamed Liese Worth, in apartment 8C at the Star Heights building in the Midlevels district of Hong Kong. He also provides her with a red E-type Jaguar sports car and lots of jewellery. Her *raison d'être* is to meet Ko's sexual needs and she has limited freedom. Even her Monday evening flower-arranging at the American Club is done in the company of Nellie Tan, an employee of Ko's China Airsea company.

The relative stability which Ko introduces into Lizzie Worthington's life is destroyed by Operation Dolphin [CIRCUS INDEX]. In February 1975 Westerby makes her acquaintance as part of his plan to panic Ko into hasty action by revealing a knowledge of his activities in Communist China. Shortly afterwards Sam Collins uses his acquaintance with her involvement in drug-smuggling to force Lizzie to betray Ko. Westerby, who has fallen in love with Lizzie, returns to Hong Kong in May and tries to rescue her from the trap into which she has fallen. He fails and in the aftermath of Operation Dolphin Lizzie is imprisoned for narcotics offences.

Lizzie Worthington is an unusually beautiful woman with long, ash-blonde hair, strong, lightly-freckled shoulders, tiny gold hairs on her spine and the kind of breasts that encourage waiters to look down the front of her dress. However, in a good light her face is marred not only by the scar on her chin, caused by a blow from Ricardo, but also by signs of strain from too much racketing about. She speaks in a stateless foreign accent, probably acquired from Ricardo, and she relates to people with an easy physical intimacy. Her walk is full of sexual promise. The first time Westerby meets her she is dressed simply in a plain dress with a halter neck and sandals. Her hair is in a pony tail. At a later fashion show she wears a glamorous strapless dress and pearl collar and earrings. On leaving she covers her shoulders with a cape. The effect of this outfit is to make her look about ten years older and six inches taller than she does in the jeans and sweater into which she changes later. Lizzie drinks Remy Martin with ice and soda and has a taste for Kobe beef. For music she prefers Duke Ellington, Cat Anderson and Louis Armstrong.

Lizzie is essentially the prisoner of other people's dreams. Her parents use her to fulfil their fantasies of fame and power, Peter Worthington tries to mould her into the perfect wife, and for Drake Ko she is the reincarnation of his beloved mother figure, Liese Hibbert. As a result Lizzie has no firm centre of self and can escape other people's definitions only through her own fantasies and/or flight. Thus, to break the wife and mother mould she tells the headmistress of Peter Worthington's school that she has a degree in Sanskrit and she deals with her experiences in South East Asia by pretending to be a Shropshire aristocrat's daughter seeking fulfilment through Buddhism and art. The real tragedy of Lizzie Worthington is that, for all that she is constantly being shifted away from reality by herself and others, she is at root a humorous, good-natured, warm and loving human being. A term in a Hong Kong prison seems unlikely to do anything to sustain her essential zest for life. (*HS*)

Worthington, Peter Schoolteacher husband of Lizzie Worthington. His origins are public school but he has gone into state education at a school in Barnsbury, London, out of a sense of mission. He is married to Lizzie for an undefined period. After she leaves him in 1972 he looks after their son, Ian, with the help of his mother, Jenny. Peter Worthington is, at age thirty-four, a large and rugged man with greying wiry hair. He has a kind and friendly face. Nervousness makes him drum or crack his fingers. He wears a heavy tweed suit that makes no concession to fashion. Although well-intentioned he is essentially a dogmatic and insensitive bore who much prefers talking to listening. Few if any of his pronouncements about Lizzie's character and behaviour turn out to be true. For all his air of authority he is a weak man unwilling to acknowledge his wife's infidelity. (*HS*)

*wrangler Code-breaker. (*HS*)

Zimin, — Real name of Commercial Boris, a former soldier who trains as a spy at Karla's private training school outside Moscow. In 1968, under the name Smirnov, he works in Switzerland as the paymaster to an East German espionage *apparat* (organization). Other postings include Vienna, where he operates under the name Kursky (not to be confused with Oleg Kursky) and perhaps West Berlin, if we can accept the theory that he is the Zimin who successfully blackmails a French senator into giving away secrets. In 1973 he is Second Secretary (Commercial) at the Soviet Embassy in Vientiane, Laos. His official name being incomprehensible, the diplomatic community refers to him as 'Commercial Boris'. Working under the name Mr Delassus, Zimin is responsible for moving the funds destined for Nelson Ko from the Banque de l'Indochine to a local bank account held by Indocharter. (*HS*)

Appendix

Notes on the 'Circus' Series of Novels

Between 1961 and 1980 John le Carré published seven novels dealing with a special department of the British Intelligence Service he calls the Circus. Brief details of their content and information on editions is given here.

Call for the Dead Our first acquaintance with the Circus and with the master spy, George Smiley, occurs in 1960 (or possibly 1959) when Smiley first resigns from the Circus in order to have a free hand in investigating the apparent suicide of a civil servant named Samuel Fennan. By the time he has completed his independent probings into what turns out to be murder, Smiley has uncovered and destroyed an East German spy ring made up of Fennan's wife, Elsa, and two Abteilung agents, Dieter Frey and Hans-Dieter Mundt. Peter Guillam of the Circus and Mendel, a retired policeman, assist Smiley during this 'Fennan case'.

A Murder of Quality Later in 1960 while Smiley is distanced from the Circus – his resignation still stands – he is asked by an ex-Circus colleague, Ailsa Brimley, to investigate a murder threat at Carne School in Dorset where Terence Fielding, the brother of Ailsa's late Circus boss is Senior Housemaster. Using his Circus skills and after uncovering a large number of unpleasant facts from the pasts of those close to the centre of the case, Smiley finally establishes that Terence Fielding murdered the teacher's wife, Stella Rode, to stop her blackmailing him about a wartime conviction for homosexuality and also killed the schoolboy Perkins, to whom he was attracted, to prevent him communicating vital evidence.

The Spy Who Came in from the Cold Following his return to East Germany after committing two murders during the Fennan case (in *Call for the Dead*), Hans-Dieter Mundt has great success in destroying the Berlin networks of a British agent, Alec Leamas. In 1961 Control, the new head of the Circus, concocts a plot aimed at discrediting Mundt by exposing him as a British spy. At the end of things in 1962, Leamas, who has carried the burden of this Fiedler–Mundt Operation, discovers that Mundt is truly a double agent, recruited by Guillam during the Fennan case, and that Control's real aim has been to eliminate the threat posed by Jens Fiedler, a senior member of the Abteilung who had begun to suspect Mundt of teachery. With the accomplishment of Control's true goal

Leamas and Liz Gold, an innocent civilian drawn into the scheme, are allowed to return to the West, but she is shot as they cross the Berlin Wall and the disillusioned Leamas decides to share her fate. Although Smiley is still officially retired from the Circus and plays a somewhat minor role here, his character – as always – pervades the story.

The Looking-Glass War In 1964 (or 1965) 'the Department', an almost defunct branch of intelligence responsible for military targets, trains a retired agent, Fred Leiser, and then sends him into East Germany to gather information on Soviet rocketry. The mission, Operation Mayfly, is a complete failure and Leiser is captured by East German soldiers. There is every reason to believe that this is exactly what Control, the head of the Circus, whose help has been crucial in getting the operation launched, was hoping would happen since the elimination of 'the Department' will increase the resources available to the Circus. The burden of executing Control's various ploys falls on George Smiley who has by now returned to intelligence work at the Circus.

Tinker, Tailor, Soldier, Spy By 1973 the Circus is in disarray. Intelligent and loyal officers such as Control, Smiley, Jim Prideaux (head 'scalphunter') and Connie Sachs (expert on Soviet intelligence) have been forced into retirement or, like Guillam, been exiled to outstations and the head of the Circus is now the mediocre Percy Alleline. Furthermore, the cleverly contrived Operation Witchcraft, initiated for receiving 'Moscow Centre' secrets, now has complete access to British secrets. All this is the result of the efforts of Bill Haydon, the mole at the Circus recruited back in the 1930s by the Soviet agent, Karla (now head of 'Moscow Centre'). However, the 'scalphunter' Ricki Tarr in Hong Kong communicates certain news to Oliver Lacon, the Minister's Adviser on intelligence, and to Guillam and Smiley. This information launches an investigation which finally exposes Haydon as the traitor. As a reward for master-minding the investigation Smiley is at last made head of the Circus.

The Honourable Schoolboy Following the discovery of a Soviet agent within its ranks (in *Tinker, Tailor, Soldier, Spy*), the Circus falls into disgrace and is stripped of most of its resources. However, this state of affairs does not prevent Smiley, assisted by Guillam, Connie Sachs, di Salis (an expert on China) and the former 'scalphunter', Fawn, from seeking out opportunities to damage 'Moscow Centre'. Research into cases suppressed by Haydon, the Circus mole, eventually yields evidence in 1974 that funds intended for a Soviet mole are being paid into a Hong

Kong bank account. A complex investigation conducted by Smiley and his assistants in Britain, and by the agents Craw and Westerby in Hong Kong, eventually reveals that the mole is Nelson Ko, a member of the Communist Chinese military and intelligence élite and that his brother Drake, the guardian of the Hong Kong bank account, is trying to bring him out of China. Pressure from American narcotics agents, who are eager to investigate Drake Ko's activities, forces Smiley to take steps to convince Drake to act quickly with regards to his brother's escape. His efforts are successful and Nelson Ko is arrested by British and American intelligence agents in 1975 while landing on Po Toi, the most southerly of the Hong Kong islands. Jerry Westerby, who has finally turned against the operation, is killed while trying to assist both of the Ko brothers. Because of a conspiracy between Enderby, a member of the Intelligence Steering Committee, and Martello, the head of American Intelligence in London, the Circus loses its prize and Nelson Ko is allowed to fall into the hands of the Americans. Smiley is forced to resign, and Enderby becomes head of the Circus.

Smiley's People In 1978, three years after his forced retirement, Smiley is called back into service to deal with the murder of his former agent, General Vladimir, by Soviet agents on Hampstead Heath. His mandate is to conduct a cover-up but the discovery that Vladimir's target was his old enemy, 'Moscow Centre's' agent Karla, persuades Smiley to pursue the investigation still further. By gathering together the evidence collected by Vladimir and his friend, Otto Leipzig, and by blackmailing a Soviet diplomat, Grigoriev, Smiley eventually discovers that Karla has committed a number of illegal acts in order to fund and protect his insane daughter, Tatiana, whom he has secretly placed in a Swiss clinic near Berne. Armed with this information Smiley is able to blackmail Karla into defecting. This major triumph over his long-time rival brings to an end Smiley's career in intelligence.

Details of Published Editions

Call for the Dead (London: Gollancz, 1961; New York: Walker and Co., 1962)

A Murder of Quality (London: Gollancz, 1962; New York: Walker and Co., 1963)

The Incongruous Spy (USA)/*The le Carré Omnibus* (UK) – an omnibus edition of *Call for the Dead* and *A Murder of Quality* (New York: Walker and Co., 1964/London: Gollancz, 1969)

The Spy Who Came in from the Cold (London: Gollancz, 1963; New York: Coward-McCann, 1964)

The Looking-Glass War (London: Heinemann, 1965; New York: Coward-McCann, 1965)

Tinker, Tailor, Soldier, Spy (London: Hodder and Stoughton, 1974; New York: Knopf, 1974)

The Honourable Schoolboy (London: Hodder and Stoughton, 1977; New York: Knopf, 1977)

Smiley's People (London: Hodder and Stoughton, 1980; New York: Knopf, 1980)

The Quest for Karla – an omnibus edition of *Tinker, Tailor, Soldier, Spy*, *The Honourable Schoolboy* and *Smiley's People* (London: Hodder and Stoughton, 1982; New York: Knopf, 1982)

All the **Circus** novels are published in paperback in the UK by Pan except for *Call for the Dead* and *A Murder of Quality* which Penguin publish. In the USA all the **Circus** novels are published in paperback by Bantam.

Index to the Circus Chapter

Note   Main geographical areas are grouped under:
Africa; Middle East; South America; South East Asia;
otherwise see individual countries.

A

above-the-line residents (legal)
   46–47
Abteilung *see* East German
   Intelligence Service
Accounts (Circus)   45,46
Acton, London *see* lamplighters at
Adriatic Working Party (Circus)   19
Africa, Circus activity in   42
   French North   17,18
   Kenya   13
   Mozambique   13
Agate, Geoff   45
agents (Circus)
   briefing/interrogating/training   14
   deep penetration   17
   double   16
   field   45,46–47
   freelance   47
   illegal residents   43,47
   legal residents   43,46–47
   local   44,47
   Occasionals   13,21,47
Aggravate (network)   17,19,47
Alleline, Percy   13,17,18,19,20,21,
   33,35,42,43,44,48
Allitson, Oscar   45
Alwyn, —   46
American Intelligence Service (the
   Cousins/Company)   10,17,18,
   19,23,24,25
American narcotics agents   22,23,
   36,37
Anstruther, —   47
Argyll, Scotland *see* stinks-and-
   bangs-school at
Ashe, William   16,31

Astrid, —   46
Austria, Circus activity in
   Vienna   33

B

BBC (British Broadcasting
   Corporation), as cover   46
baby-sitting (Circus)   44
Banking Section (Circus)   9,31,45,
   49
Bath, Avon *see* wranglers at
Bayswater Library for Psychic
   Research   31
Belgian arms dealers   17
below-the-line residents (illegal)   47
—, Ben   47
Berlin Wall *see* Germany
Bilova, Hanka   47
blackmail (Circus)   17,24,25,27,39,
   40,43
Bland, Roy   9,17,19,21,33,42,44,
   47,49
Blatt and Rodney Bank   46
'Blondie' *see* Mundt, Hans-Dieter
—, Boris   34
Bream, Miss   46
Bretlev, Ivan Ivanovitch   22
bribery (Circus)   17,43
Brimley, Ailsa   13,45
British Airways, as cover   46
British embassy/consulate, as cover
   46
British Intelligence Service
   (the) Circus   *passim*
   (the) Department   10,18
Brixton, London *see* scalphunters at

Brod, — ('Ivlov')   34
Bryant, P.   10,46
Bulgaria, Circus activity in   17
Bywater Street, London   7

C

Cabinet Office, Whitehall   41
Cambridge Circus, London *see*
   Circus Headquarters
Camden Town, London (safe house)
   see Lock Gardens
Canada Bill 44
Canterbury, Kent *see* long-arm radio
   transmission base at
charm-school (Circus)   44
China   13,21,22,23,24,36,38,42
   Amoy   13
   Peking–Hong Kong shuttle   17
   Shanghai   36,37,38
   Wenchow   12
Chronologies of Major Operations
   28–40
Churayevs, the   47
Circus, the   *passim*
CIRCUS DEPARTMENTS
   Non-Operational
Accounts   45,46
Housekeeping   9,42,46,49
janitors   46,49
maintenance   46
(the) Mothers   46
Personnel   46
Registry   9,46,49
Resettlement   46
Secretariat, secretaries   46,48
Services, general   46

CIRCUS DEPARTMENTS
   Non-Operational *cont.*
(the) shuttle   46
Special Despatch   46
CIRCUS DEPARTMENTS
   Operational
Adriatic Working Party   19
Banking Section (for espionage
   activity)   9,31,45,49
code-breaking *see* wranglers
coding   13,45,49
duty-officers   9,20,45,49
experimental audio-laboratory (at
   Harlow)   45
'fifth floor, the' (senior
   administration)   9,48
forgers (shoemakers)   45
interpreters   45
lamplighters (at the Laundry,
   Acton)   19,25,42,43–44
baby-sitting   44
listening (electronic surveillance)
   25,44,49
pavement artists (surveillance
   specialists)   27,44
post boxes   44
postmen   44
safe houses   14,19,20,25,34,35,
   38,44
transport   44
watching (surveillance) 25,44
London Station   19,20,42,49
long-arm radio transmission base
   (at Canterbury)   45
nuts and bolts (technical/scientific
   services)   45
Oddbins   45
research   45

CIRCUS DEPARTMENTS
  Operational *cont.*
Sarratt (the Nursery at)   20,35,
    41,44–45
  agents (briefing/training)   14
  charm-school   44
  combat techniques   44
  contact procedures   44
  courier routes   44
  dead letter boxes   44
  interrogation   44
  memorization of phone numbers
    44
  tradecraft   15,44
  word codes   44
Satellites, Satellites Four   14,42,49
scalphunters ('Travel'), (at
    Brixton)   13,17,19,24,25,43,44,
    49
  blackmail   17,24,25,27,39,40,43
  bribery   17,43
  hit-and-run jobs   43
  kidnapping   43
  murder   43
shoemakers (forgers)   45
Soviet Attack, Director   43
special travel   45
stinks-and-bangs school (at
    Argyll)   45
technical and scientific services
    (nuts and bolts)   45
tradecraft   15,44
tradesmen   45
transcribers   45
'Travel' *see* scalphunters
vetting   45
water school (at Helford estuary)
    45

CIRCUS DEPARTMENTS
  Operational *cont.*
  Western Europe, Director   43
  wranglers (code-breakers), (at
    Bath)   41,45,49
Circus doctor   46
Circus Headquarters   7,8,13,45,46,
    48–49
Circus Hierarchy   41–47
Circus mole *see* 'Gerald'
Circus Operations, History of
    12–27
  Chronologies   28–40
code-breakers *see* wranglers
coding (Circus)   13,45,49
Collins, Sam   13,17,19,20,21,22,23,
    24,32,33,34,35,36,37,43,47,48
Colonial Office, Whitehall   41
combat techniques (Circus)   44
communism, communist   13,16,17
contact procedures (Circus)   44
Contemplate (network)   17,47
Control   8,10,12,15,16,17,18,19,31,
    33,34,42,43,48
courier routes (Circus)   44
Cousins/Company, the *see* American
    Intelligence Service
Craddox, —   44
Cranko, —   44
Craven, Villem   25,26,39,40
Craw, William   22,23,36,37,44,47
Czechoslovakia, Circus activity in
    13,17,33, (map 77)
  Aggravate network   17,19,47
  Brno   19

D

DDR Defence Ministry,
   E. Germany 14
dead letter boxes (Circus) 44
Defence, Ministry of, Whitehall 42
de Gray, Brian 13,14
de Jong, — 13,14
Delaware, Mo 19,42
Department, the *see* British
   Intelligence Service
de Silsky, Nick 19,21,42
di Salis, Doc 13,21,22,37,42,45,49
Dolphin, Diana 46,49
Dolphin, Operation 21–24,25,32,
   43,44,45,48,49
  chronology 35–38
'Dolphinarium', the, Maresfield,
   Sussex (safe house) 38
Doolittle, — 45
duty-officers (Circus) 9,20,45,49
  logbooks 20,34,39

E

East German CP Praesidium (SED)
   14
East German Intelligence Service
   (Abteilung) 14,15,16,29,31
  Ways and Means Committee 31
East German Steel Mission, London
   14,15,29,30
East Germany *see* Germany
—, Ellen 46
—, Elvira 31
Enderby, Saul 24,25,27,39,40,41,
   42,43

Esterhase, Toby 17,19,20,21,26,27,
   33,35,37,39,40,42,43,44
Europe, Eastern 21,47
  southern 13
experimental audio-laboratory,
   Harlow (Circus) 45

F

Fanshawe, P.R. de T. 12
Fawley, — 46
Fawn, — 21,23,24,43
Feger, Fritz 14
Fellowby, — 45
Fennan Case, chronology 28–30
Fennan, Elsa 14,15,28,29,30,42
Fennan, Samuel 14,15,16,28,29,30,
   42
Ferguson, — 44
Fiedler, Jens 16,31,32
Fiedler–Mundt Operation,
   chronology 30–31
Fielding, Adrian 12,13,41
Finland, Circus activity in
  Helsinki 47
'fifth, floor, the' (Circus) 9,48
Ford, Arthur 16,30,31
forgers *see* shoemakers (Circus)
Foreign Office, Whitehall 41,42
France, Circus activity in 13
  Paris 20,24,25,27,35,39,40,46,47
Frau Marthe 14
Frey, Dieter ('Mr Robinson') 9,15,
   28,29,30
Frost, J. 10,21,23,37

G

Gadfly, Operation 18
'Gerald' (Circus mole) 18,19,20,32,
    33,35,45
Germany 12,15,47
  Berlin 14,15,18,27,31,32,47,
    (map 77)
    Dürer-Strasse (safe house) 14
    Wedding, girl from 14
  Berlin Wall 14,17,32
  East Germany 8,14,15,16,17,31,
    32, (map 77) see also DDR
    Defence Ministry; East German
    Intelligence Service (Abteilung)
    Görlitz 32
    Leipzig 32
  West Germany
    Hamburg 13,25,26,39,40
—, Ginnie 46
Gold, Liz 16,17,31,32
gold seam ('laundering') operation,
    Soviet 21,23,37
Grigoriev, Anton 27,39,40,44
Guillam, Peter 7,8,9,10,13,14,15,
    17,18,19,20,21,23,24,28,30,32,
    34,35,37,43,46,47,48,49
  Guillam's parents 13

H

Habolt, Max 19,20,32,33,35,44
Hackett, — 14
Haggard, — 45
Hammer, — 42
Hampstead, London (safe flat)
    25,44

Hankie, Teddy 34,44
Harlow, Essex see experimental
    audio-laboratory at
Haverlake, — 13,14
Haydon, Bill 8,12,13,14,17,18,19,
    20,21,32,33,35,36,37,41,42,43,
    44,45,48,49
Haydon Case, chronology 32–35
Helford estuary, Cornwall
    French fishing smacks at 13
    water school 13
Hibbert, Rev., — 22,37
—, Hilary 45
hit-and-run jobs (Circus) 43
Holland, Circus activity in 13,16
  The Hague 32
Hong Kong 10,20,21,23,24,32,34,
    36,37,38,46,47, (maps 99,100)
    High Haven (Circus HQ) 21
    Peking–Hong Kong shuttle 17
    Po Toi Island 24
Hotel Islay, Sussex Gardens,
    London 17,34
housekeeper, Housekeeping (Circus)
    9,42,46,49
Hungary (Plato network in) 17,47
Hyde, — 45

I

illegal residents see agents (Circus)
India, Circus activity in 17
Indocharter 21,22,23,36
Intelligence Steering Committee
    22,41
Inter-Ministerial Steering Committee
    (the Wise Men) 42,43,44

interpreters (Circus) 45
interrogation (Circus) 44
'Irina' 20,34
Italy
  Tuscany 37
'Ivlov' *see* Brod

J

janitors (Circus) 46,49
Japanese Intelligence (Toka) 17
jargon terms 11
Jebedee, — 12,13,41
Jensen, Peter 46
—, John 42
—, Juliet 46

K

Karla 9,12,13,14,19,20,22,24,25,
  26,27,35,38,39,40,45
  (daughter) Tatiana 26,27,39,40
  deep-penetration agent techniques
  17
Karla Case, chronology 38–40
Kaspar, Spike 19,21,42
Kensington, London (safe house)
  44
kidnapping (Circus) 43
Kiever, Sam 16,31
Kirov, Oleg *see* Kursky, Oleg
Knightsbridge, London (Circus HQ,
  pre-1945) 12,13
Ko, Drake 21,22,23,24,37,38
Ko, Nelson 22,23,24,36,37,38
'Komet' 27

Kretzschmar, Claus 25,26,27,39,40
Krieglova, Eva 47
Kursky, Oleg (Kirov) 24,25,26,38,
  39

L

Lacon, Oliver 20,26,32,33,34,35,41
Lambeth, London (safe house) 44
lamplighters, Acton (Circus) 19,
  25,42,43–44
Landsbury, Lord John 13,45
Landkron, — 47
Ländser, — 14
Lark, — 45
Larrett, — 45
'laundering' operation *see* gold seam
Laundry, the (Acton) *see*
  lamplighters at
Leamas, Alec 8,13,14,15,16,17,28,
  30,31,32,41,45,47
legal residents *see* agents (Circus)
Leipzig, Otto 24,25,26,39,40,47
listeners, listening – electronic
  surveillance (Circus) 25,44,49
Lock Gardens, London (Witchcraft
  safe house) 10,19,20,34,35,44
London 9–10, (map 120) *see also*
  individual place names
London Station (Circus) 19,20,42,
  49
long-arm radio transmission base,
  Canterbury (Circus) 45
Luff, — 41
—, Luke 25
Lusty, Pete 43

M

McCall, — 46
McCraig, Millie 13,44,49
MacFadean, — 46
Mackelvore, Steve 20,46
Magnus, Bill 41,45
maintenance (Circus) 46
Maresfield, Sussex ('Dolphinarium'
    safe house) 38
Marshall, Charlie 23,36,37,38
Martello, Marty 23,37
Martindale, Roddy 13,41,45
—, Mary 46
Masterman, Mary 45
Masters, Major — 36
Maston, — 13,14,15,41,42
Mayfly, Operation 18
Meakin, Mollie 43,45,46
Meinertzhagen girls 44
Mellows, — 46
memorization of phone numbers
    (Circus) 44
Mendel, Inspector — 14,15,20,28,
    29,30,33,34
Merlin, Source 18,19
Middle East, Circus activity in 13,
    17
  Egypt 17,18
—, Mikhel 25,26,39,40
Miller, Vladimir see Vladimir,
    General
Minister's Adviser, the (chief/head
    of Circus) 9,20,41
Moscow Centre (Soviet Intelligence)
    10,12,13,18,19,20,21,22,26,39
Mostyn, Nigel 25,26,39,45
Mothers, the (Circus) 46

Mundt, Hans-Dieter ('Blondie'/
    'Freitag') 14,15,16,17,28,29,30,
    31,32
  Fiedler–Mundt Operation
    chronology 30–31
  murder (Circus) 43

N

Norway, Circus activity in 13
Nursery, the see Sarratt
nuts and bolts – technical/scientific
    services (Circus) 45

O

Occasionals see agents (Circus)
Oddbins (Circus) 45
Operations, History of Major 12–27
  Chronologies 28–40
Ostrakova, Maria 25,26,27,39,40
  (daughter) Alexandra 25,27,39
Overseas Committee for Academic
    Research, Oxford 12
Oxford 9,12
  training school 41

P

Paul, — 41
pavement artists – surveillance
    specialists (Circus) 27,44
Peking–Hong Kong shuttle 17
Pelling, Cess 22,37
Pelling, Humphrey (Nunc) 22,37

Personnel (Circus) 46
Peters, — 16,32
Pitt, — 16
phone numbers, memorization of
    (Circus) 44
Plato (network) 17,19,47
Poland, Circus activity in 17
police see Special Branch
Polyakov, Aleksey A. 18,19,20,34
Porteous, Phil 19,42,46,49
Portugal, Circus scandal in 18
post boxes (Circus) 44
postmen (Circus) 44
Pretorius, — 42
Pribyls, the 47
Prideaux, Jim 12,13,19,20,21,33,
    34,35,43,45,46
Purcell, Molly 45

R

Registry (Circus) 9,46,49
research (Circus) 45
Resettlement (Circus) 46
Ricardo, Tiny 21,22,23,36,37,38
Riemeck, Karl 14,15,16,31
Riga Group (Baltic nationalists) 24
Roach, Bill 33
Rolling Stone, Operation 16,32

S

SED (East German CP
    Praesidium) 14
Sachs, Connie 9,12,19,20,21,24,26,
    34,37,40,42,45,49

safe houses/flats for mainline
    operations (Circus) 14,19,20,
    25,34,35,38,44
St James's, London (safe house)
    44
—, Sal 10,46
Saloman, — 14
Sarratt, Hertfordshire, the Nursery
    at (Circus) 20,35,41,44–45
Sarrow, — 14
Sartor brothers 44
Satellites, Satellites Four (Circus)
    14,42,49
scalphunters – 'Travel', Brixton
    (Circus) 13,17,19,24,25,43,44,
    49
Scarr, Adam 14,15,16,28,29,30
Scotland
    Argyll see stinks-and-bangs school
    at
    Western Isles 37
Secretariat, secretaries (Circus)
    46,48
Security Service, Whitehall 42
Sembrini, Pete 43
Sercombe, Lady Ann see Smiley,
    Lady Ann
Services, general (Circus) 46
Sheridan Theatre, Hammersmith
    15,30
shoemakers – forgers (Circus) 45
shuttle, the (Circus) 46
Skordeno, Paul 17,19,42
Slingo, Harry 44
Smiley, George passim
Smiley, Lady Ann (née Sercombe)
    10,13,33
Source References code note 6

South America, Circus activity in
    13,17
  Brazil   17
South East Asia   8,17,23,42,45,47,
    (map 171) *see also* Hong Kong
  Borneo   13
  Burma   13
  Cambodia
    Battambang   23,38
    Phnom Penh   23,38
  Laos
    Vientiane   17,21,22,36,37
  Malaysia   13
    Kuala Lumpur   34
  Thailand   17,23,36,38
    Bangkok   23,38
  Vietnam (South)
    Saigon   36,38
Soviet Attack, Director (Circus)   43
Soviet Intelligence *see* Moscow
    Centre
Soviet Union   13,17,19,21,42
  British Intelligence in   21
  Georgia (Contemplate network
    in)   17,47
  gold seam (laundering) operation
    21,23,37
  Moscow   12,39
  Ukraine (Contemplate network in)
    17,47
Spain, Circus activity in   17
Sparke, —   12,41
Sparrow, Ben   13
Special Branch police   13
Special Despatch (Circus)   46
special travel (Circus)   45
Stack, Karl   43
Stanley, —   44

Steed-Asprey, —   9,12,13,41
Stevcek, General —   19,33
stinks-and-bangs school, Argyll
    (Circus)   45
Strickland, Lauder   43,45
surveillance *see* listeners; pavement
    artists; watchers
Switzerland, Circus activity in
  Berne   27,40, (map 58)
  clinic near   27,39
  Thun   40

T

Tarr, Ricki   13,17,20,21,32,34,35,
    43
—,   Tatiana (Karla's daughter)   26,
    27,39,40
Taverner, Felix   15
technical and scientific services *see*
    nuts and bolts (Circus)
Testify, Operation   19,20,21,32,34,
    35,48
Thatch, —   44
Thesinger, Tufty   18,40
Thruxton, Ben   12,45
Thursby, —   45
Thursgood's school, Devon   34
Tiu, —   22,23,24,36,37,38
Toka (Japanese Intelligence)   17
tradecraft (Circus)   15,44
tradesmen (Circus)   45
transcribers (Circus)   45
transport (Circus)   44
'Travel' *see* scalphunters (Circus)
Treasury, Whitehall   42

V

Vanhofer, Cy   43
vetting (Circus)   45
Viereck, —   14
Viktorov, Colonel Gregor *see*
    Polyakov, A.A.
Vladimir, General ('Miller')   24,25,
    26,38,39

W

watchers, watching – surveillance
    (Circus)   25,44 *see also*
    pavement artists (Circus)
water school, Helford estuary
    (Circus)   45
Watford, Hertfordshire (Sarratt staff
    quarters)   45
Wayfarer, Phoebe   17,22,23,37,47
Westerby, Clive Gerald (Jerry)   10,
    11,13,19,20,21,22,23,24,33,34,
    35,36,37,38,45,47

Western Europe, Director (Circus)
    43
Weybridge Repertory Theatre,
    Surrey   14,29,30
Whitehall, London *see* individual
    Ministries and Offices
Wilbraham, Chris   41
Wise Men, the *see* Inter-Ministerial
    Steering Committee
Witchcraft, Operation   18,19,20,32,
    33,34,35
word codes (Circus)   44
Worthington, Elizabeth ('Liese
    Worth')   21,22,23,24,36,37
Worthington, Peter   22,37
wranglers – code-breakers, Bath
    (Circus)   41,45,49

Y

Yugoslavia
    Belgrade network   17,18